THE MOTH AND THE STAR
A Biography of Virginia Woolf

Virginia Woolf

THE MOTH
AND
THE STAR

A Biography of Virginia Woolf

by
AILEEN PIPPETT

LITTLE, BROWN AND COMPANY
BOSTON   TORONTO

Published September 1955
Reprinted November 1955

Published simultaneously in Canada
by Little, Brown & Company (Canada) Limited

The more we know of people the less we can sum them up. Just as we think we hold the bird in our hands, the bird flits off.

An essay by Virginia Woolf on "Mrs. Thrale"
(From *The Moment,* February, 1941)

It seems then that a profound, impartial and absolutely just opinion of our fellow creatures is utterly unknown.

Virginia Woolf in *Jacob's Room* (1922)

Do we then know nobody? Only our own versions of them, which, as likely as not, are emanations from ourselves.

A letter from Virginia Woolf to Vita Sackville-West (1926)

The truth of one's sensations is not in the fact, but in the reverberation.

A letter from Virginia Woolf to Vita Sackville-West (1929)

Preface

BEFORE I began to think of writing this book, all I knew about Virginia Woolf was that I had read everything I could by her and about her and that in this way she had become a part of my life. I met her once, in a Bloomsbury attic, by candlelight, unexpectedly, at a small party some time in the middle nineteen-thirties. To me it was a memorable occasion, though I did nothing to make it so, being more than content to admire and observe and remain quieter than the mice behind the wainscoting, for I believed then, as I do still, that anything of importance an author has to say to a reader is to be found in books and heard in the privacy of the mind.

I continued to read her books as they were issued, not as the devotee of any cult but confident they would go on giving me the same sense that they were the real thing, part of English literature, with their roots in the past and their branches spreading out to the future. Each one was an invitation to enjoy with her more adventures in the world of the imagination. She was one of the host of friends who knew nothing whatever about me but made me freely welcome to use their eyes and ears, to listen to their discussions, quiver with their rages and share their jokes.

In this feeling about Virginia Woolf I knew, of course, that I was not alone, but I was rather surprised by the frequency and ease with which it was expressed. Her name could be expected to occur in memoirs, autobiographies and essays by her friends and contemporaries. What delighted me was to find it coupled with that of Dickens, as though she were a friend of the family, or Margaret Mead, as though she might be heard from again any time now: and this from people who could have had no opportunity of knowing her in person.

But this did not at all square with the evidence that the cold war between highbrows and lowbrows still goes on. "Bloomsbury" has been revived as a term of abuse, defying definition and puzzling people like me who have lived or worked there without being in the least incommoded by knowing that famous and talented artists were just around the corner. Nor do the words "Ivory Tower" make any sense as applied to Virginia Woolf and her friends when one remembers how they were in the very thick of all the controversies which raged in the exciting years of change between the two World Wars, and when one considers that her life span covered the vastly different Edwardian and late Victorian days.

Who is right? Those who maintain that the Bloomsbury Circle deliberately shut itself off from contact with ordinary life, or those who feel that it is part of the history of our times? Does the fact that it is dead and can never be revived prove that it has no influence today? Did it appear without cause and disappear without effect? How has it happened that Virginia Woolf has not been buried deep under a load of adulation and then promptly forgotten? Why is she still talked about, why are her books still read, and why do more and more people feel the continuing stream of the life force flowing through them?

It seemed to me that answers to some of these questions might lie in the personality of the woman herself as apart from the literary artist and the social thinker. In trying to reconstruct this very elusive and complex personality, fragile as a moth and enduring as a star, I received great assistance from talking with many of her friends, who knew her at different times in their lives and hers, who differ about the smokeability of her cigars but who agree that she was a rare human being, not perfect but always tenderly remembered, as though some bloom and freshness refuse to fade.

The extracts from her journal, published under the title *A Writer's Diary*, have been an invaluable guide. I am deeply indebted to Leonard Woolf for his kindness in allowing me to study this book before publication, for his permission to draw upon it and to quote from letters written by his wife, of which he holds the copyright, and for his frank and impartial attitude throughout.

Many of the letters I have been privileged to see were sent by Virginia Woolf to Lady Nicolson, referred to in the following pages by her maiden and pen name of Vita Sackville-West. They fill many chronological gaps in the *Diary*, since they cover the period from 1922 to 1941, and also cast light on attitudes and opinions not elsewhere so directly expressed.

It is a piece of the greatest good fortune to me — though Virginia Woolf often bewailed it as the greatest ill-luck to her — that the two friends were so frequently prevented from meeting. Vita Sackville-West spent much of her time traveling with her husband, Sir Harold Nicolson, on his Foreign Office missions; and it seemed that no sooner was she back in England than Virginia Woolf was either on a holiday in Europe or visiting booksellers in Britain or temporarily too ill to receive visitors but happy to while away the boredom of convalescence by writing letters. Even when they were both in the same country, one would be busy in London while the other was in Kent or Sussex, not great distances apart as the crow flies — but English roads and railroads are not crows. These circumstances explain the very frequent references to Vita Sackville-West in this biography. Other close friends of Virginia Woolf's either lived nearer her, traveled less, or for other reasons were not such regular correspondents.

I owe grateful acknowledgments to all friends who have permitted me to quote their words, and to the publishers Harcourt, Brace and Company for allowing me to give extracts from Virginia Woolf's books. Many others have contributed to my book in various ways, by encouragement, criticism and practical help in the work involved, or by telling me what part Virginia Woolf played in their lives. I thank them all.

Finally I must record my gratitude to her for her share in making me a receiver and, I hope, in turn a transmitter of the haunting and mysterious music of the world.

New York
December, 1954

THE MOTH AND THE STAR

A Biography of Virginia Woolf

Chapter I

AN AMBASSADOR'S life is not an easy one. But sometimes he finds among the papers demanding his attention on his desk an invitation that is not only an honor to receive but a pleasure to accept.

This was certainly the case when, early in 1882, James Russell Lowell, United States Minister to the Court of St. James's in London, was asked to stand in "quasi-sponsorial relation" to a child. In less jocose but also less accurate words, would he be a godfather? He gladly agreed, for the request came from one of his closest friends, a very distinguished Englishman and one, moreover, who deserved well of the United States for his part in promoting friendly understanding between Englishmen and Americans.

Lowell at once ordered the usual precious trinket to be sent to the baby for her naming ceremony; and, never at a loss to turn a compliment, always able to show that New England understood the amenities of gracious living as well as old England, he followed the gift with "Verses Intended to Go with a Posset Dish to my Dear Little God-Daughter." In these lines, full of good wishes, he hoped the child would inherit her father's wit and her mother's beauty; but immediately realizing this was a tall order for a quite exceptionally brilliant future, he decided not to demand too much of fate. So he settled for the simple wish that

the child would be
A sample of heredity.

This was a safe draft, duly honored on the bank of time; for the frail baby, named Adeline Virginia Stephen, born on January 25, 1882, at Hyde Park Gate, London, was destined to become as Virginia Woolf even more famous than her father in the world of letters; and though she would never rank as a Hollywood starlet nor parade at Atlantic City, every artist who saw her, everyone with the slightest aesthetic sensibility, and every friend she had, celebrated her beauty.

In case heredity was not sufficient capital endowment, there was environment to swell the account with compound interest, for Leslie Stephen, her father, was a magnet for the famous and distinguished of his day. The list of eminent Victorians who were either related to him (or to his wife), happy to be his friends or proud to be associated with him in his work, is so dazzling as to become boring. These celebrities are like the crown jewels, which are nice to think of as being on show and strongly guarded in the Tower of London, but which, to tell the truth, are not nearly so impressive when seen all together as when a few are worn on suitable occasions. Let the glittering names, like the precious stones, take their turn at being displayed.

A few must, however, be mentioned right at the beginning, for the sake of the record.

Julia Stephen was Leslie Stephen's second wife. His first was Thackeray's younger daughter Minnie, who died suddenly in 1875, leaving him with a young daughter. It was Julia's second marriage also; she had been a widow, with three young children, for eight years when she and Leslie married in 1878. They had known each other for a long while — her first husband, Herbert Duckworth, a barrister, being an acquaintance of Leslie Stephen — and had first met through Tom Hughes (of *Tom Brown's Schooldays* fame) when she was Julia Jackson, a strikingly beautiful girl, courted and admired by eminent artists, and chosen by Burne-Jones as the model for his painting of the Annunciation.

Not only Julia Jackson's background but her forebears were fascinating. Her mother was one of seven sisters, all famous for their beauty and charm, whose grandfather was a French nobleman, the Chevalier de l'Etang, a page to Marie Antoinette who had survived the Revolution and emigrated to India. Virginia's own description of her mother's family was that they had all been "extremely frivolous and art-loving and sociable"; whereas on her father's side, she declared, they were "all lawyers, or country gentry and clergymen since the time of Elizabeth and before."[1] There is a faint note of mockery and even a hint of disapproval in this summing up, but also a secret pride.

The mother represented romance, the father achievement. The first stood for the accidental, the undeserved but appreciated element of beauty; the other for moral worth, intellectual integrity and hard work.

Leslie Stephen was fifty when Virginia was born; Julia was thirty-six. In that half century he had not only changed his career from don and parson at Cambridge to journalist in London but had witnessed great changes in the social scene. He was born five years before the accession of Queen Victoria, in the year of the Great Reform Act, first of the many steps towards making Parliament representative of all classes. Already the process had begun by which the landed aristocracy was gradually supplanted by an intellectual aristocracy continually drawing fresh vigor and more members from the middle classes. The prestige of the hereditary nobility was still very high. Their wealth, conserved by the system of entail and primogeniture and supplemented by advantageous marriages with heiresses within their ranks, was still very great. But their powers and privileges were steadily dwindling. They were more and more often marooned on their estates, stranded in honorary positions at court. Glamour was theirs, and ease, but dominance was passing to men who relied not on birth but on brains for their success in the professions; whose money might be earned by their own efforts or drawn from industrial or trading sources without exciting contempt or derision; whose tradition was one of moral courage; whose marriages to women

[1] *Virginia Woolf* by Winifred Holtby.

of their own kind linked them with other families by a system more resembling interlocking directorates than dynastic alliances.

If this seems too glowing a picture of a class, consider the astonishing brilliance of the Victorian sky, crowded with stars newly discovered and continuing to shine. It was an historical development. The Stephen family and their like were not exceptional but typical. They were the elite, it is true, but the sort of elite that could not have established itself at any other time. They commanded respect because they worked to deserve it. Careers were open to the talents as they had never been before. Competition was keen but not cutthroat. Doors previously shut were now open; but not to beggars, idlers or flatterers. Scholars, poets and wits no longer depended on the patronage of a few rich men. They did not live in squalor, meet in coffeehouses and taverns, and die in poverty. They could bring up large families and send their sons to public schools and universities. They looked for support to the increasing numbers of their own kind.

Virginia's playground could be Kensington Gardens, as it had been for her father and uncle, not because the five-storied stuccoed house in Hyde Park Gate was an ancestral mansion but because the Stephens could afford to live there.

Kensington was no longer flanked by market gardens and country lanes; it was fashionable and expensive. The young queen who had responded in the Gardens with a curtsy to the bows of little Leslie and his brother was now the stately Widow of Windsor, with a Jubilee looming ahead, and Kensington's rural character had been altogether changed by tributes to the memory of her dead husband by the time Virginia was born. The public museums, colleges and art galleries of the cultural and educational center the Prince Consort had sponsored to commemorate the 1851 Exhibition had almost all been completed. The Albert Memorial and the Albert Hall were about ten years old, dominating the scene and assaulting the imagination. Even larger, but newer and much more prolific of its kind, was the towering block of apartments known as Albert Hall Mansions.

Little has changed architecturally since then. But the ideas and circumstances of the people who now live behind that imposing late-Victorian façade, or hurry, so far as traffic will allow of speed, along Knightsbridge and Kensington Gore or walk in the Park and Gardens, have altered almost beyond recognition. A man making his living by his pen could not have lived there in the eighteenth century; no successful author is likely even so much as to consider having a whole house full of children and servants there in the twentieth.

Leslie Stephen was editing the *Cornhill Magazine* in 1882. This was a monthly designed to appeal to upper-middle-class family circles. Thackeray had been a previous editor; Hardy had contributed serials. A prodigious amount of miscellaneous writing was behind Virginia's father, and even more important work ahead. But before embarking upon journalism as a profession, he had already made a reputation. A delicate child, extremely sensitive to poetry, shy and emotional, he survived an Eton education and toughened at Cambridge into a noteworthy and enthusiastic athlete. Rowing and walking were his favorite pursuits. Too tall and awkward to be a good man in a boat, he was a remarkable coach. As a walker he was unrivaled. Distance was no object — thirty miles, fifty miles, to London and back, by roads or cross country — it was all one to him. He took academic studies in his stride too, becoming a Fellow of Trinity Hall, an award which required the holder to take holy orders. A change in his religious beliefs, without any decline in his moral fervor, made him resign his office and return from Cambridge to London. He is probably better known as a leading agnostic than as one of the founders of muscular Christianity. While still a don and a parson he also established other records in the new sport of mountain climbing. An early member of the Alpine Club, later its president and editor of its journal after leaving Cambridge, he was the first man to climb the Schreckhorn, and was recognized as one of the great climbers of his day.

This passion for storming up mountain peaks was not shared by his daughter Virginia. Her devotion to him made her not mind "walking my little legs off trotting beside him round the Serpentine" in Hyde Park, but "How could I think mountains and climbing romantic?" she wrote in 1924 to a friend [1] visiting the Dolomites. "Wasn't I brought up with alpenstocks in my nursery, and a raised map of the Alps, showing every peak my father had climbed? Of course, London and the marshes are the places I like best." She probably kept her counsel about this at the time, however, as children know how to do when called upon to admire some adult activity in which they cannot share, and there is no record that she went so far as to agree with the opinion of the famous Swiss guide Melchior Anderegg, who came to England as Leslie Stephen's guest, that the London chimney pots were more impressive than Alpine peaks and the waxworks in Madam Tussaud's more beautiful than the effigies in Westminster Abbey.

Her father set up still other records. He was famous for his silences. Not only could he and did he remain silent throughout his own dinner parties, if he felt so inclined, but he could and did walk all day long, from breakfast at dawn to supper at night, without exchanging one word with his invited companions. This was not churlishness or bad temper; just a preoccupation with his own thoughts which his friends learned to respect. Virginia, too, could be silent, when she was listening intently. She could fade out of a conversation when she was tired or unwell. But she recognized the social necessity of "beating up the waters of talk so that life mayn't be wasted." She never learned, as her father did, the technique of protecting herself completely from interruption of her thoughts by an impenetrable wall of silence.

His unsociability sometimes found more positive expression than mere withdrawal into his own thoughts or his own room. He had a disconcerting habit, when bored by a visitor, of enquiring audibly, "Why can't he go?" Such outbursts of irritation were more comical than frightening, more temporarily startling than lastingly offensive, for he was loved as well as respected. Once his

[1] V. Sackville-West.

friend, always his friend. Not easy to know, he was impossible to forget. A craggy character, a Schreckhorn of a man, exerting no easy charm but the fascination of the difficult.

That he could be tactful when necessary is sufficiently proved by his making and keeping so many American friends. When he visited the United States in 1863 he was welcomed in Boston because of the known record of his father and grandfather on the issue of slavery in England and its colonies. But he must have faced many awkward social situations because the London *Times*, which was thought to express prevailing British opinion, was misrepresenting and sneering at the North and indicating that all Englishmen worthy of the name were naturally on the side of the gentlemen of the South. Leslie Stephen's fundamental honesty and sincerity, no less than the clarity of his intelligence, resulted in introductions to such men as Charles Eliot Norton, Oliver Wendell Holmes and James Russell Lowell, leading to friendships that lasted all their lives.

On his return to England he challenged the right of the London *Times* to speak authoritatively about American affairs and denounced it for fostering bad feeling between the two nations by its ignorance and interference. His vigorous pamphlet had an excellent effect on the British public; and his regular contributions for many years to the *Nation* were also helpful in promoting understanding and friendship. For these services alone, if for nothing else, Ambassador Lowell would have thought it no less a duty than a pleasure to send a posset dish and dedicatory verses to his dear little goddaughter.

Virginia was the third of four children born to Julia and Leslie Stephen in the first few years of their marriage. Close in age, they were very closely linked in feeling. First came Vanessa, so dearly loved by Virginia that no words could ever express her feelings. She was the elder sister to whom one went for protection and comfort when clouds darkened a childish sky. She was the rock, the refuge, as well as the playmate, the friend, the co-conspirator, the secret sharer. Then came Thoby, whom Virginia adored,

whose approval she sought, whose praise she treasured, whose
memory remained always bright, the golden, glorious brother.
And then Adrian, the merry, mischief-loving, incomparably comical younger brother, to whose defense Virginia was ready to rush
if ever he should be in need. Come the four corners of the world
in arms, the four young Stephen children were ready.

Between them and their stepbrothers and stepsister there was
not, of course, the same extremely close tie. There was, in the first
place, the difference in age, and this gap in the years was fortunate, since it tended to reduce the inevitable tensions and jealousies between the two groups.

The Duckworths were part of the machinery of life to the
Stephens; they could be useful or they could be a nuisance; they
could be looked to for fun or fuss, as the case might be, but for
the most part they were just incomprehensible. Sometimes they
impinged, and then again they vanished. They had their own
orbits around the joint center of their expanding universe. They
can scarcely have remembered their own father, whereas Mr.
Stephen, with the long legs and the red beard, was a familiar
figure and had been practically their next-door neighbor ever
since they had learned to distinguish one adult from another. As
for babies, well, babies were plentiful in those Victorian days; you
couldn't expect to avoid them. Stella Duckworth, the eldest of the
three, was already beginning to be a young lady by the time
Vanessa was born; not too old to appreciate having a live doll to
play with, nor too young to feel the thrill of responsibility for a
helpless infant which is the basis of most sisterly affection. Her
two brothers, Gerald and George, were away at school a good deal
of the time, but when at home no doubt often felt called upon to
assist in the education of Thoby and Adrian, the teasing and
toughening of youngsters being considered a very important part
of the arduous business of growing up, and the prerogative of
older members of a family to pass on to the younger ones some of
the lessons they had learned.

There was certainly plenty of rough-and-tumble in such a

household, as well as a great deal of love and tenderness. Julia, a wise woman, faced many problems in the varied demands made upon her. It cannot have been an accident that her eldest daughter, by her first husband, being named Stella, the eldest child by her second husband was called Vanessa. Thus, if any rivalry for parental affection should occur between the stepsisters, the matter could be settled by remembering Jonathan Swift — a name as familiar as that of Father Christmas in such a literary household. Could anyone say whether Stella or Vanessa was the Dean's real and only love? Of course not. Both were equally dear.

But it was necessarily a male-dominated home; not an easy growing-up place for an extremely sensitive and fragile girl. Virginia's father was convinced that he had overcome his own early physical weakness and emotionalism by sheer determination and will power. Any tendency in his sons to be dreamy and impractical distressed him and must, he considered, be dealt with by similar methods; not by brutal external disciplines and strict rules of formal conduct, but by an inner understanding of the ideal of true manliness. No sentimental humbug, of course; no sanctimonious self-righteousness — prigs are an abomination. Above all, no laziness, no faltering on the road to perfection. That was all he asked, as loving parents continue to ask and then are surprised if the results are not exactly what they expect and their children make their own mistakes, learn by their own experiences, follow their own inner compulsions or conform to a new social pattern.

For Virginia, being a girl and delicate, exceptions could be made; and this she always resented. It was so reasonable, so kind; and so infuriating. The boys must not be mollycoddled, but it was necessary to cosset her. She was not strong enough to go to school; her brothers had to fit themselves for university honors and success in a chosen profession. She was the darling, the pet, the elected companion; but her inferiority was always subtly stressed. So, at least, she fiercely felt and continued to feel. The fact that only other women of her kind and generation could understand

this feeling was another source of exacerbation in later life. She
always aroused the protective instincts in her friends; and this,
she confided to her diary and in letters, was what she hated —
caring and being taken care of. The caring because it exhausted
her, physically and emotionally; the being taken care of because
she so often needed it and immediately felt guilty about enjoying
it. She did not want to be an invalid; she possessed, indeed, quite
astonishing reserves of physical energy at times, and had constantly to be warned against overtaxing her strength. This problem
she learned to face realistically, to admit that there are limits to
the hours one can work or the miles one can walk or the sleep one
can do without. But if anything less than the utmost was expected
of her as an artist, on the grounds that she was a woman, she flew
into a fury. She was prepared to do battle for other women, too,
if she suspected the slightest snub, often to their surprise and embarrassment if circumstances had made them less sensitive than
she to any hint of masculine condescension, any implied insult to
women as a sex.

A great deal of the acerbity she sometimes showed, the aggressive quality of her feminism — as it strikes today's women — and
the uncertainty of her response to male friendship and admiration,
in short, what she called her "angularities," can only be understood in terms of early concessions to weakness, early teasings,
early jealousies. Surely, one asks, if ever a family was ahead of its
time as regards sex equality, it was the Stephen family. If ever
young women were able to mix freely with young men without
tiresome questions and troublesome restrictions, they were
Vanessa and Virginia Stephen. If ever a writer had reason to feel
sure that her work would be criticized on its merits and not
greeted with astonishment as though she were some sort of super-
performing flea, that writer was Virginia Woolf. All quite true.
And all missing the point that as a little girl she would like to
have been the one thing she could not be, a tomboy.

If only her head had been screwed on right, she wrote, after
one of the headaches that laid her low for days on end, headaches

that seemed to start with a cloud at the top of her spine ("fourth knob down on the left"); if only she had not had that annoyingly intermittent pulse ever since she was a baby; then she could have gone to school like other girls, and been more like the sort of woman her friends apparently urged her to be.

"I agree about the lack of jolly vulgarity," she wrote in 1926. "But then think how I was brought up! No school: mooning about alone among my father's books; never any chance to pick up all that goes on in schools — throwing balls; ragging; hockey; vulgarity; scenes — jealousies — only rage with my half-brother" (note, no special incident recalled, just a generalized remembrance of a large male obstacle frustrating her in some way) "and being walked off my legs round the Serpentine by my father."

Her relationship with her parents, particularly with her father, was extremely complicated. She tried over and over again to write them out of her system, but their ghosts continued to haunt her. In newspaper articles she would tell true, charming, amusing anecdotes about the home life of the Great Man of Letters; what a delightful companion he was to his children, drawing comic animals, or making odd but very pertinent comments sometimes on the flyleaves and in the margins of books (and he the president of that almost sacred institution, the London Library!); reciting reams of poetry at the top of his voice in Hyde Park, to the delight of his chorusing daughters and the bewilderment of parkkeepers and nursemaids wheeling perambulators; how patient and understanding and tolerant he was, sincerely believing in freedom and justice and reason. With an admirable detachment and lack of sentimentality she brought out the foibles and the qualities that made him beloved. They are studio portraits. The Old Gentleman wears his medals and his coat has been brushed; the pose is relaxed but characteristic; the background is just right; the light is kind.

When she comes to portraying him in a novel she uses no camera, but paints on a canvas with a powerful brush. She is con-

cerned with truth on a different level. She has to be fair to him
and at the same time faithful to her own vision. Only if she can
achieve that will his unquiet spirit have rest.

In her diary and letters the case again is altered. Here she gives
pen-and-ink sketches of quite startling vividness; and the pictures
are not of him alone but of herself, too. For him there is the placa-
tory tribute of flowers on his tombstone; for her the relief of being
free of his domination.

She remembers with gratitude his lugging home great volumes
for her to read. "I think of it with some sentiment," she writes in
her diary in 1929, "— father tramping over the Library with his
little girl sitting at H. P. G." (Hyde Park Gate) "in mind."

And here is an extract from a letter. "I am sometimes pleased to
think that I read English literature when I was young; I like to
think of myself tapping at my father's study door, saying very
loud and clear, 'Can I have another volume, father? I've finished
this one.' Then he would be very pleased and say, 'Gracious, child,
how you gobble,' and get up and take down, it may have been the
6th or 7th volume of Gibbon's complete works, or Speddings,
Bacon, or Cowper's *Letters*. 'But, my dear, if it's worth reading,
it's worth reading twice,' he would say.

"I have a great devotion for him — what a disinterested man,
how high-minded, how tender to me, and fierce and intolerable." [1]

When *To the Lighthouse* appeared, with its unmistakable
portraits of her mother and father as Mr. and Mrs. Ramsay, she
wrote that her mother had haunted her: "But then so did that old
wretch, my father. Do you think it sentimental; do you think it
irreverent about him, I should like to know? I am more like him
than her, I think, and therefore more critical; but he was an
adorable man, and somehow tremendous."

He continued to haunt her. In 1928 she remembered his birthday in her diary: "He would have been 96, 96, yes, today; and
could have been 96, like other people one has known; but mercifully was not. His life would have entirely ended mine. What

[1] To V. Sackville-West (1929).

would have happened? No writing, no books; — inconceivable."

A few months before her death, in the dark war year of 1940, the ghosts were again with her, but kindlier now.

"How beautiful they were," she wrote in her diary in December, "those old people — I mean father and mother — how simple, how clear, how untroubled. I have been dipping into old letters and father's memoirs. He loved her; oh and was so candid and reasonable and transparent — and had such a fastidious, delicate mind, educated and transparent. How serene and gay even, their life reads to me: no mud; no whirlpools. And so human — with the children and the little hum and song of the nursery."

Yes, serene and gay, but not always, even to an outsider. Thomas Hardy, so close and valued a friend that he was asked to witness the deed in which Stephen renounced holy orders and who could recall in his extreme old age how quiet and pleasant was the street in which their house stood, could also note in his diary that he had called one day and found Stephen in a mood of self-reproach and misery: "just the same or worse . . . suffering under some terrible curse which prevents his saying any but caustic things."

Others noted signs of gloom. There was little Susan Grosvenor, for instance, who lived nearby. "The darkest house in London, we used to say. Something to do with the lighting perhaps. So melancholy, so romantic. We loved it. The old man, you know, with all those children to bring up." This is Susan, Lady Tweedsmuir, speaking in 1953, recalling early days.

But there was more to it than shaded lamps and a silent old man to make the Hyde Park Gate house somehow frightening and yet alluring to a young visitor.

"Our parents were great friends. My mother and Virginia's were very fond of one another, and they wanted us to be the same. But unfortunately they let us know it . . . well, you know how it is with children," said Lady Tweedsmuir, speaking with the wisdom of a grandmother. "And Virginia and I were both painfully shy; so I can't say we knew one another well when we were young.

She would be very silent, and I felt she was critical. *Farouche,* somehow, if you know what I mean. As a girl. Later on, of course, when we were both grown up and married, she had all the ease of a woman of the world, and we were able to become great friends. We used to have tea together in Tavistock Square, and Virginia would toast homemade scones over the gas fire — very good scones they were, too — and we would talk about the past, and laugh, and sometimes not turn on the lights until it was really too dark for anything. I always loved her, always enjoyed our talks. Sometimes, perhaps because of the past and because I was a little bit in awe of her still, she reminded me so much of that great man, her father, I used to find her conversation faintly alarming. But always most stimulating. Yes, most stimulating. But I did love her. Don't forget to say that. I *did* love her." And Lady Tweedsmuir, gentlest and kindest of women, turned away and walked back along the brightly lit corridor of her London club, ghosts thick about her, reassuring that shy girl, Susan Grosvenor, that modest middle-aged woman, Mrs. John Buchan; murmuring, "did love her."

There is no doubt about it; Virginia was no angel-child. Delicate, beautiful, enchanting when she so pleased, she was no Little Eva, waiting to be wafted aloft. The clouds she trailed were not all rosy-tinted. She could be more than just somehow faintly alarming. She could be a little fury when aroused.

A faded snapshot still exists, showing her when she was between four and five years old. She is playing cricket in the garden at St. Ives, on the coast of Cornwall, where the Stephen family spent its summers. It is a highly unorthodox game of cricket, naturally. In fact, one may doubt whether it is cricket, or a game, at all. For Virginia, crouched behind the three stumps of the wicket, is a tigress. From the flat shoes and wrinkled black stockings to the wide-brimmed sun hat which seems to quiver in every frill, she is alert, on guard, facing an enemy. Her legs apart, she bends forward, her little thin hands clutching the hem of her loose frock and spreading it out to catch the ball. (Let's hope it was a soft ball, not merely a smaller version of the projectile used in the real game.) Someone is going to throw something at her, or towards her, at any rate; and she has to do something about it. The theory is (does she know it?) that the gesticulating lunatic — out of the picture — who is going to hurl this ball in her direction at any moment now is her friend, on her side, co-operating with her to get the batsman out. The batsman is little Adrian. Does he care? No, he clutches his bat, stands in the correct position, his body and hands properly placed, looks towards the bowler; and is one mass of giggles. But Virginia is serious. She is not to be taken in by all that nonsense at the other end of the pitch: that bowler means mischief; that ball is peril. Well, she is ready, let a hundred bowlers, a thousand balls come her way. And let anything hit or hurt Adrian, and she will exact a terrible vengeance.

There is another family photograph, taken in 1892, in the same luxuriant, terraced garden, with the flowering bushes always tapping at the windows and trying to sneak in at the doors. Seated in a wicker chair in the background, but somehow dominating the group, is Mrs. Stephen; pensive, under a wide hat, a shawl round her shoulders; her head is supported by her left hand (an attitude Virginia often assumed, probably in the kind of unconscious imitation so often observed in families). The lovely line of the cheek and chin, the exquisite placing of the features, are clearly to be seen, though the mouth looks tired and the eyes are shadowed. She is the Mrs. Ramsay of *To the Lighthouse*, whose beauty was a burden she could never lay down.

Beside her are the two Duckworth boys. The elder (has he just come down from London for the week end?) is already a stylish young man, in a dark suit, shirt cuffs showing a fraction of an inch, his hands clasped over a cane, a small mustache over a smiling mouth, a light Homburg hat on his head. The younger has not yet reached this stage of elegance. His belted Norfolk jacket bulges; he sprawls, does not know what to do with his legs, except to use them to hold still for the camera a handsome flop-eared spaniel between his ankles, so that his feet look disproportionately enormous.

In front, seated on a bank, are the four Stephen children. Vanessa, already strikingly beautiful, with a wide forehead, candid eyes, a controlled smile, long hair over one shoulder, sits with hands relaxed in her lap. Thoby, not sure whether to sulk or to laugh, is still a schoolboy, with an Etonish sort of turn-down collar. He has taken off his floppy white hat and flung it on the grass; he has also opened his coat to show the watch chain looped through the bottom button of his vest. Virginia, already very tall for her age, remarkably like her sister and mother, is watchful and unsmiling. Her hair is less tidy than Vanessa's, her skirt rather crumpled, toes slightly turned in, stockings wrinkled, knees tightly pressed together. Only young Adrian, wearing breeches that button below the knees, a turn-down collar like Thoby's and a jacket which has, it seems, become too short almost overnight, thinks it is all a lark.

But Virginia disliked old photographs of herself: salutary, but not gratifying, she remarked. For real pictures of life as it was at St. Ives one must go to her novels. *To the Lighthouse,* of course; for though the scene is supposed to be a Hebridean island, the characters are the Stephen family and friends, and they carry their world with them, so that it really matters very little whether they are to the north of Scotland or the west of England. In *Jacob's Room* one reads about the young men sailing their boat from Falmouth to St. Ives, stripping and diving overboard into the sea and, after six days of adventure, rejoining polite female society ashore. In this comparatively early book Virginia Woolf was precise about locating her characters; mentioning, for instance, the Scilly Isles, Gurnard's Head, steamers on their way to and from Cardiff; sketching in the Cornish landscape, the white cottages on the cliff edge, "saved from the salt breeze only by the depth of a brick, and between the lace curtains you saw the gannet drop like a stone, and on stormy days the gulls came shuddering through the air, and the steamers' lights were now high, now deep." She added small touches of local color to fix that rocky coast more firmly in the reader's mind — the granite boulders piled by primeval man — the old woman bringing out of doors the cream pan to be scoured. But although such details indicate the scene is in Cornwall, Virginia Woolf never tried to pretend to be Cornish; the old country-woman standing at her cottage door is not a county symbol, or even a national one. She is the universal peasant, listening patiently, with half an ear, to the strange talk of the rich summer visitors, waiting submissively enough for them to go their way and leave her to continue her daylong, yearlong, lifelong tasks.

The accuracy of register in such a scene shows that even as a girl Virginia observed minutely and felt deeply the otherness of other people. In later books she eliminated detail in order to strengthen design. The children playing in the garden at the beginning of *The Waves* may be envisaged as hiding in the currant bushes at St. Ives by any reader who happens to know or remember that the author spent the first thirteen summers of her life there. But it makes no difference if we have never even heard of Cornwall before; it is the surge of an ocean vaster than the Atlantic which bears us up in this book.

That they were happy summers there can be no doubt. For one thing, there was the continuity with the life in London; the same family circle, the same visiting friends; the same talk about books and religion and politics; the same domestic crises, handled in the same sure way by Mrs. Stephen. The outer life changed with the season; the inner life continued, with its own seasons and storms and glories.

But there were family troubles, not all of which could be concealed from the children, in spite of Julia's efforts to protect them. When Virginia was about seven or eight years old her father's habits of persistent overwork began to catch up with him. His usual cure for too much reading and writing was strenuous physical exercise, but when a man is nearing sixty even the Alps in wintertime may not be able to restore youthful vigor. He had to give up his editorship of the monumental *Dictionary of National Biography* after a mere twenty-six volumes had appeared, though he continued to write occasional articles for the quarterly issues, to a final total of 378 contributions. It was too late for him to learn to take life easily; he had believed for too long that any relaxation of effort was shameful weakness, to be overcome by a fresh expenditure of will power.

Neither the will nor the imagination, however, can banish all troubles. In the late 1880s, when Leslie Stephen's own health was beginning to fail, his favorite nephew, James K. Stephen, son of his elder brother, began to show alarming symptoms of mental instability. This extraordinarily brilliant, handsome and charming young man, the most amusing and witty of companions, became unpredictable in his behavior, veering between the extremes of wild gaiety and deep gloom. His oddities were so marked that he was expelled from his club and later committed to a mental home, where he died in 1892. Virginia was ten years old. She need have known nothing about it, though children often know a great deal more than their elders think about what is going on supposedly beyond their ken; except for the unfortunate fact that, before his illness was diagnosed, the young man made violent advances to her half sister Stella Duckworth.

Her Uncle Fitzjames broke beneath the strain; he turned into an old man; had to retire, deteriorated more and more rapidly as the months went by, and died in 1894. This also was the year in which her father was forced to admit a defeat; he promised his wife that he would go no more a-roaming in his beloved mountains. In a short time senility, madness and death had made themselves known in the children's paradise.

Julia fought to the last to protect her husband and her brood. And then, in 1895, she committed the crime for which Virginia never quite forgave her; she died. She felt tired; she felt ill; and then she died. She went away; she left them; she deserted; suddenly there was no more Mother.

Virginia was never able to describe, to admit, or to recover from this shattering blow. She tried and tried and tried; every known device, to numb the pain, avert the horror. All to no avail.

She tried illness and madness, retreating into that dream world where there is no death, the glorious, terrible, unimaginable world where one is completely united with Love itself, beyond the possibility of fear and pain and anguish, never again to be forsaken and alone.

But the really terrible thing about hallucinations is that they depart. One struggles awake from this deep sleep of the mind and discovers that the world is going on much as before. So, since the great miracle has not yet occurred, the final victory is not yet achieved, one must try other means of denying and defying death.

When health and sanity returned Virginia was, she thought, secure behind the defense she had automatically erected in the very moment of anguish. No, she did not really feel anything; was incapable of feeling anything; everybody was, but very few would admit it; people who cry and make gestures, they are just pretending; because, in fact . . . well, the fact is . . . but don't ask me any more questions, don't let me ask myself any more questions!

About her father she could think and write with a kind of detached, if tremulous, gaiety. The mixture of her feelings about him is odd and interesting to her, not terrifying. She could be fierce and tender about him in one breath. His ghost could be faced. After all, she had escaped him, he had not left her. The victory was hers. He was a mountain she had climbed. Whether its peak was starkly clear against the sky or wreathed in storm clouds, she knew the way up, and the way down to safety.

That other mountain, her mother, had far gentler slopes. Only, all at once the path crumbled — an avalanche had crashed down into the valley long ago — the easy upward way was barred. There was a precipice. One slip, and another avalanche would crash. But no: there was a parapet — quite a high one, really. It was all perfectly safe. You just went straight on, rounded a curve, and everything was quite all right. Why the panic? All you needed to remember was that the parapet was there. But don't go too close. Don't look over the edge!

We all do it, in some form or another; say No to death. The more it could hurt us, the louder we cry: No. Virginia's defiance resounds through her books; becomes a positive affirmation of life. Its force is the measure of the steepness of that precipice. By the quietness with which she picks her steps onwards, past the danger spot, with no more than a sidelong glance towards the parapet, we know how vital it is for her to reassure herself that the barrier is there.

There is a scene at the beginning of *The Years* in which a family is summoned to the bed of a dying mother. It's only another false alarm, thinks Delia. Nothing's going to happen, nothing whatever. Surely her sister can't be going to cry again? But she joins the procession upstairs to the bedroom. She notices everything; what they are wearing; the dog who wants to come too; two nurses crying, including one who had only arrived that afternoon; her brother on his knees.

Ought I to kneel too? she wondered. Not in the passage, she decided. She looked away; she saw the little window at the end of the passage. Rain was falling; there was a light somewhere that made the raindrops shine. One drop after another slid down the pane; they slid and they paused; one drop joined another drop and then they slid again. There was complete silence in the bedroom.

Is this death? Delia asked herself. For a moment there seemed to be something there. A wall of water seemed to gape apart; the two walls held themselves apart. She listened. There was complete silence. Then there was a stir, a shuffle of feet in the bedroom and out came her father, stumbling.

"Rose!" he cried. "Rose! Rose!" He held his arms with the fists clenched out in front of him.

You did that very well, Delia told him as he passed her. It was like a scene in a play. She observed quite dispassionately that the raindrops were still falling. One sliding met another and together in one drop they rolled to the bottom of the window-pane.

Unnatural, unfeeling girl? No. It actually happened.

"Remember turning aside at mother's bed, when she had died, and Stella took us in, to laugh, secretly, at the nurse crying. She's pretending, I said, aged 13, and was afraid I was not feeling enough. So now," she wrote in her diary in September 1934, when another death had left her feeling "dazed; very wooden . . . The substance gone out of everything. I don't think this is exaggerated."

She goes on to quote, with agreement, Maupassant's analysis of the writer's temperament: unable to suffer or enjoy simply and easily like everyone else, even despair becoming, in the fraction of an instant, a subject of observation and dissection.

All the references to her mother in her diary and letters show the same sudden wincing away from too close an examination, except of herself. And that self is a supposedly dispassionate observer, condemned, because she is a writer, to observe herself observing, prevented from having any deep feeling. That self is never the child suddenly alone, in the dark. That child is hidden, hidden somewhere, over a precipice; still crying — but one cannot, must not, will not hear.

Could anything be more revealing than the apparent calmness with which she wrote, "I don't know if I'm like Mrs. Ramsay: as my mother died when I was 13 probably it is a child's view of her"? [1] So rational a statement, skirting such an abyss of unreason. So politely grown-up a disclaimer of the compliment that she, a child, could really have known her mother well enough to bring her to life for someone who had never seen her.

And then the quivering joy beneath the surface surprise with which she noted in her diary her sister's comment on Mrs. Ramsay:

"Nessa enthusiastic — a sublime, almost upsetting spectacle. She says it is an amazing portrait of mother; a supreme portrait painter; has lived in it; found the rising of the dead almost painful."

[1] To V. Sackville-West (May 1927).

Yes, the parapet was there. Her "damned 'method' " is how she described it: "The one thing that justifies my faults as a writer. Because I don't think one could have reached those particular emotions in any other way." [1] The mature woman speaks. The practiced writer, the artist who has labored in the service of her gift, goes confidently on her way.

AFTER Julia Stephen's death the St. Ives house was given up. Leslie Stephen was inconsolable. He had loved Minnie Thackeray tenderly, but that feeling was as nothing compared with the deep devotion he felt for the woman who had rescued him from the melancholy and despair into which Minnie's death had plunged him. Life and work went on, honors were showered upon him; but the glory had departed. He was getting old, and tired, and deaf; his children were growing up; valued friends were in the same sad plight or were passing from the earthly scene; the young men were not the giants he had known when he was young.

Stella Duckworth took over the management of the household. When Vanessa was considered old enough for this responsibility Stella married. "Prue Ramsay, leaning on her father's arm, was given in marriage," is how Virginia refers to this in To the Lighthouse. "What, people said, could have been more fitting? And, they added, how beautiful she looked!"

But on the next page we read: "Prue Ramsay died that summer in some illness connected with childbirth, which was indeed a tragedy, people said, everything, they said, had promised so well."

The effect of this death on Virginia has to be imagined. Partly it can be measured by the apparent flippancy with which it is mentioned; partly by the fact that it is printed inside the same kind of square brackets which enclose the reference to her mother's death.

[1] Letter to V. Sackville-West.

[Mr. Ramsay, stumbling along a passage one dark morning, stretched his arms out, but Mrs. Ramsay having died rather suddenly the night before, his arms, though stretched out, remained empty.]

But, forgetting "this damned 'method,'" consider the situation. Stella was in love. Stella postponed her marriage until someone else could take her mother's place in the family life. Then there was a grand wedding; bridesmaids, with bouquets and pretty dresses; bells ringing, sun shining; toasts drunk; happiness ahead. Soon there was to be a baby — lots of babies, lots of fun. Life was winning all along the line. And then — Stella died.

It was all so meaningless. Hope had been renewed. Joy had beckoned. A promise had been made. And then, that promise was not kept. Life was like that, it seemed. Doors opened; and then were slammed in your face. Bridesmaids and babies not wanted.

But the routine at Hyde Park Gate continued, though the house seemed strangely empty now. Thoby Stephen went up to Cambridge in the autumn of 1899 and found new friends. Four of them, Lytton Strachey, Saxon Sydney-Turner, Leonard Woolf and Clive Bell, and Thoby himself, used to meet regularly on Saturdays at midnight in Clive Bell's rooms and called themselves the Midnight Society. They were serious but by no means solemn young men, interested in poetry and in politics, in literature and in life, given to abstract discussion and also enjoying fun. There was nothing sinister or especially purposeful about their society. They just liked one another, without being particularly alike, and, feeling life expanding before them in all sorts of distracting directions, made this little knot as a reminder of the pleasures of friendship.

Vanessa did not find running the London house a dull job: in fact, there were times when it was all too exciting, with their father insisting at intervals that she would ruin him with her extravagance and carelessness about the accounts. These charges were, of course, quite unfounded, being expressions of his own

anxiety and unhappiness such as elderly people often display, and
having no necessary connection with her comparative inexperi-
ence or with the actual financial position. But the fact that his
complaints were unreasonable did not make his querulous out-
breaks easier to deal with. Fortunately they did not last long, and
fortunately there was a sensible and kindly cook in whom Vanessa
found an ally when the only way to appease him was to make a
fool of him. The male-dominated home had become a female-
dominated home, but with a male head of enormous power. The
growing Virginia learned many practical lessons from the experiences of this time. She was not only confirmed in her faith in
Vanessa as a winner of all their battles, just as she had been in
their childhood, but in her conviction of the fundamental stupidity
of men, especially clever men; in the superiority of women in all
matters of making life easier. She resented the indignity of having
to be devious; she resented it on behalf of women as a whole, not
for herself in particular. In theory she had an enormous amount
of freedom to do and think as she pleased. In practice she had at
times to walk very carefully, to choose her moment, get what she
could. Nothing unusual in this, of course. It is the kind of adjust-
ment to the society in which one lives that everyone, male or
female, has to learn how to make. The acceptance of circumstances beyond one's control is often a habit acquired in childhood, at school if not at home. Some people enjoy the little tricks
and subterfuges by which they get their own way. In others the
rebellion against authority is so deeply repressed that they are
unconscious of showing it. They do not realize, for instance, that
an attitude of amused tolerance for the idiosyncrasies of the opposite sex may actually cover a hidden contempt.

Virginia was both proud and analytical. When her father made
a scene and almost reduced Vanessa to tears, it was terrible for
Virginia to have to excuse him for being so majestic and so unreasonable. It was also belittling to his real dignity that they knew
he would be sorry later on and would reproach himself bitterly
and need to be comforted because he was such an unkind father.

There was no longer a mother to bear the brunt of these storms and these repentances. But there was still the cook, who could be relied upon to say, "Never mind. We'll drown this in the milk and smother this in the gas. It's as broad as it's long. It'll all come out in the wash. He'll never know the difference." The cook was a woman. Experience proved that women could usually be trusted to be more sympathetic and understanding than men. You didn't have to do so much explaining to them. They didn't talk the hind leg off a donkey about Morals and Truth and so on; they just produced a practical solution of an immediate problem; and that was the end of that. All the same, when you came to think of it (and, not being the cook, you did think of it) it was not very pleasant to be a conspirator. Why did there have to be a conspiracy of women to circumvent men?

Oh yes, Virginia was free; quite remarkably free for the turn of the century. Virginia had an eager and inquiring mind. Very well, she should be enabled to learn. All the resources of her father's library, the London Library, the British Museum, should be at her disposal. The very best people should come and teach her Greek, if that was what she wanted. (But her brothers went to the university, as a matter of course.) Vanessa wanted to study art, did she? Odd propensity, that. Still, it could be managed. It should never be said of Leslie Stephen that he stood in his children's way. But this business of smoking; he really did have to ask the girls to draw the line at that. He didn't wish to be unreasonable or unkind or old-fashioned; but he must say, he did not like to see women smoking. Permission to choose your own career and promise of help so long as you took your chosen profession seriously, that was worth thousands of cigarettes, Virginia very rightly agreed. Why, then, did she after her father's death take to smoking cheroots, cigars and even a pipe? The obvious explanation is that she still harbored some lingering resentment against her father because he had the power to prevent her from doing as she wished; the awful power of expressing his disapproval. Her rational mind said he had a perfect right to say what he did and did

not like. But if his liking or not liking was based on his feeling of
what was suitable to women and what was not, then she was up
in arms. Her freedom, and Vanessa's, on important matters was
bought at the price of uncounted concessions to his masculine-
Victorian prejudices.

There was no argument about Virginia's becoming a writer.
Her bent in that direction had been clear from her early years.
Her "scribbling" would have aroused no particular surprise, since
in the Stephen home reading and writing were as normal as talking and walking, and when her continued absorption as she grew
older showed that she was serious about it and not merely imitat-
ing her elders, her father probably was gratified and encouraging.
In any event writing was a "reputable and harmless occupation"
for women. "The family peace was not broken by the scratching
of a pen. No demand was made upon the family purse," as she
rather acidly commented in a lecture to the Women's Service
League.[1] The only equipment required was paper, pen and ink.
The only training was the practical one of learning by doing. The
only master was the inner drive.

She had her copybooks, in which she practiced various styles,
notably the Elizabethan prose writers, whom she "loved first and
most wildly." Even as a "little creature" at St. Ives (that is, before
she was thirteen years old) she had tried her hand at a story in
the manner of Hawthorne, as she records in passing in her diary in
1938. One would like to know more. Why was Hawthorne her
model at that time, for instance? Had Godfather Lowell been
recently attending to his spiritual duties of making sure she was
being trained up in the way she should go? And which particular
Hawthorne volume had struck her childish fancy so forcibly? *The
Scarlet Letter* or *The House of the Seven Gables* or *Twice-Told
Tales?* Alas, those old copybooks disappeared long ago. Unless
there was some secret hoarder, some inveterate tidier-up who
could not bear to throw anything away, we shall have to remain
satisfied with the glimpse the diary gives us of the child sitting on

[1] See "Professions for Women" in *The Death of the Moth.*

the "green plush sofa in the drawing-room at St. Ives while the adults dined" in the soft summer twilight, with the sound of the waves breaking on the shore below. Perhaps future generations may yet discover something of what was going on in that little bent head. Those childish scribbles may possibly still exist somewhere and prove to be as delightful as Jane Austen's *Love and Freindship*, as startling and revelatory as the early Brontë manuscripts. But it is useless to speculate about them now. Virginia herself advocated the ruthless scrapping of anything that did not come out right, but fortunately preserved early drafts and later revisions of work in progress which enabled her husband to publish several important posthumous volumes. She also advised her "Young Poet" [1] not to publish anything until he was thirty, when it was too late for her to follow this self-denying ordinance.

What the diary tells us of her writing when she was in her teens is revealing, because it is so exactly what one would expect: "a long picturesque essay upon the Christian religion, I think; called Religio Laici, I believe, proving that man has need of a God; but the God was described in process of change; and I also wrote a history of Women; and a history of my own family — all very long-winded and Elizabethan in style." These are less likely to come to light, for, as she was fifteen or sixteen at the time, she was old enough — and self-conscious enough — to have decided that they were rubbish and to have made sure they were destroyed before anyone else could see them and possibly laugh at her for being so ambitious. Her father would not have laughed; he would never have been so unkind. But he would have applied to them the same standards of criticism which he used in the biographical essays for which he is famous; and that would have been even more paralyzing and crushing than ridicule, however kindly meant to encourage her to persevere.

Her first published writings are not hopelessly irrecoverable, but are hard to trace. As she could never bear to read what she had written in the past (any issue of a journal in which an article

[1] *A Letter to a Young Poet.*

by her appeared was completely ruined for her, she declared),
she deliberately tried to obscure the trail that leads to these early
efforts. She did this by a display of apparent candor.

The "simple story" of her beginnings as a journalist is related
in "Professions for Women." She was "a girl in a bedroom with a
pen in her hand." She "had only to move that pen from left to
right — from ten o'clock to one." This she did, then slipped a few
of the pages into an envelope and dropped the envelope into the
red box at the corner of the street. Result: on the first day of the
next month she received a check for one pound ten shillings and
sixpence, which she promptly spent, not on anything useful but
on buying a beautiful Persian cat which got her into a lot of
trouble with her neighbors.

What could be more factual? But what was she writing about,
and when was this, and where did her contribution appear?

This is where the obscuring begins. According to her own account, the article, "I seem to remember, was about a novel by a
famous man." But directly she came to write she discovered she
had to do battle with a phantom. "I encountered her with the very
first words. The shadow of her wings fell on my page; I heard the
rustling of her skirts in the room. She slipped behind me . . . she
made as if to guide my pen . . . I turned upon her and caught
her by the throat. I did my best to kill her." What was this phantom? "I called her The Angel in the House. In those days — the
last of Queen Victoria — every house had its Angel."

This intensely sympathetic, immensely charming, utterly un-
selfish, completely pure, absolutely paralyzing phantom tried to
tell the young girl in the bedroom she must conceal that she had
a mind of her own, so that no man should be shocked or offended.
The Angel was finally disposed of, only after a prolonged and
severe struggle. But there was still another obstacle to free expression.

Virginia then goes on to describe, very seriously and beautifully and simply, a genuine experience; the creative writer, in the
throes of imaginative labor, being brutally interrupted by the dis-

covery that she has not only a mind but a body, and that though she may have established her right to say what she thinks, there are still many, many things she may not freely say about what she physically feels, or she will arouse severe masculine disapproval.

It is a profound, moving and memorable statement. One is completely convinced of its literal truth. But later, as the magic fades, the young woman of today is not at all sure that she knows quite what Virginia Woolf was really talking about.

Remembering the clear warning to the reader of *A Room of One's Own* that the supposedly factual, hour-by-hour account of what happened is largely imaginary, one begins to suspect that the facts in "Professions for Women" were similarly adjusted to suit the occasion. This would be perfectly justifiable. The truth lies not in the literal facts, but comes from what the writer has to say about them.

So we are left, at this stage, with several unanswered questions, which have ceased to have any great importance.[1] We still do not know whether Leslie Stephen ever saw his daughter's writings in print. But we know a great deal more about her as a young woman, understand much more about why there is so much passion in what she writes about men and women. We feel, too, the gulf between her times and ours; but are unable to explain, as yet, why that gulf does not really separate us, how it can be that her voice sounds so clearly in our ears, abolishing the abyss, linking the generations.

VIRGINIA was not abandoned to her own devices at Hyde Park Gate. She continued to educate herself by practicing in her notebooks or by spending strenuous intellectual hours studying Greek,

---

[1] Her husband is under the impression that this first article may have appeared in *The Speaker,* which was a predecessor to *The Nation.* Leonard Woolf knows that his wife did write reviews for *The Speaker,* but is not certain this was actually the first journal to which she contributed.

or by "mooning about" in her father's library, waiting until he brought her home some more books from the London Library or was ready to go walking with her in the Gardens and the Park.

There were hordes of relations, by blood and by marriage, always ready to descend on the house, without the slightest intention of minding their own business, not to be intimidated by Leslie Stephen when they felt it their social duty to see that the girls were not "mewed up" or "buried alive." Queen Victoria was celebrating her Diamond Jubilee, or the boys were home for the holidays, or there was some other compelling reason why Vanessa and Virginia should be seen, suitably chaperoned and escorted, at various semiformal parties and dances.

It mattered very little to these kind aunts that Vanessa and Virginia detested these affairs. They were both extremely shy, and also very beautiful though not in the then current style, which, in the Naughty Nineties and nineteen hundreds, tended to the opulent and needed a great deal of dressing up for its effectiveness. In later years, when she could give her own parties and had all the social poise imaginable, Virginia would tell young friends how miserable and bored and awkward and uncertain she and Vanessa felt at these parties, and how they were as rude and haughty and unapproachable as they dared, in consequence. She would make it all sound very amusing.

"You can imagine them," said Lord David Cecil, to whom she related some of these anecdotes, "standing grimly silent, proud but drooping, like two beautiful Circassian slaves paraded for sale, gold chains dangling from their wrists . . . But I must say I should have hated to be one of the young men who had to go up and ask them to dance. Of course, they danced beautifully, were quite remarkably graceful. But getting your name on their dance program must have required considerable courage."

Virginia felt as out of place in such an atmosphere as her father did when her mother had gathered all sorts of artistic people to her At Homes, but she did not feel free, as he had, to rush out of the room. She had been properly brought up, knew what was expected of her and behaved accordingly, enduring all this "pleasure" to the bitter end, waiting until Thoby was ready to take her home and she could get her ridiculous ball dress off and relax with Vanessa or a book. She knew that the same standard of manners was not demanded from grown men and from young women. Her comments on this difference are expressed airily enough in, for instance, her novel *Night and Day*, which is full of pictures of the kind of life Virginia Stephen lived at this time. Of an old lady rudely interrupted by a young man she writes, "Happily she belonged to a generation which expected uncouthness in its men." And again: "He strode out of the room, leaving in the minds of the women a sense, half of awe, half of amusement, at the extravagant, inconsiderate, uncivilized male, outraged somehow, and gone bellowing to his lair with a roar which still sometimes reverberates in the most polished of drawing-rooms."

That roar continued to reverberate in Virginia's mind too, long after women of later generations stopped expecting uncouthness in men and had succeeded in making it plain that a little less formal politeness and a good deal more real thoughtfulness was in order.

That uncivilized male, that fierce, intolerable but tender, loving and beloved father continued to work almost to the end and to receive honors from various universities (Oxford, Cambridge, Edinburgh, Harvard) with "amused gratification," as Sir Walter Raleigh said when delivering the first Leslie Stephen Lecture at Cambridge. After Queen Victoria's death in 1901 he was in the Honors List of the new king, Edward VII, acquiring the title of Sir when he became a Knight of the Bath in 1902.

There is a portrait of him with Virginia, taken in 1903. His face is that of a man who has already said his farewell to the world. He looks in the direction the photographer requested in order that the picture shall record his profile — the large forehead, lined with age and pain and concentrated thought, the high cheekbones barely covered with flesh, the fierce nose, the full underlip just visible through the cascading mustache and the beard which quite obscures the chin. But his eyes, sunk in their sockets and shadowed by straggling eyebrows, do not see what he looks at: the gaze is turned inward.

Virginia looks in the same direction, and her face is partly in shadow. A gleam of light on the smooth hair marks the shape of the scalp. Her cheek is soft, the chin is firm, the mouth sensitive, almost tremulous, the nose emphatic but straight and well-proportioned; and her eyes, enormous, under exquisite brows, look outward, with wonder and a slight touch of apprehension. He is the eagle, worn with watching. She is the nestling about to take flight.

Chapter II

SOON after the death from cancer of Sir Leslie Stephen in the early part of 1904, the four young Stephens, Vanessa, Thoby, Virginia and Adrian, left the Kensington mansion at Hyde Park Gate and set up house at 46 Gordon Square, in the northern corner of Bloomsbury.

This district, part of the parish of Holborn, had been — and still is — the home of innumerable persons whose names, for one reason or another, have been scratched on the untidy palimpsest of London's history. But what part of that sprawling city has not its share of illustrious ghosts? It was not with any sense of taking refuge in an artistic colony that the four orphans moved to Bloomsbury. They could have followed Carlyle to Chelsea or William Morris to Hammersmith or Keats to Hampstead, where they would have had a river or a heath to delight them, in place of the park they were leaving. They chose Bloomsbury because it was cheap, convenient and pleasant. All of them must have had, with the confidence of youth, the assurance that they would make their mark or, at the least, not disgrace the name of Stephen by failing to rise above the level of mediocrity. But they could have had no idea that it was quiet, shy, delicate Virginia whose name was to be forever associated with their new home.

Bloomsbury is one of the first examples of town planning and one of the last to indicate a state of mind. About what it was intended to be, what it was and is, how it came to be regarded, it is impossible to be exact. Unnecessary, too. It has always exercised a siren attraction, and what song the sirens sang is something best left to conjecture.

It is a district of squares — very seldom square, of course — such as began to crop up in London after Inigo Jones first laid out Covent Garden as early as 1635. These open spaces express the English love for a room with a view, the desire to look out, even from behind curtains, on something besides bricks and mortar, something leafy and reminiscent of the country, somewhere for the cat to prowl and the dog to be taken for a walk, for birds to nest and children to play.

They combine mateyness with privacy. One is comfortably aware of neighbors, whose screened lights gleam at interesting intervals through the tracery of summer leaves or bare wintry boughs, while property and propriety are (or were until the desperate days of World War II), guarded by enclosing every neat patch of trees and bushes, mown lawns and graveled walks, with iron railings. Gates could be locked against intruders after dark, and during the day there was, within living memory, often a beadle in a tall hat and long coat to see that children and animals, nursemaids and their attendant sweethearts, behaved in a seemly manner.

In fact, these squares are legitimate descendants of the orchards and walled gardens that once surrounded the palaces of the nobles and prelates in the old city and along the Strand, when that higgledy-piggledy thoroughfare was recognizably what its name indicates, a riverbank.

During the prolonged struggles for power between the monarchy, the church, the nobility and (at last) the commons, these mansions of the nobles, swarming with their relations, servants, armed retainers and all sorts and conditions of dependents, were replaced by warehouses and wharves and shops, the homes of merchants, the halls of guildsmen. The population increased steadily, in spite of the Black Death, the falling sickness, the sweating sickness, the plague — call it what you will — which struck again and yet again in the crowded and insanitary metropolis.

The Restoration of Charles II meant the final defeat of the old system and the establishment of centralized government. Thereafter the chances of a peer's dying quietly in his bed were very greatly increased, and only two more kings, James II and Edward VIII, were removed from their thrones. It also marked the beginning of the process which has been going on ever since, the expansion of London, now a county in its own right. The Roman walls can be traced, by excavation; the medieval gates have left their names only; but the modern boundaries exist, in the realm of administration, as invisible as the equator.

The first big wave of the tide that was to sweep away the ancient landmarks occurred when the nobles found it convenient to return from their distant country seats and build new mansions in town. About 1660 the last Earl of Southampton decided to rebuild the old Manor House on his Bloomsbury estate, and laid out a square to the south so as to leave an open view from the great house. This was Southampton Square, later called Bloomsbury Square, and it rapidly became fashionable. For by this time, instead of armed retainers, poor relations and attendant clerics, all needing to be housed and fed under one roof, there had sprung up a new class around the nobility. These were the professional men, the lawyers, the civil servants, the men who had their brains and imagination and art to sell, not the wool or leather or spices of the merchants nor the skill of hands and labor of muscles of the working folk. These men kept their own state, lived in their own houses. It was for them that the squares were first built.

John Evelyn, the diarist, mentioned Bloomsbury Square in 1665; Alexander Pope considered it a good address. In 1678 Montague House was built, and a country lane became Great Russell Street. This was accounted in 1720 a "very handsome and well built street." Now it is narrow and dingy, though still dignified in a stubbornly decrepit way. At present it has the grim job of outfacing the British Museum, which crouches behind its great colonnaded courtyard, built in the nineteenth century on the site of Montague House.

The decline from graceful courtier to surly watchdog has not been eased by its having acquired in the late nineteenth and early twentieth centuries two embarrassingly frisky ends. To the east it received, at an odd angle, the curious and charming tesselated short cut for pedestrians and shoppers known as Sicilian Avenue. To the west, just before it dwindles into Tottenham Court Road, it sports the baroque headquarters of the Y.M.C.A., whose outbreak of cupolas, stone balls and exuberant nude statuary is mutely apologized for by the prim brick box housing the Y.W.C.A. on the other side of the street.

This is the kind of fate that has befallen many a country lane turned city street; Great Russell Street merely summarizes what has happened. The visitor or, for that matter, the native Londoner, does not need to know anything about history or architecture or even to be particularly observant; the very slightest sensitivity to his surroundings will give him London's invitation to wander, to find out what can happen next. He may be startled or amused, but seldom stung into scornful derision, for what he is seeing, whether he is aware of it or not, is the poetry of endeavor, the indomitable attempt of urban man to make his home beautiful, even if it be expressed by a sort of housewifely, "I know this room is filthy and full of junk, but I'm going to tidy up this corner."

The district north of New Oxford Street and High Holborn was not fated to become the really fashionable part of London. As Anatole France remarked, all great cities turn westward. In the east, where the sun rises, the poor get up early and go to work; in the west the homes of the rich receive the last gleams of sunset. But Bloomsbury, grimly interrupted by the forbidding Tottenham Court Road to the west, and the even more daunting Theobald's Road to the south and Gray's Inn Road to the west, could only move northward, over the meadows of the old Southampton Manor House, until it finally reached, in the nineteenth century, the bleak cliffs of the great railroad stations to the north, Euston, King's Cross and St. Pancras. It declined from fashion to respectability to downright dinginess.

The basic plan of squares and tree-lined streets, however, remained, imposing on successive architects the need for aiming at an appearance of restraint without rigidity, for a degree of formality and elegance, for avoiding the caprices of romantic fancy which are fundamentally poetic but which so often strike later generations as comic or vulgar.

The characteristic Bloomsbury house, which still persists, is in the style usually known as Georgian. It has a weathered brick face, rarely ornamented apart from stone facings on fanlight doorways; neatly spaced and well-proportioned windows narrowly inset, except for the dormer windows which light the attics and vary the line of the steep, slate roofs. Dispensing with a front garden because it shares the plane trees and lilac bushes of the square with its neighbors, it would be flush with the sidewalk were it not for the plunging "area" steps leading to the cellar and kitchen in the semibasement. It is dignified and discreet. It manages to avoid fussiness and flamboyance, to escape the pompities of caryatids, pillars and porticoes. It is never coy or quaint, makes no pretense of being rustic, does not set out to charm or intimidate, is content to be the kind of house which a logical, self-respecting citizen could expect to enter without slinking or being announced by a flourish of trumpets.

When the four young Stephens moved to Bloomsbury the process of decay and change was already marked, but it was still a pleasant, gracious, airy and comparatively quiet neighborhood.

Quiet was important for all of them, because they had been brought up to respect it. It was particularly important to Virginia, who had learned from her scholarly father that absence of conversation did not mean withdrawal of companionship. "Taking his hat and his stick," she wrote of him many years later, "calling for his dog and his daughter, he would stride off into

Kensington Gardens. . . . He was not then in the least 'alarming'; he was very simple, very confiding; and his silence,
though one might last unbroken from the Round Pond to the
Marble Arch, was curiously full of meaning, as if he were thinking half aloud, about poetry and philosophy and people he had
known."

No unearthly hush can ever have pervaded a house as crowded
as theirs had been, but when their father tramped upstairs to
his study, chanting as he went any kind of verse that came into
his head or suited his mood, then one knew better than to be
rowdy; at least one was quiet enough on the floor below to note
with affectionate respect and amusement the sound of the books,
being dumped unceremoniously around him as he read and wrote.
Since Virginia already knew that she was going to read and write,
the new home must contain a room in which she could work un-
disturbed. Vanessa needed a studio, with good light and plenty
of space; her demand, as an artist, was less for quiet than for
elbow room. The two young men, Adrian and Thoby, were studi-
ous but sociable; more used from school and university life to
racket and distraction, they were also more secure than their
sisters in their traditional masculine immunity from domestic
uproar.

For even in the best run household, in the most select neighborhood, peace and quiet were as hard to get in the early years
of this century as they are today. The idea that cities get noisier
and noisier is part of the cherished illusion that in the old days
everything was more pleasant and easy. Cities may register
more in decibels as the decades go by, but what really changes
is not the quantity but the quality of sounds measured in terms
of their power to distract, to interrupt and eventually to drive to
frenzy.

A house in a London residential district in Edwardian times
vibrated all day long with some kind or another of strident
clamor. Most of the household necessities we now buy in super-
markets or order by telephone were trundled through the streets

by traders screaming their wares or offering their services. The steady throb which rises from a big city today is far less insistent and disturbing than the hundred small cries, forever threatening to break into intelligibility, which assailed the ears of anyone trying to concentrate. Particularly if she were a woman and therefore automatically invested with some degree of domestic responsibility. Virginia, the girl who found her father's silences full of meaning, became in Bloomsbury the young woman for whom household sounds had meaning, became the writer who transmuted these irritations remembered in tranquillity into her own kind of poetry.

For example, here is a passage from *Jacob's Room* (published in 1922). Betty Flanders, widow, mother of two sons fighting in World War I, wakes in the night.

"Not at this distance," she thought. "It is the sea."
Again, far away, she heard the dull sound, as if nocturnal women were beating great carpets.

It is an image that would never occur to a man. If he ever heard that peculiarly horrible and ominous thud of carpets being beaten he would probably interpret it correctly as a warning that some woman was on a cleaning rampage again and he had better make himself scarce. In these days of vacuum cleaners it is not an image that would present itself to anyone.

Another example from the same novel shows how Virginia used the intrusion of a sound to sharpen a picture. Jacob, on a boat between the Scilly Islands and Cornwall one sunny day, looks shoreward.

The mainland, not so very far off — you could see clefts in the cliffs, white cottages, smoke going up — wore an extraordinary look of calm, of sunny peace, as if wisdom and piety had descended upon the dwellers there. Now a cry sounded, as of a man calling pilchards in a main street. It wore an extraordinary look of piety and peace, as if old men smoked by the door, and girls

stood, hands on hips, at the well, and horses stood; as if the end
of the world had come, and cabbage fields and stone walls, and
coast-guard stations, and, above all, the white sand bays with the
waves breaking unseen by any one, rose to heaven in a kind of
ecstasy.

Here a sound, heard far off, not understood, not needing to be
understood, comes at first like a cruel interruption; cleaves the
still air, is enfolded again by a repetition of the "extraordinary
look of piety and peace": it is no longer an interruption, but the
dark downstroke a painter might use to tie his composition together, to fix on his canvas a picture almost unbearably bright,
almost quivering away into invisibility.

Such mastery over words, such technical skill as these two
quotations and innumerable other passages show, is not easily
acquired. It is possible that the young Virginia had this power
at her command much earlier than we know, since miracles do
happen and genius is not like measles or senility, something
likely to manifest itself at certain periods of growth. If the old
copybooks in which she scribbled romances, practiced styles and
drafted essays had not disappeared, there might be evidence
that she was a child prodigy. But nothing seems to have been
preserved to suggest she was ever such a little horror; and literature has probably benefited by the fact that she was not in
her very early years surrounded by adoring relatives unused to
manifestations of youthful brilliance. She was the daughter of a
critic, a critic herself, trained to intellectual honesty, aware from
her acquaintance with the celebrities of the day and her knowledge of the great writers of the past that literature is not produced easily and automatically, but results from hard work and
long practice.

Duncan Grant, the artist, recalling her as she was at this early
period of her long and self-imposed apprenticeship to her craft,
this opening stage of her life without Father, indicates that she
seemed, in fact, slow in developing to maturity. "I do not think,"
he wrote in *Horizon* in 1941, "that her new existence had 'be-

come alive' to Virginia's imagination in those first years. She gave the impression of being so intensely receptive to any experience new to her, and so interested in facts that she had not come across before, that time was necessary to give it meaning as a whole. It took the years to complete her vision of it."

So, paradoxically, her workroom had double windows, not to keep out the street sounds (which was impossible) but in order that she might hear them better, so that the man calling fish was not an intruder but an integral part of her picture.

Far from wishing to cut herself off from contact with the busy life around her, she was eager to share it. All her life she loved to take long walks, to ride on buses through crowded thoroughfares, noting, listening, above all enjoying. What she observed and experienced during these hours of mingling with all sorts and conditions of men and women became the raw material of her writing. In theory she never worked more than two hours a day. In practice, as her work sheets and time schedules and diary show, when she was in good health she found it advisable to work no more than two hours at a stretch at any one job. Actually she was working all the time, secreting, storing, sorting, digesting. Those two hours were hours of furious concentration when what had been filtered through her imagination was made to give up its poetry and its significance. They were hours when she tried to tear the very heart of truth out of the world of appearances. These alone were the hours when the actual sounds had to be muffled.

There was all the difference in the world between a Cornishman announcing in his soft West Country accent that there was a run of pilchards or mackerel freshly caught and a London fishmonger indicating that he was around if you happened to want cod or kippers or herring in a hurry; he was no sweet Molly Malone to sing "Cockles and mussels, alive, alive-oh" in perfect tune, with a pleasant piano accompaniment.

London street cries are beautiful enough when we think of the pretty eighteenth-century colored prints used to decorate hotel bedrooms or to advertise soap. In fact, however, no pretty girl, neatly shod, with a perfect complexion and wearing a large hat, delicately proffered her wares. More often one heard the distressful growls of a tired old woman, dressed in filthy rags to indicate gypsy origin, although she probably emerged from a slum, who inquired mournfully, off key, and without any apparent hope of success, "Who'll buy my lav-en-der? Sixteen branches for one penny." The costermonger or greengrocer employed no choir of children to sing "Cherry ripe." He just yelled that he had carrots "penny-a-bench" or "lovely rhubarb" or "strorbries, tanner-a-pahnd," or whatever else was going cheap at Covent Garden market that day, or the previous day. The milkman rattled his churns to announce that if you wanted milk you had better have your jugs ready at the area door, when he would crash open the side gate, clatter down the side steps on his iron-tipped boots and engage in cheerful conversation with the cook about the weather — an inexhaustible topic at all times. The chimney sweep was a horror to see, a nightmare to hear; but he must not be missed, for someone was always sure to be complaining that the drawing room fire did not draw properly or that the flues of the kitchen stove were choked again, and goodness alone knew when the grinning monster, white teeth flashing in a soot-grimed face, would be along again. The worst offender was the coalman, always terrifying, always unintelligible; one could listen in anguish to find out just what kind of coal he had for sale and in the end make nothing of his cry but a sad — and obviously non-sensical — "mauvais temps."

What did the artist, tormented by these shrieks, bewildered by these howls, do with all this kind of gravel that London kept unloading on the lawns and flower beds of her mind? She turned it into poetry. Here is Peter Walsh coming out of Regent's Park, recalling his old, unhappy love for Clarissa Dalloway:

A sound interrupted him: a frail quivering sound, a voice bubbling up without direction, vigour, beginning or end, running

weakly and shrilly and with an absence of all human meaning
into

ee um fah um so
foo swee too eem oo —

the voice of no age or sex, the voice of an ancient spring spouting
from the earth; which issued, just opposite Regent's Park Tube
station from a tall quivering shape, like a funnel, like a rusty
pump, like a wind-beaten tree for ever barren of leaves which
lets the wind run up and down its branches singing

ee um fah um so
foo swee too eem oo

and rocks and creaks and moans in the eternal breeze. . . .

Still remembering how once in some primeval May she had
walked with her lover, this rusty pump, this battered old woman
with one hand exposed for coppers the other clutching her side,
would still be there in ten million years, remembering how once
she had walked in May, where the sea flows now, with whom it
did not matter — he was a man, oh yes, a man who had loved
her. But the passage of ages had blurred the clarity of that
ancient May day; the bright petalled flowers were hoar and silver
frosted; and she no longer saw, when she implored him (as she
now did quite clearly) "Look in my eyes with thy sweet eyes
intently," she no longer saw brown eyes, black whiskers or sun-
burnt face but only a looming shape, a shadow shape, to which,
with the bird-like freshness of the very aged she still twittered
"give me your hand and let me press it gently" (Peter Walsh
couldn't help giving the poor creature a coin as he stepped into
his taxi), "and if some one should see, what matter they?" she
demanded; and her fist clutched at her side, and she smiled,
pocketing her shilling, and all peering inquisitive eyes seemed
blotted out, and the passing generations — the pavement was
crowded with bustling middle-class people — vanished, like
leaves, to be trodden under, to be soaked and steeped and made
mould of by that eternal spring —

ee um fah um so
foo swee too eem oo

Cheerfully, almost gaily, the invincible thread of sound wound
up into the air like a smoke from a cottage chimney, winding
up clean beech trees and issuing in a tuft of blue smoke among
the topmost leaves. "And if some one should see, what matter
they?"

This is not Ophelia turning everything to favor and to prettiness; it is Prospero releasing Caliban so that his wretchedness, his ugliness, his spite change from a persecution of the spirit to a benediction.

Not all the street sounds were unpleasant. The most welcome announcement was the bell of the muffin man (who sold crumpets from a covered tray balanced on his head and wore a green baize apron) because that was just one regular clang and it was, as a rule, only heard on dull Sunday afternoons in winter, just as it was getting dark, when one had recovered from the torpor following midday dinner and the fire was just right for toasting something for tea on long forks, skirts out of the way of any falling cinders, cheeks just beyond the scorching range.

And then there were the sounds which, while not reminding a woman of household chores to be done or to see about having done, were just plain maddening — the hurdy-gurdies, the barrel organs, the brass bands, the hymn singers, all needing to be bribed to go away, at their amiably remorseless snail's pace. The horses, too. Doubtless the horse is a noble animal, to be loved and admired and tended faithfully, and the work horse is a patient beast, often the pride and joy and main support of his owner, a friend of the family, to be sleeked up and adorned with ribbons and paraded annually so that he can win more ribbons and more praise. It is not his fault that he is shod with iron and draws iron-wheeled carts along stone-paved streets; nor that he is started and stopped by traditional growls, groans, grunts and, frequently, curses; nor that children delight to shriek "Whip be'ind, guv'nor!" to warn his driver that other urchins are trying to board the vehicle from the rear. Neither can he be blamed if he occasionally responds to all this goading by throwing back his head and emitting what sounds like a scream of demonic laughter. All the same one has to admit that as a user of the streets and as an occupier of a mews or stable he is noisier and less predictable than his modern successor. A Bloomsbury Square, having its garden in the front, almost always had a mews at the back, picturesque, smelly, housing poor people and poor horses; at the turn of the century it had not yet become a garage, a studio or an elegant home.

London also was at that time a city of innumerable churches, almost all of them equipped with peals of bells arid chiming clocks. Big Ben had hundreds of competitors in announcing the time every quarter of an hour. True, they did not all agree with one another about the time, but then, as the Irish porter asked Lord Dunsany, what would be the good of two clocks telling the same time? At least they were useful as weather prophets, since you could tell from which direction the wind was blowing according to whether it was the church around the corner or the one along the street whose iron notes cleaved the air most forcibly. Little wonder that Virginia's thoughts so often turned to time, since she was so constantly reminded of its passage.

There was still another persistent sound. Owing to its large number of open spaces, so that, seen from any hilltop, the city seems lost in trees, London is a Babel of birds. Enchanting as it is to hear, as you ride on a bus or walk past a garden, the song of a lark or a thrush, the inanely cheerful or inanely mournful notes of sparrows and pigeons can become almost unendurable. These impudent little beggars, who could pick up an easy living all the year round from the nosebags of horses if housewives were not generous with crumbs or trees with insects and worms, throve exceedingly and seemed convinced it was their business to arouse all sleepers at the first crack of dawn. Of recent years they have become less numerous, either because they find automobiles an unacceptable substitute for horses from their point of view, or because they dislike the millions of starlings which now infest the city and defy all attempts to dislodge them. Poison, electrocution, supersonic sound, nothing seems to discourage them. During the day they go out to the suburbs for food, and when the workers go back home in the evenings, the starlings return to town and carry on all night long a deafening chatter, a ferocious caricature of human discussion about nothing at all.

This last manifestation of natural idiocy Virginia was spared. In her time the starlings had not multiplied beyond all bearing, they had not become so strangely urbanized, had not adopted the queer counter-commuting pattern they now follow. For some reason not yet explained they were largely limited to colonies in the trees of the Inner Temple, and their version of what goes on in a court of law was less devastating than their present performance around the Admiralty and Trafalgar Square.

Also, by the evening work had been put aside by mutual consent and the brothers and sisters gathered for social life. There would have been, of course, plenty of coming and going during the day, for the horde of relations and family friends would be not only interested but concerned to make sure everything was all right. It was not that the young people were considered incompetent to look after themselves, particularly as the cook Sophie and the maid Maud were still with them, and Vanessa had shown her ability to run a large household in a way to satisfy the most exacting critic.

But what was novel, and therefore faintly perturbing in those days, was that the new household in Gordon Square had no boss, revolved around no central male. This would be, to an Edwardian, as odd as having a village without a church. In spite of Leslie Stephen's recurrent pretense that bankruptcy was imminent and that the family would have to retire to the outposts of Wimbledon (a highly flourishing and respectable suburb, by the way, even before international lawn tennis made it famous), he was able to leave each of his children comfortably provided for. Even if it had occurred to either of the brothers to start ordering his sisters about, he could not have enforced his will against theirs, since they were all financially independent. Thoby might be "pressing and exacting" with Virginia about reading Shakespeare, but that was because he wanted her to share his enthusiasm. But he would not, for instance, say, "I do not like Persian cats and therefore you shall not have one," or "I consider your clothes not at all becoming or suitable for a young woman, and they are much too expensive in any case."

No crises implying the supremacy of the male will or whim interfered with a regime based on affection, tolerance and mutual respect; they all knew from experience what devastating domestic storms can blow up when one person controls the purse strings and he, however beloved and benevolent and believing in freedom, is old, sick, disappointed and deaf. But not disappointed in his children, nor fearful of their future. In the last entry of his journal their father had written: "It comforts me to think that you are all so fond of each other that when I am gone you will be the better able to do without me."

By pooling their resources the young people presented a united, if unconventional, front. It was an arrangement so sensible, so logical and so successful that it was bound to be bewildering to a society still dedicated to the ideal of the Victorian Papa, in practice if not in theory. By pooling their friends as well as pursuing their own separate avocations they brought into being, without conscious intent, what later became the famous Bloomsbury Group. It was they and their friends who, without in the least desiring or planning it, were in the first place responsible for turning Bloomsbury into a state of mind.

Chapter III

THE ODD thing is that it was not to these residents of Bloomsbury that Bloomsbury was a state of mind. To them it was not
anything in particular except somewhere to live and work. It
aroused in them no violent local patriotism, any more than St.
Ives inspired Virginia to write purely Cornish novels. Away
from Bloomsbury, as they frequently were, they experienced no
great pangs of nostalgia. Call it Gloomsbury, for all they cared.
It never caused them to write romantic ballads in its praise;
Southampton Row never appeared in their dreams transformed
into the Swanee River but remained obstinately a convenient
street where one could always catch a bus. They did not debate
the difference between the various squares, whether Woburn's
lilac was more lovely than Torrington's iris, or Gordon's chrysan-
themums more glorious than those in Kensington Gardens. They
did not occupy themselves with exploring Bloomsbury's antiqui-
ties or form a society for preserving its amenities or celebrating
the anniversaries of its former famous inhabitants. Nor did they
send out expeditions to identify the statues with which it
abounds, nor seek to make the first successful ascent of the steeple of St. George's Church and bring back proof that it was true,
as alleged, that the stone figure crowning that neat but improbable stepped pyramid shows King George I as England's dragon-
slaying saint. Though this last was the kind of exploit that might
have appealed to young men from Cambridge; indeed, it is hard
to believe that it did not, and one waits for the discovery by

some future historian that they did in fact succumb to this temptation.

The suggestion that there was any special geographical significance connected with the work they were doing or the ideas that interested them would have seemed fantastic, and as a matter of fact no such suggestion was made until the growing reputation of Virginia and her friends had made them objects of envy, malice and all uncharitableness so that "Bloomsbury" became a convenient term of abuse among their detractors and a suitable symbol to their would-be imitators.

But this was far in the future, long after the first Bloomsbury Group — if such it could be called — had broken up and the surviving members had come together again, with new friends, in a state of society vastly changed by World War I.

What happened in the first place was, quite simply, that Thoby Stephen, having entertained his friends at Hyde Park Gate, now had a home of his own in London and entertained his friends there. The original members of the Midnight Society of his Cambridge days gathered when they could in Gordon Square. Vanessa and Virginia acted as hostesses and joined in the talk. Such evenings were very different from the semiformal dances, at which you dressed like a fool, felt a fool, and were expected to talk like a fool; and then pretend you were enjoying yourself. Virginia was still extremely shy, but at last she had a real opportunity to enjoy male society on terms of frankness and equality. She was not now oppressed in spirit by the aged celebrities who had visited her father and had either made her feel nervous because of her admiration of their achievements or seemed to her pompous bores. She began to blossom, particularly if Thoby approved.

The friends were interested in all manner of things, but certainly not in forming any sort of group. This was a time of expansion, not of settling down. They wanted fun and freedom and adventure. They had to experiment in ways of living, choose careers. They knew that the "changes and chances of this mortal life" loomed ahead.

So this early Bloomsbury Group began to break up almost as soon as it formed. Leonard Woolf, for instance, took a job in the Ceylon Civil Service in 1904, and was away from London until 1911.

The fatigues and excitements of the new way of life caused Virginia to have a mental and physical breakdown in 1905. When she recovered the family decided to take a holiday traveling in Europe.

Greece was their goal. What Greece meant to them, especially to Thoby and Virginia, is more than can ever be told, since she herself failed, in spite of many efforts, to analyze the reasons for the compelling fascination that Greek had for her. Greece was much more to them than sunshine and honey and ruins. They sought the Greece of the poets, philosophers, sculptors, lawgivers, heroes: a more glorious Greece than the ancient Greeks can ever have known, since they merely lived in it and can never have guessed what their struggles and defeats and attempts to understand the world and to expound a way of living would mean to countless generations long after their temples were overthrown, their gods and heroes entertainment for children, even the pronunciation of their language a matter of debate.

What the young Stephens found was, naturally, disillusioning as well as stimulating, for the Greece of the imagination can only be visited by the imagination, and remains inviolate even if there are bugs in the beds and the hotels are crowded with tourists and the language one has struggled so hard to learn is different from what one had been led to believe. The reader can discover a great deal about what they hoped to see in the essay "On Not Knowing Greek" (*The Common Reader*, Vol. I); and what they actually saw in the novel *Jacob's Room*.

There was the Acropolis; but had they [Jacob and Sandra] actually reached it? The columns and the Temple remain; the emotion of the living breaks fresh on them year after year; and of that what remains? As for reaching the Acropolis, who shall say that we ever do it, or that when Jacob woke next morning he found anything hard and durable to keep for ever?

Virginia visited Greece again twenty-seven years later. "It was so strange coming back here again," she wrote to Vita Sackville-West in 1932. "I hardly knew where I was; or when it was. There was my own ghost coming down from the Acropolis, aged 23; and how I pitied her."

But whether the Virginia of twenty-three was melancholy because she doubted one can ever really reach the Acropolis; or whether the Virginia of fifty pitied the girl because she was happy and therefore vulnerable to the malice of the jealous gods, this is uncertain.

The next thing to happen was a very heavy blow indeed. Modern Greece breeds ancient pests. There was no World Health Organization in those days to make inoculation a prerequisite to obtaining a passport visa. A vicious typhoid germ attacked; and Thoby failed to survive. Once more Virginia's world was laid in waste around her. Thoby, the magnificent, adored Thoby, whom everybody without exception loved, vanished.

But not from her memory. He came back to her in dreams and visions and in the person of her favorite nephew, Julian Bell. He is the Jacob of *Jacob's Room*, and the mysterious, symbolic Percival in *The Waves*. Death preserved his image as on a Grecian urn, "forever young, forever fair."

R. F. Harrod, the biographer of Lord Keynes, describes him thus: "Handsome, gifted, winning, idolized by a group of the most brilliant youth of Cambridge, entirely unspoilt, taking all admiration with unselfconscious gracefulness, a man of affairs, one who might make a great mark in the world. He deserves to be remembered."

Though his loss to the world cannot be measured, his loss to Virginia can be gauged. In a way he replaced her father; that is, she valued his approval. But she did not have to resist his domination. There is a great deal more freedom in a happy relationship between brother and sister than between parent and child or between husband and wife. There is no need to placate or charm. So much is taken for granted, without emotional stress, so much understood without explanation. Brothers and sisters may quarrel — they frequently do; or drift apart, in space or in feeling — which happens more often than they care to admit. But even when they remain closely linked by affection and understanding in adult life, they do not, as a rule, impinge to any great extent on one another. The sufferometer is not overworked, seldom indicates an uncomfortable nearness to the danger mark.

If Thoby had lived he could have helped Virginia to overcome her shyness and her annoyance with herself for her "angularities." She needed, particularly at this time, all the assurance she could get that men were not secretly as ill at ease with her as she was with them, or that their expressed admiration did not really mask an insufferable condescension, or their indifference reveal an appalling insensitivity. She would in later years have suffered far fewer agonies of apprehension about criticism of her work if she had been able to outgrow her exaggerated fears that men would be kind to her because she was a woman, or dismiss her as negligible for the same irrelevant reason. Her cloistered adolescence had left her unfitted for easy social intercourse; she knew all the rules without being able to enjoy the game. Love and marriage she was not ready for yet; they would have interfered with the freedom and solitude she required for her development. Thoby's gay acceptance of life as it came would have been of great help to her in facing a world she felt to be brutal and rough and fundamentally indifferent — which, of course, it is — and at the same time full of glories and adventures — which, of course, it is. The casual offer of a brother's helping hand now and then was what she needed to encourage her to step right out from her father's library and join the fun. As it was, she had to nerve herself to do it, always fearing that the "pallid bust of Pallas just above the chamber door" would come crashing down on her head as she crossed the threshold. And Thoby was not there to laugh and brush her down and say, "Silly old things, these plaster casts; fall apart as soon as you look at them. Come on. You look a mess, but who cares?"

An enormous amount of the peevish irritability and exacerbated pride which her diary shows to have been one of her regular fluctuations in mood would have been spared her if she had had for some years the continued assurance by an elder brother that practically none of the things that bothered her really mattered. Her reason told her this was so; experience taught her that it was. But that is not the same thing. What she needed was someone to get her into the habit of laughing things off. It had to be a man, so that she could get rid of the notion that men were all basically stupid and patronizing; and it had to be a man with whom there was no question of emotional entanglement, no extra love demand such as her father had made on her. Thoby could have eased her path very considerably, without knowing he was doing it. But she lost him too soon. She formed very bad mental habits in these Edwardian days. She preferred, she told herself, to trudge along her way, footsore and dusty, cursing the people who offered her a lift in case they did it out of kindness because she was a woman, and equally cursing those who did not even trouble to notice her. Sometimes she would pick up a stone and hurl it at a passing car and grin if her aim was good and then feel quite friendly to the outraged driver — if, say, he was Arnold Bennett. And if she had a car of her own, or had accepted a lift, then she would be apt to torment herself with thoughts of other women, on other roads, who still had to trudge alone with blistered heels, whom she could do nothing practical to help — which is her basic feminist attitude.

It was a generous attitude, but a wasteful one, either when it was expressed in self-reproach (a very bad mental habit carried over from her father) or in futile explosions of anger.

Having found at the outset of her writing career that she must do battle with the Angel in the House, she was inevitably a feminist. But, since she was on the winning side in that long war and had nothing to complain of personally, why not forget it? asks the young woman of the 1950s. Her own friends were puzzled and regretful to find her so extremely touchy still in the 1930s. Why did she have to continue to suffer on behalf of women as a whole? She herself was astonished and finally bored by Dame Ethel Smyth's outpourings on the subject. Why could she not see that her own readiness to suspect a sneer and resent an implied insult was also out of date, unnecessary, and a waste of time?

The probable explanation is that these friends were younger women, and that Dame Ethel Smyth was older. Only women just coming to maturity in the first decade of this century can understand how fierce were the battles about women's rights in those days.

We are accustomed to looking back on the years before the 1914-1918 war as a period of stability and peace, a glittering if not golden age. Fond illusion. Internationally it cannot have been true or the war would not have broken out. Nationally it is never true that life is peaceful and quiet: in every country there is always a tremendous row of some kind or other going on. Domestically the Edwardian uproar was awful.

Women like Ethel Smyth were old enough and physically vigorous enough to decide whether or not they should abandon their art and their careers and fling themselves into the militant movement for women's suffrage. If they decided in the affirmative they usually went to prison, were forcibly fed or otherwise maltreated, and in any case met with so much contumely and derision that they lived thereafter in an intermittent state of near paranoia which no amount of future honor and respect could really cure.

Schoolgirls found it fun. They enjoyed arguments among themselves and were perfectly used to being told to make less noise. They also enjoyed provoking their elders by asking awkward questions. If Mother gave one answer and Father another and they could quote Teacher as giving a third and a newspaper a fourth, the confusion that followed was most amusing. If they were serious and none of the answers satisfied them, this merely confirmed the low opinion they already had of the honesty or intelligence of their supposed betters. And if the "children should be seen and not heard" rule was finally invoked against them, that was easily shrugged off. Very rarely was any permanent injury done in such skirmishes with authority.

But women of Virginia's age and state of development were continually being annoyed and interrupted by the incessant discussions. They could not be indifferent because they were seldom let alone to do what they wanted without being teased and tormented and advised and adjured and expected to agree with someone or another (man or woman) that some other woman was either a disgrace to her sex or an ornament. They could seldom give the right answer; agreement might leave them feeling disloyal to a friend or cowardly for evading an issue; disagreement might lead to an exchange of unforgivable insults or to smoldering resentment that might break out later at the slightest provocation. Sufficient heat was engendered in nearly every household at this time to keep the witches' caldron continually on the boil.

Virginia was not far enough advanced in her chosen career to be able to sacrifice it for any other interest. She was not physically strong enough to be any use defending a barricade. She respected, perhaps envied, women who were cast in a heroic mold; but she had no impulse to emulate them. Her job was to perfect herself as a writer; of that she was sure. She was too analytical and had too much common sense to imagine that she would be any good as a crusader. She was too skeptical and intelligent to believe that her adherence to any particular cause would make much difference in bringing about heaven on earth. She did not think she was above the battle, but she could not avoid thinking the battle cries were rather ridiculous. It was un-

fortunate for her peace of mind that she never quite ceased to
hear them.

IF THE group of friends and relations who were constantly
meeting in Bloomsbury in this prewar time had begun to form
a world of their own, it was a world in a state of flux. In 1907
Adrian and Virginia moved from Gordon Square to Fitzroy
Square, when Vanessa married Clive Bell, one of Thoby's oldest
friends, who later made a brilliant name for himself as an art
critic by his provocative, persuasive and influential writings.
Thus the imaginary circle acquired a second center.

A few doors away from Adrian and Virginia in Fitzroy Square
the artist Duncan Grant shared rooms with John Maynard
Keynes, the economist. Later these four shared a house in
Brunswick Square for a short time. Duncan Grant was a cousin
of Lytton Strachey. Keynes was a friend of Lytton Strachey and
Leonard Woolf. Desmond MacCarthy, the critic, who for many
years used the pen name of Affable Hawk, was a close friend,
and it was his wife who coined the name "Bloomsberries" round
about 1910 or 1911, for private convenience, not for public
mystification. Music was represented by Sydney Saxon-Turner;
mathematics by H. T. J. Norton. Roger Fry, artist and art critic,
became an intimate and beloved friend some years before he
opened his famous Omega Workshop in Fitzroy Square. E. M.
Forster was an occasional and much appreciated addition to the
group, whenever he came to London.

They were all brilliant, all different, all free to come and go.
On Thursday evenings Adrian's study on the ground floor of the
Fitzroy Square house was the place where they met, informally.
They drank whiskey, or cocoa, and ate buns. And talked. There
was no set entertainment, no agenda, no minutes; just conver-
sation. But it must have been absorbing conversation, since it

very often went on until one or two o'clock in the morning. Anything and everything could be discussed freely, even in the
presence of "the ladies." This was a notable break with the conventions of the times. It was not a descent into rowdy Bohe-
mianism. Virginia was shy and never attempted to lead the conversation. She did much more listening than talking. But any
young man who was less than honest in his expressions of opinion because women were in the room, or who was not prepared
to hear a woman reply as frankly as if she, too, was an intelligent
and educated human being, would very soon find that he ceased
to be welcome.

Miss Virginia Stephen was definitely at this time not willing
to appear as a beautiful Circassian slave; nor was she yet ready
to laugh at herself for the fierceness with which she rebuffed
any young man who attempted to conciliate her with an ill-
advised compliment on her success in that superfeminine role.
She was still the little tigress behind the wicket in the old St.
Ives garden snapshot. And Adrian was still a mass of giggles.

One of his friends at Cambridge was William Horace de Vere
Cole; usually known simply as Horace Cole, "Molar" Cole to his
intimates, and, to newspapers, as the "world's champion hoaxer."
While they were still undergraduates they had the bright idea of
dressing up as German officers, taking command of a detachment of troops and marching them across the frontier into
France. However, it occurred to them in time that the Kaiser
might not be amused and that the complications following
upon such an international incident might be disproportionately serious to the ease of such a simple exploit. They next
thought of impersonating the Sultan of Zanzibar, who was then
visiting England, and paying a state visit to Cambridge. Caution
again prevailed: to these wild young men the chancellor of the
university was more formidable when angered than the Emperor
of Germany. So they invented an uncle for the sultan and
played their trick on the mayor of Cambridge, not on the university authorities. The story leaked out and made newspaper

headlines. They were traced, and everyone in England enjoyed the joke, except the mayor and corporation of Cambridge. These irate officials demanded vengeance, but the vice-chancellor of the university persuaded them that the least said was the soonest mended; and the incident was considered closed.

A few years later the irrepressible Cole had another proposition to discuss with Adrian. This time Virginia was brought in on the mischief. The idea originated in the wish of one naval officer to pull the leg of another naval officer, who happened to be a cousin of Virginia's and Adrian's and also happened to be chief of staff to the admiral in command of the Channel Fleet, then assembled at Weymouth. Cole's characteristic suggestion was that the Emperor of Abyssinia and his suite should visit the Admiral's flagship, the *Dreadnought*.

Six people took part in the masquerade. Theatrical costumiers came to Fitzroy Square to arrange convincing make-up. Anthony Buxton posed as the emperor; Virginia, Duncan Grant and Guy Ridley as his attendants. This meant having their faces blackened, gumming on false beards and mustaches, and wearing elaborate Eastern-looking robes. Adrian was to act as interpreter; he needed only a little sunburn powder and some false hair as a disguise, it was considered, though his height (he was six feet five inches tall) made him eminently recognizable at a glance. Cole, who was to play the part of a young gentleman from the Foreign Office, just had to wear a top hat and tail coat in order to look thoroughly convincing.

After they had left London by train for Weymouth a telegram was sent to the admiral to warn him of their coming. It was signed in the name of the permanent head of the Foreign Office, but was actually sent by a fellow prankster with the believe-it-or-not name of Tudor Castle. On the journey Cole tried to teach Adrian a few words and phrases of Swahili, taken from a grammar issued by the Society for the Propagation of the Gospel, and Adrian also practiced speaking in an unnaturally deep bass, with a supposedly German accent, instead of in his normal voice.

Everything went well, though they had several narrow escapes from detection. They were met at the station with appropriate ceremony and conducted to the harbor, where a smart steam launch was waiting to take them to the *Dreadnought*. On board, the marines were lined up on deck, and the admiral and his staff, all in full-dress uniform, were ready to receive them. Flags were flying; the band played.

Almost the first person Adrian met was his cousin, who stared hard at him, but decided not to believe the evidence of his own eyes. The next person to whom he was introduced by Cole was the captain of the ship; he turned out to be a man Adrian knew well and had taken long country walks with. But once again the disguise held; plus the inconceivability of any-one's daring to have the impudence to try and fool the Royal Navy.

When called upon to convey the admiral's welcome to the emperor, Adrian could remember only a few even faintly Swahili-sounding words. But at school he had had to memorize whole stretches of Latin and Greek, so he called Virgil and Homer to his aid and rattled off a lot of classical poetry, remem-bering to take care to make it into meaningless nonsense by mispronouncing and breaking up words, hoping that no one would trace to its source this babble of schoolboy double talk. No one did, though he overheard two officers commenting on the "oddness" of the "lingo." Soon after, he was told there was one man in the fleet who knew Abyssinian; but he was on leave.

They were pressed to eat and drink, but dared not, for fear of disturbing their make-up, and had to make excuses about their religious beliefs and the necessity for quite special prepa-ration of food for members of the royal family. Then the wind began to blow and rain to fall. Their complexions and Duncan Grant's mustache were in grave danger; Cole explained that the emperor found England chilly, and they were shown below, where they had an opportunity of making suitable repairs.

Then there was the problem of the salute; what was the correct number of guns to be fired in honor of the Emperor of Abyssinia; it was regrettable that no one knew, because this was such an unprecedented occasion. But the emperor, through his interpreter and the representative of the Foreign Office, graciously signified that it was not necessary at all. The French fleet had not saluted him and his party at Toulon, so why should the British? As a matter of fact Cole would have loved a salute, but Adrian thought of all the work the sailors would have to do cleaning up the guns again after firing them.

Next they had to receive an apology because the bandmaster had been unable to get a copy of the Abyssinian national anthem, so had played the anthem of Zanzibar instead. Adrian replied that this was just fine, please think no more about it.

Back on shore, Cole tipped the sailors royally, but still had two more tricks up his sleeve. He tried to pin a fancy-dress order on a young officer — who shyly refused it, lacking the permission of his superiors — and insisted that the waiters who served them dinner on the train wear white gloves, although, as these were not standard equipment and had to be specially bought, this meant a delay before the famished hoaxers could get anything to eat.

This story, like the sultan story, leaked out, probably through Cole, who was never one to hide his light under a bushel. A full-page photograph of the group in all their regalia appeared in the newspapers, though the names of the jokers were not known. Questions were asked in Parliament. Was it or was it not a fact, and so on? A fine state of affairs, when anybody could get aboard a battleship and be shown Britain's most secret weapons of defense! What did the First Lord of the Admiralty have to say about that?

While some politicians tried to make capital out of the affair and other politicians tried to hush it up, the public enjoyed the

joke played on the Navy. An assistant in the theatrical costumiers told the newspapers that he had overheard the expression
"Bunga-Bunga." This delighted music-hall comedians and rude
little boys, much to the annoyance of naval officers on shore
leave. The captain of the ship, meeting Cole and Adrian in the
street one day, laughed. But Adrian's cousin did not. Did
Adrian know, he demanded, what the officers in the mess had to
say about the identity of the mysterious woman in the case?
"They are saying she is a common woman of the town — and *I*
have to sit and hear this in silence!" Another relation, who
had thoroughly enjoyed the Cambridge story, was horrified at
the Weymouth affair. He offered help if legal proceedings were
taken but implored Adrian, whatever happened, "for God's sake
keep Virginia's name out of it." Miss Stephen, naturally, very
much appreciated this concern for her reputation.

But here was more than a woman's honor to be safeguarded:
the honor of the Navy had to be upheld. In a story entitled "A
Society" which she wrote some years later, she gave a very color-
ful, spirited and inaccurate account of how the Navy took its
revenge. This story appeared in the volume *Monday or Tuesday* in 1921, but was omitted from later reprints of this material after her death, in accordance with her own wishes.

One reason for this decision was that in the meantime the
actual facts of the whole affair had been related by Adrian in
a little book, now extremely rare, after Horace Cole died, in
1936. The task devolved on him, he explained, because it was
well known that he could not tell a lie; with him the reader
could feel safe from deception. This was his characteristically
charming and tactful way of referring not only to Cole's delight
in mystification and rumor but to Virginia's technique of taking
hold of an anecdote as though it were a painted top, tossing it
in the air, setting it spinning, and then describing, not the
top, but the radiations it gave off as it whirled around. What began as a plaything, made of colored wood or metal, of a definite
size and ascertainable cost at a toyshop, might end, once she got

her hands on it, as the great globe itself, the very platonic form of a top.

Later, when she was more sure of herself, she would perform this trick before your eyes, in conversation. She would take a story right out of your mouth, improvise and fantasticate upon it, and then hand it back to you, pretending the new version was entirely your own. But in these early days she was more interested in what other people had to say; her thoughts were private, mainly expressed in the notebooks which most young writers seem compelled to keep in an attempt to teach themselves how to write, how to find the right word, to describe what they see. Because the right word *must* be found. "Nothing can exist unless it is properly described."

THE THURSDAY evenings at Fitzroy Square were times of relaxation. The talk might be serious but never dull; the ideas discussed might be abstract, but the thoughts were never dim. There was always somebody to puncture pomposity with a timely question or a comical instance disproving an inflated theory. How could the gathering not be gay when Lytton Strachey, for one, was there? "Inert" was a word Virginia used more than once to describe his way of sprawling his immensely long limbs so that he looked like some old rug or shawl that had been dropped over a chair and forgotten. "Cadaverous" was another word frequently used to describe his appearance. But out of the mouth of the fantastically elongated figure would come, in a high, thin drawl, remarks of explosive force that would shatter any portentousness and have the whole company rocking with laughter.

He might look the epitome of laziness, with barely enough energy to stand upright. In fact he was, like the rest of them, hard at work. They were all getting established, contributing to magazines, writing books, painting pictures, gradually making reputations. They were not in any great hurry, not expecting immediate success. There was ample time ahead, it seemed in those days, to win fame and fortune; perfecting their craft, discovering the world and their place in it and their own potentialities and weaknesses, those were the overriding considerations. When they achieved recognition it was because there was solid work behind them, good foundations quietly laid.

E. M. Forster actually wrote his first four novels between 1905 and 1910. The first three excited little attention; the fourth, *Howard's End,* made it clear to a small but discerning public that here was a noteworthy talent, and probably much more. Time (considerable time) would prove the rightness of this judgment.

Lytton Strachey's first book was not published until 1912. It was a little book, one of the volumes in the Home University Library, easy to handle, easy to read, cheap to buy; a precious discovery for any young reader who wanted something for more than the passing moment and who could be led to delve further into any subject once his interest was aroused. The title was *Landmarks in French Literature.* It was not a runaway best seller, as understood today; but it made Lytton Strachey's name, prepared the way for his later fame.

Virginia Stephen was at work on a novel. It took her seven years to finish, and when it appeared it attracted little notice, because by that time the First World War had broken out. But the point is that while she was writing it no one among her friends was nagging at her to complete it or was unduly surprised that it took so long. That was her affair. The important thing was that she should be satisfied it was as good as she knew how to make it before she offered it to the public.

She wrote regularly, every morning, for two hours, in her workroom on the third floor, using an ordinary steel pen, standing at a high table rather like that used by an architect. This habit of standing while she wrote was a marked deviation from her father's way of sprawling on his spine in a low rocker. She could, and did, write in other positions, crouched over a fire, with a pad or notebook on her knees, or propped up in bed. But what she wrote then were diary entries or letters to friends, rapidly composed when she had some time to spare or when there was need to hurry to catch the post. When she was concentrating on a book or an article, she found too much comfort was uncomfortable. Discipline and ease did not go together. In order to get started she needed the ritual of the right posture.

She was almost like a monk at work on a missal, so great was her absorption, her feeling of dedication to her task. Nothing from the outer world could be allowed to interfere. Everything had to be absolutely what she was used to: the table at the right height, her pens and ink handy, her time schedule and watch in sight. Often her work was "a battle," but she had to fight it alone.

"Why can't I write except in sordid rooms?" she asked. "Furniture that people can sit in implies people, and I want complete solitude — that's at the back of my mind." [1]

She continued to use an ordinary steel pen long after fountain pens had come into general use, but the momentary pause to dip the pen in the ink did not disturb the rhythmic flow of words — if they were willing to flow. Then they might appear on the page, in her thin, upright, elegant, but not very legible handwriting, "faster than the fastest typewriting." Sometimes they refused to come, and a morning's battle might produce no more than fifty words. But, even if the pen had been "diseased" or she emerged with ink-stained lips, indicating prolonged struggle, the physical contact with her chosen materials and the repetition of habitual gestures had yielded at least once the infinite satisfaction of writing a sentence, of feeling it "form and curve under my fingers."

Afterwards would come the revisions and rewriting on the typewriter, over and over and over again, making sense out of

[1] Letter to V. Sackville-West (February 1927).

the notebooks that often looked like a lunatic's dream; polishing for the printer but taking away the bright glow these phrases had had for her when she first captured them and wrote them down.

Typing brought its own kind of satisfaction. It was laborious but salutary; it marked a stage toward the final completion of a job, which meant release to do something else, capture some other idea that was hovering almost within reach. But, she noted, a typed sentence was somehow different from a written one. "For one thing it is formed out of what is already there; it does not spring fresh from the mind."

Correcting proofs was the sheerest misery. "It's all buzz and jerk; I want to spin a thread like a spider."[1] But it had to be done, even if she ended changing commas into semicolons in a daze of despair, finding the whole book flat, false and profitless. "I suppose there may be half a paragraph somewhere worth reading, but I doubt it"[1] is a typical comment.

To reread her own books was a sort of self-flagellation, they seemed to her so awful, so crude. And yet there was sometimes a light on the printed page which had never shone before. "What are they, I wonder, the very intimate things one says in print? There's a whole family of them. It's the proof, to me, of being a writer, that one expresses them in print only."[1]

To the end of her life writing remained a mystery to her, in the classic sense, a mystery to which she was dedicated. The Delphic Sibyl stood by her tripod, inhaled the incense fumes, and the Oracle spoke. Virginia stood at her table or sat by her fire, with paper and an inkpot before her, took a pen in her hand, and words came. Where they came from, why she had no peace until they were written, what they were to mean to those who read them — these were unanswerable questions. They were her life. But she could also stand apart from them and wonder.

Because there was so much else in life to enjoy and experience. Love and friendship, in their innumerable forms; walking

[1] Letters to V. Sackville-West (1926).

and laughter; food and clothes; looking at pictures; listening to music. Why did everything under her sun have to be offered up as incense so that words might get written on a page? Was it worth it? Did Nature really know what she was up to? But what was the use of arguing?

SHE DID, of course, enjoy herself, in usual, conventional ways. She went to the opera, for instance. Not that she particularly liked opera — on the contrary — but there happened to be a very good Wagnerian season in 1908, and one of the advantages of Bloomsbury is that it is within very easy walking distance of Covent Garden Opera House. Chance mention of an almost forgotten name reminded her nearly thirty years later of "my first love. I remember sitting opposite her at supper at the Savoy about 1908 between the acts of the Valkyrie and adoring her." [1]

Queen Alexandra went to the opera too, and so did Jacob Flanders. This is how Virginia described the occasion in *Jacob's Room:*

The autumn season was in full swing. Tristan was twitching his rug up under his armpits twice a week; Isolde waved her scarf in miraculous sympathy with the conductor's baton. In all parts of the house were to be found pink faces and glittering breasts. When a Royal hand attached to an invisible body slipped out and withdrew the red and white bouquet reposing on the scarlet ledge, the Queen of England seemed a name worth dying for. Beauty, in its hothouse variety, flowered in box after box; and though nothing was said of profound importance . . . the lips (through an opera glass) remained red, adorable. Bald distinguished men with gold-headed canes strolled down the crimson avenues between the stalls, and only broke from intercourse with the boxes when the lights went down, and the conductor, first bowing to the Queen, next to the bald-headed men, swept round on his feet and raised his wand.

[1] Letter to V. Sackville-West (January 1937).

Then two thousand hearts in the semi-darkness remembered, anticipated, traveled dark labyrinths.

But the *Valkyrie* is more a test of endurance than *Tristan and Isolde*. Both audience and performers need a break longer than usual in order to get some fresh air, some food, an opportunity to stretch their legs. If Virginia, instead of going downhill and across the Strand to eat at the Savoy, had turned in the opposite direction she would have been part of the beauty (human variety) that flowered in Bow Street and Long Acre and Drury Lane on such autumn evenings.

These narrow, busy streets would be quiet at this time. The workers who would be bringing in the loads of hothouse blooms, ripe fruit or common or garden cabbages for sale in Covent Garden market early next morning had not yet arrived on the scene. The strollers from the opera would be likely to encounter only a few office workers making their way to the nearest tea-shop still open for the sustaining but indigestible meal — quite different from that supplied by the Savoy — they usually ate before going home. A tired typist could, in one swift glance, observe the young man in his dress suit, the young woman in her filmy dress, all white and shimmering in the twilight, her cloak like folded wings; and wish, perhaps, that these visitors from another world, where women were fresh and clean and wide-eyed at this hour, came more often that way. A newspaperman, slipping in or out of a pub, might wonder when he would get a chance to cover the opera and think of the story he could write and how it would probably appear next day as no more than a list of names of those present at the performance. A policeman might hope these strangers knew where they were and that they realized there were some tough characters lurking in dark corners of Seven Dials; he might even warn them that he thought he'd heard the first bell and that the Opera House was this way.

It is unlikely that any of them guessed this tall young woman, so fragile, so mothlike, was seeing even more than she was seen. When the Valkyries ceased riding the whirlwind and the last curtain call was taken, she came out from under that Niagara of sound, shook off the spray of that tremendous tumult and, slightly blinded, somewhat deafened, rather stiff, noted:

Of all the carriages that leave the arch of the Opera House, not one turns eastward, and when the little thief is caught in the empty market-place no one in black-and-white or rose-colored evening dress blocks the way by pausing with a hand upon the carriage door to help or condemn.

So she wrote, in that incomparable guidebook to London, *Jacob's Room.*

Virginia loved London, as only one who knows it intimately can be said to love a city. She hated it too, at times; which is only another proof that she knew it thoroughly. Her knowledge of it came from her tireless tramping of its streets at all hours, riding on the tops of buses or threading the mazes of the underground railway, talking and listening to people in shops and restaurants, to blind beggars or street singers. Her interest was not confined to Bloomsbury or her own set. She had an insatiable curiosity about other people, from the Queen to the scrubwoman. How did they live? What did they think about and hope for? What was the reality behind the smiling mask which public duty imposed on the great lady, or beneath the gray veils of apathy and fatigue which years of dull work had draped about the kneeling figure of the cleaner of doorsteps?

All her references to London have a note of authority and authenticity — she knew, she was there. She wrote as a poet and a lover — sometimes an outraged lover — never as an antiquarian or a romanticist. She could truthfully claim, "I covered the whole street, Oxford Street, Piccadilly Circus, with the blaze and ripple of my mind, with vine leaves and rose leaves." [1] She saw "the lamps of London uphold the dark as upon the points of burning bayonets," and also saw that "The street market in Soho is fierce with light. Raw meat, china mugs, and silk stockings blaze in it. Raw voices wrap themselves round the flaring

[1] *The Waves.*

gas-jets. . . . Shawled women carry babies with purple eyelids; boys stand at street corners; girls look across the road — rude illustrations, pictures in a book whose pages we turn over and over as if we should at last find what we look for. Every face, every shop, bedroom window, public-house, and dark square, is a picture feverishly turned." [1]

She carries most conviction to a Londoner when she writes about the Thames and about St. Paul's Cathedral, whether she shows it as seen from Waterloo Bridge as it "swells white above the fretted, pointed, or oblong buildings beside it. The cross alone shines rosy-gilt," or "floating on the uneven white mist" when the bonfire blazed on Parliament Hill one Guy Fawkes night. For, "if there is such a thing as a shell secreted by man to fit man himself here we find it, on the banks of the Thames, where the great streets join and St. Paul's Cathedral, like the volute on the top of the snail shell, finishes it off." [1]

These descriptions could only be written by someone who knew, by direct experience, not hearsay, that St. Paul's is to London what St. Peter's is to Rome. Regardless of religion, it is a symbol in a way that Westminster Abbey is not (so that when William Morris can exclaim, "Anyone who prefers St. Paul's to Westminster Abbey would prefer his lady bald," the real Londoner, while admitting the force of the comparison, is shocked by the brutality of the statement).

Until Hitler's bombs unburied it by destroying its surrounding huddle of streets, the great church was practically not to be seen, except from a distance. But St. Paul's has a dome. It lifts up to the sky, and the Londoner's heart is uplifted by the sight or the thought of it. This is the symbol, undefined and attached to no dogma (apart from the cross), representing, maybe, the struggle out of disorder and dirt. It is not only a landmark for the wanderer, but the standard of measurement which every Londoner admits. Sea level is one thing, but "as high as the dome of St. Paul's" is another; and very important. The New

[1] *Jacob's Room.*

Yorker has a thrill of pride in his skyscrapers; he will pick them out and name them as a mountaineer will name the Alpine peaks. The Londoner is not necessarily proud of St. Paul's — only very glad to see it. Other London churches, with their spires and steeples and sometimes very unexpected ornaments, have their special connotations, their appeals to affection and memory; the names of the saints to whom they are dedicated mix with the chimes of their clocks or bells like music in the mind. But St. Paul's, that tea cozy, that snail shell, means something at once special and communal.

Two THINGS occurred in 1910 that were to be important to Virginia and her friends. The first was a lawsuit, the second a picture show.

The lawsuit provided sensational newspaper reading for six days in February of that year. It was concerned with inheritance of a fortune and succession to a peerage, with a romance some fifty years previously between a beautiful Spanish ballerina and a young English nobleman, with a marriage between cousins, with mysterious attempts to falsify records in Madrid. It was an old story for the family concerned and for the lawyers who had for years been laboriously tracing witnesses and taking depositions from bullfighters and parish priests in odd corners of Europe. For the public it had all the elements of melodrama except a villain; which made it all the more romantic. The English lord had been a faithful lover and an honest father. He had acknowledged and provided for his children. The point at issue was whether he had been successful in marrying his lovely dancer or was her previous marriage properly attested and therefore still valid? Was his legitimate heir the son who had been farming in South America or the nephew who had married his daughter, lived with him in his historic mansion and borne the burden of administering his vast estates during his declining years? The plight of the lady who had to listen while the private life of her mother and father was revealed when her husband and her brother were forced to submit their rival claims to the decision of the English law courts made a particular appeal to popular sympathy. When her brother's case collapsed the towns-folk and the tenantry turned out *en masse* to give her and her husband and child an enthusiastic welcome home.

The full story is told in a book published in 1937, entitled *Pepita,* written by a woman who was a young girl at the time of the lawsuit and who was with her mother and father when little girls offered bouquets, boy scouts stood at attention, and the fire brigade unhitched the horses and dragged the carriage through the park and the courtyards to the main door of the great house on the day of that triumphant return. It is an entrancing story and Virginia would have been less than human if she had failed to share the general interest aroused at the time, when only a few of its salient points, expressed in dry legal question and answer in the court or screaming headlines in the newspaper, were revealed. Knowing her passionate desire to understand the reality behind any kind of life that seemed glamorous to her be-cause it was different from her own, we may be sure the news-papers did not scream in vain for her attention.

But something more than the fascination of the story emerges from the book, and that is the character of the writer. One has to admire the masterly handling of complicated detail, the ease and strength of the writing, the strong common sense side by side with humor in the narration, the amazing detachment and yet real human warmth and understanding displayed, the po-etic clarity of the whole. And, beyond all that, one is left with the conviction that here is a woman of quite massive integrity and courage and vision. More than her grandmother and her mother are here portrayed; she herself stands before us. Michel-angelo might have carved her in marble strength and supple-ness; Leonardo da Vinci might have captured her dreaming grace on canvas. Actually it was Virginia Woolf who gave the world her picture in *Orlando*.

For the author of *Pepita* was Vita Sackville-West. She and Virginia did not meet until 1922. *Orlando* did not appear until 1928. It was the kind of biography that only Virginia Woolf could write and Vita Sackville-West inspire. The lawsuit in 1910 was a hint of what was to come. To use Virginia's own symbol, it was the first glimpse of a "fin in a waste of waters."

THE SECOND fin to show in 1910 belonged to quite a different fish, which surfaced much more rapidly. Virginia and her sister met Roger Fry and immediately recognized him as a kindred spirit and destined friend. He was much older than most of their friends (forty-four to their average of thirty or less), and he already had an international reputation as an art critic, lecturer and expert on art. But he was at this time reaching a crisis in his affairs, finding it necessary to rebuild his life. He had recently returned from the United States and was considerably disillusioned by his experience of buying old masters for the Metropolitan Museum of Art in New York when it was directed by or (as he felt) tyrannized over by the millionaire Pierpont Morgan. He was tired of being employed to purchase from impecunious aristocrats works of art they had inherited and did not love, on behalf of rich men who were, when it came to the point, equally indifferent to the beauty of these masterpieces and cared only for his assurance that they were genuine and worth the money. He also had a bitter domestic tragedy to surmount; he was, after years of hoping a cure could be found for his wife's recurrent illness, forced to accept the doctors' decision that it was beyond their powers to prevent the increasing pressure of her skull on her brain. She would live a long while, but his children were already motherless. In spite of his reputation and his achievements he was back where he had started twenty years before, looking for a real home and a real outlet for his energies, his acquired knowledge and his brilliant natural gifts.

A comparatively trifling commission provided the opportunity. A private picture gallery in London, the Grafton, decided to put on a show of modern French art. Roger Fry went to Paris with a free hand to choose pictures that he liked, and he brought back examples of the work of Cézanne, Gauguin, Van Gogh, Matisse, Picasso and others. Most of these pictures are now in public galleries. They change hands for immense sums. Acquisition of a new example or the arrangement of an international loan exhibition draws flocks of people to see the originals of reproductions with which they have long been familiar and which have brightened their rooms for many years. Sometimes these reproductions are even apologized for as being slightly old-fashioned, showing the artist in an early period when he used a style and technique he later abandoned, but having for the owner a sentimental value, in spite of what the youngsters say about its being old stuff these days.

But when the first Postimpressionist Exhibition opened in November 1910, the public was outraged. The gallery was crammed with visitors who were either incredulous or insulted, seemed to be threatened with attacks of hysteria or apoplexy. They reeled home in various stages of exhaustion or excitement to talk about it or to write to the newspapers. The hunt was up. The hounds bayed, the horses galloped, riders tried to take impossible fences and were thrown into muddy ditches; and that sly fox, art, slipped away once more.

Of course not all the passions that were aroused were angry ones; not everyone felt that the whole thing was an impudent swindle and that civilization would come crashing down about our ears unless this kind of nonsense was denounced and the people who perpetrated such a hoax, together with those who defended them, were boycotted from decent society. Quite a number felt the excitement in the form of an intense curiosity, a desire to understand.

Roger Fry himself, far from being discouraged by the uproar or dismayed by the insults and catcalls, was stimulated in various practical ways. He himself began to paint, to encourage other young artists and to find opportunities for their work to be seen and enjoyed. For him art was not simply a matter of squares of painted canvas to be hung on walls; it was part of daily life. Beauty was to be found not in a useless object with a lot of frilly ornament on it, but in something that was well designed for its purpose. All the arts were related. The same basic principles applied to architecture and to clothes, to pots and pans and poetry, to furniture and fabrics and factories, to teacups and to statuary. His ideas were profound, and he examined them closely and expounded them incisively. He was a formidable controversialist and also a practical demonstrator of what he meant. He could find the right words, but they were not mere catchwords; he could produce beautiful objects, brought from the ends of the earth or made in his own workshops, to show that he knew what he was talking about. His influence has been more pervasive than is generally realized; his ideas, though fiercely debated at the time, have come to be taken for granted. The mass manufacturer of today, using new plastic materials, produces better articles and sells them in a much wider market to satisfy a far more critical public because of a man whose name he may never have heard, because that man proved that the so-called new art was merely an extension of the old art.

There was no Roger Fry school or cult; he never demanded agreement, much preferring frank discussion which led to further clarification of his own thoughts, and opportunities to show what he meant by references to, say, the Russian ballet or peasant art or a shop window or a factory or a hat. The world spread its riches before him; his delight was to invite others to open their eyes and share what he saw.

Vanessa Bell and Duncan Grant were among the young artists

who worked with him. Desmond MacCarthy was the secretary of the 1910 exhibition of postimpressionist pictures from France, and Leonard Woolf for the second (which showed two years later what contemporary artists had been doing in the interval). Lytton Strachey understood the importance of the visual arts, though he did not care about Matisse or Picasso. Maynard Keynes was willing to learn and able to talk about pictures, and later bought many either for the National Gallery or for himself. Clive Bell was an active opener of eyes and influential exponent of the ideas about art and life which he shared with Roger Fry and expressed in his own words. Virginia was delighted to listen when Roger Fry explained to Henry James or Arnold Bennett how Cézanne and Flaubert were both trying to catch the moment of beauty and truth in their different nets.

So it was through his close friendship with this group of young people that postimpressionism came to be linked with the nebulous "Bloomsbury Circle" in the public mind. Ironically enough, it was a feud between artists themselves that helped to fix the notion that there was something peculiar going on in Bloomsbury. Four artists considered they had not been fairly treated in the display at the 1913 Ideal Home Exhibition of modern domestic art objects produced in the Omega Workshops, the co-operative founded by Roger Fry, and they aired their alleged grievances in a circular sent to the press. In this document they referred to "This family party of strayed and dissenting Aesthetes" who needed help to do the "rough and masculine work" if their efforts were to "rise above the level of a pleasant tea-party." The sidelong reference to Virginia and her sister is obvious. They also complained of the appearance of "a new form of fish in the troubled waters of Art." This was the "Pecksniff-shark, a timid but voracious journalistic monster, unscrupulous, smooth-tongued and, owing chiefly to its weakness, mischievous." This, presumably, was an expression of annoyance that Clive Bell and Desmond MacCarthy, among others, were so clear and persuasive in their articles in the influential literary magazines.

Already the myth was forming that there was a special, exclusive group of people, with a special, exclusive outlook, beyond understanding and therefore not worth examining; and all these special, exclusive people lived in a close huddle and admired one another and cared nothing about anyone else, and so could be conveniently attacked by referring to them in one word — Bloomsbury.

Chapter IV

ON OR ABOUT December, 1910, human character changed."
This is Virginia Woolf being deliberately provocative, beating a
drum to announce that the show is about to begin.

Having secured silence, she readily admits that the assertion
is disputable, the date arbitrary. She chose it, in fact, because it
marked the end of the reign of Edward VII and the beginning
of the reign of George V and so gave her a convenient opportunity
to discuss the difference between the Edwardians and the Geor-
gians and to explain why she and her like could not write and
would not try to write as Arnold Bennett, John Galsworthy and
H. G. Wells had written and were still writing when she challenged them in 1924.

A change in her life occurred in 1912; for most people the
change came in 1914, when the Germans invaded Belgium and
immediately all Europe was ablaze with war.

The first, the private date marks the year of her marriage to
Leonard Woolf. She was thirty years old. She was no longer
the shy girl seeking, half fearfully, to escape from her father's
domination. The last ten years had taught her how to stand on
her own feet and speak for herself. She knew what she wanted,
and her choice of life partner proved to be exquisitely right. She
changed her name, she changed her home; but she was more
herself as Virginia Woolf than she had been as Virginia Stephen.
Her marriage was no break with the past, no repudiation of old
values, but a vindication of all that was wise and sound in those
values and an opportunity for further vigorous and continued

development of her gifts as an artist, a thinker and a woman.

When Leonard Woolf returned to London in 1911 after seven years in Ceylon it was to a city very little changed outwardly but inwardly very different. While he had been in charge of a huge territory that was relapsing into primitive jungle, inhabited by people so impoverished, underfed and ignorant that even the hope of finding a better way of life was almost extinct and the means of achieving it beyond effective comprehension under alien rule, the people of England were vigorously and stubbornly continuing the fight against their native rulers, to assert their democratic will against an oligarchy that blocked their progress. Leslie Stephen had been born in the year of the first Reform Act; Leonard Woolf came back from a British colony in the year when, at last, the House of Lords limited its powers to obstruct, hamper, delay and destroy the work of the House of Commons.

The difference between London and Ceylon was not only that one exchanged paved streets for pathless jungle, motorbuses for bullock carts. In the outposts of empire palaces, temples and cities crumbled and were forgotten, signs of former magnificence were obliterated as easily as the traces of irrigation channels that had once made a desert fertile and civilization possible. In the heart of the empire the maintenance of a pure water supply was one of the many matters which were the concern of local government bodies made up of elected representatives, employing skilled technicians, people who knew what was needed and how to go about getting it. There was plenty of dirt, disease, ignorance, poverty, apathy and crime, but there was also an increasing number of people anxious to come to grips with these problems. Women were demanding the vote, not as an empty privilege but in order to make themselves heard on important points of social welfare, housing, sanitation, divorce law reform, education, child care. Ireland was demanding home rule, and there seemed reason to hope that this might yet be achieved without bloodshed, for had not an independent Union of South Africa been established the previous year, a source of congratulation instead of the shame of the Boer War? Labor was emerging more clearly every year as a definite force; trade unionists not only wanted higher wages but expressed themselves in favor of peace and brotherhood, were discussing practical ways and means of establishing the reign of law to replace anarchy in international affairs.

All these things interested Leonard Woolf mightily. Fresh from his experiences of seeing the effects of imperialism superimposed on conquest, he could discuss with his idealist friends the next step to this or that goal, new ways of repaying the community for the expensive education they had received at the universities and public schools. They could tell him things too, for they were not just dreamers. Maynard Keynes, for one, could show him the reverse of the government medal. It was not only in the colonies themselves that one was frustrated by apathy, indecision, vested interest, downright stupidity; have a job at the India Office or the Treasury and see what one may be up against; work on municipal affairs at Hampstead or Hammersmith, or go with Lytton Strachey to a women's suffrage meeting; learn what happens inside a working men's college.

Naturally Virginia was drawn more and more into practical affairs from which she had hitherto held aloof, feeling herself inadequately equipped to deal with them. She was not the stuff of which an active committee member or an organizer of a new society is made, and both she and her husband knew that these were not the ways she should attempt to express herself. But her admiration (amounting, observers said, almost to awe at times) of his abilities and devotion to public affairs made her feel far less of an "outsider" who could only help a cause she believed in by signing a check. Many years later, when she was sitting and talking with Elizabeth Bowen, she paused, hearing steps outside her door. "They put me to shame," she said, "these young men, tramping upstairs to see Leonard. No, shame is not the right word. Only, they are able to do so much I could never do."

One of her husband's interests was in the Co-operative Movement; and this opened to her many doors on which, without his encouragement, she would not have dared to knock, the doors of working-class housewives. She went with him on a tour of the industrial north of England (hitherto almost unknown territory to her) and attended as a visitor, not a delegate, a congress of the Women's Co-operative Guild in Newcastle in 1913. Seventeen years later she told the story of her experience at this meeting in an introduction to *Life As We Have Known It*, a volume of memoirs and letters written by Co-operative women, edited by her old friend, Margaret Llewelyn Davies.

This is an extremely important document for anyone who wishes to understand Virginia Woolf's complex character. It reveals her limitations and also her awareness of her blind spots; her fastidiousness and irritability when faced with something she could not understand or felt shut out from, and at the same time the honesty with which she criticized herself for the egotism of this kind of response. It shows, above all, the strength of her desire to achieve the impossible — to be herself and to be every other kind of woman as well.

At the time of attending this conference she had known only a very sheltered middle-class life, and her feelings of humiliation and rage were understandable. She admired the vigor of body and independence of mind which these practical working women showed, but felt oppressed because, not having shared their experiences at the washtub and the cooking stove, she feared she could not share their thoughts, nor could they share hers. She approved of their aims, but was not her sympathy fictitious since she already had what they were demanding, baths and electricity? Must she, in order to understand them with her blood and her bones as well as her eyes and her imagination, limit herself to such desires, think only about higher wages and shorter hours and laborsaving appliances and a raising of the school-leaving age? It was impossible. When she relaxed in an armchair, she could see Greece or Italy, hear Mozart or Shakespeare. What had they been able to see out of their windows but slag heaps or rows and rows of slate roofs, what did they listen for but the clamor of children coming home from school or the steps of a husband returning tired and dirty from work, demanding a meal? There must be more, but what was it?

Her instinct was right. She was fortunate in having friends who were patient with her impatience and who showed their faith in her by asking her to read these memoirs of women's early struggles, knowing she would discern the underlying poetry in them and realize that there was not the impassable barrier between her and women of quite different background and up-bringing she had once imagined. She was even more fortunate in marrying a man whose fundamental honesty matched her own, who recognized her true quality as she recognized his, who could appreciate the beauty of the palaces as well as understand the importance of keeping the irrigation channels in good repair.

ABOUT this time the early Bloomsbury Group were tending to forsake Bloomsbury. The Stracheys moved to Hampstead, the Woolfs to Clifford's Inn, a small, quiet, eighteenth-century court off Fleet Street, near the law courts, where Samuel Butler had once lived and written *Erewhon*. Here Virginia continued to work on her novel. According to her diary she seems to have completed it in July 1913, though it was not actually published until 1915. In the meantime the fateful date of August 4, 1914, had changed everything.

Many of those who lived through both the First and Second World Wars agree that the first was, in various ways, the grimmer experience. This is not merely a personal judgment, based on the fact that they were young in 1914 and a sudden hole was torn in their lives just when they were leaving school or starting on a career. There was a widespread feeling of shocked incredulity in 1914 very different from the acceptance of the inevitable in 1939.

Among the minority who had foreseen the coming clash and warned the unheeding majority of its consequences, there was a very considerable measure of hope that it could be avoided. The country as a whole was psychologically unprepared. Even those who opposed war in general or this war in particular were far from unanimous about their reasons for doing so.

Virginia remembered the Boer War at the turn of the century, how her father had imagined he heard the booming of guns in far-off South Africa, how he shrank from all news about the campaign because to him it meant lives of young men thrown away in a shameful cause. In the ensuing years she had come to believe there was hope that men would settle their national differences by other means than relapsing into the barbarism of war. Personal courage she admired, personal anger she understood. But arguments were not settled by fighting. Surely it was obvious that war was as out-of-date and absurd as dueling? But how could she express her opinion? As a woman she had no political voice. And, since she was not called upon to be an active participant, had she any moral right to attempt to influence any young man who was debating what he ought to do?

Few of her friends had any doubts; but they reached a great variety of different conclusions, and acted in different ways. But even when they agreed with one another, the same course of action might have different results. Maynard Keynes believed in the rightness of the war, but was prepared at all costs to resist being conscripted to fight. Lytton Strachey was strongly opposed to the war, but was found physically unfit for soldiering. Two younger men, David Garnett and Francis Birrell (both of very impressive literary lineage), refused to fight but shared the perils of the front line by doing Friends' Ambulance work in France until drafted for agricultural labor under the National Service Act. Another young friend, Rupert Brooke, with whom Virginia had gone swimming and had discussed poetry when they were with a group of friends on a camping vacation, enlisted. He was so strikingly handsome that Henry James, seeing him when he was at Cambridge, was much relieved to hear that his poetry was not very good yet. "With that appearance, if he had also talent it would be too unfair," said the famous old man. After Rupert Brooke's death his lines about "some corner of a foreign field" being "forever England" were on every tongue. He became the symbol of gallant British youth giving his life for his country. This posthumous fame and the sight of his portrait in shop windows was not much consolation to his friends. To those who sought any opportunity for a speedy end to the appalling carnage he was a symbol of the wasted life and unfulfilled promise of his generation. But advocates of an early peace, whether they were of military age and fitness or not, were derided, denounced and disgraced. Bertrand Russell was almost literally thrown out of Cambridge and later went to prison for expressing pacifist views.

Thus Virginia Woolf found herself among the thousands of women who were condemned to wait helplessly for what bad news might come next. She was not among the wives and mothers who could find what solace there was in the thought that they had "given" their sons and husbands to their country. She was among the minority who were not comforted by vicarious glory but were forced to swim against the tide of popular feeling. Only those who have experienced it can know the extreme loneliness of this position. Cut off from the flow of mass emotion one feels empty, hollow, bloodless.

Virginia Woolf was particularly sensitive to crowd feeling. There are several pages at the beginning of *Mrs. Dalloway* which are quite unmatched as an evocation of this irrational, subconscious response to some symbol of national pride. A car passing down Bond Street and along Piccadilly attracts attention because all traffic makes way for it. Nobody knows whose car it is, nor who is inside. The King, the Queen, the Prince of Wales, the Prime Minister?

Yet at once rumors were in circulation . . . falling invisibly, inaudibly, like a cloud . . . falling indeed with something of a cloud's sudden sobriety and stillness upon faces which a second before had been utterly disorderly. But now mystery had brushed them with her wing; the spirit of religion was abroad. . . . The car had gone, but it had left a slight ripple. . . . Something so trifling in single instances that no mathematical instrument, though capable of transmitting shocks in China, could register the vibration; yet in its fulness rather formidable, and in its common appeal emotional. . . . For the surface agitation of the passing car as it sunk grazed something very profound.

In the last war, when danger threatened everyone, not merely the men fighting overseas, when the source of the danger, the nature of the threat, the need for courage were fully understood and unanimously accepted, there was strength to be found in the very heart of peril. In the First World War there was very little to relieve the awful strain of inaction. Except within the circle of a few intimates one was alone; passers-by were strangers, enemies, not comrades and sharers.

It is little wonder that Virginia's health broke down again during these war years. She and Leonard moved from the center of London to the outskirts, where life flowed more quietly and there were fewer inducements to overexciting and exhausting social intercourse. They also took a cottage in the country so that at week ends they could be near her sister Vanessa, and a few very special friends such as Maynard Keynes and Duncan Grant, who were either occasional visitors or war workers in the neighborhood.

THE TOWN HOUSE was in Richmond-on-Thames, to the southwest of London proper, which, technically speaking, ends where Hammersmith meets Chiswick in a turmoil of traffic at Young's Corner or where the looping river marks the boundary between the counties of London and Surrey. Richmond is a town rich in historic and artistic associations and with a character of its own,

and yet is often regarded as a London suburb. Hordes of office
workers leave it every morning and return to it at night; still other
hordes use it as a playground every fine, or semifine, week end.
It is easily reached, by many routes. There is no sharp dividing
line separating it from London; nothing lies between the two
except more houses and more history.

A choice of buses from Bloomsbury would have carried Virginia past her old home at Hyde Park Gate to her new destination. She could cross the river at Hammersmith or at Gunnersbury. Another link was the District section of the Underground
Railway, which is only theoretically underground for the greater
part of this westward stretch. Whichever way she chose she would
be hurrying through time, past and present nudging her elbow
to attract her attention all the way. Hammersmith might mean
William Morris, the pre-Raphaelites and the Kelmscott Press, or
Cobden-Sanderson and the Doves, or the Oxford and Cambridge
Boat Race and her father coaching his crew of rowers. Chiswick
might recall Becky Sharp and Miss Pinkerton's Academy on the
Mall, and all the rest of *Vanity Fair* and Thackeray. Bedford
Park was neither a park nor a mansion, but the red-brick nest of
that wild swan, William Butler Yeats. Gunnersbury, now built
over, was in those days still an oasis of orchards, and part of the
fun and glory of going to Kew in lilactime was to see the apple,
pear and cherry trees heavy with their bright blossoms in
the thin spring sunshine, and the pink sprays of almond
in the tiny gardens of the cottages that crowd up to the District
line.

It is really best to continue by train for the rest of the way;
the traveler who succumbs to the temptation to walk over Kew
Bridge and on through the Gardens to his destination is liable to
be hours late for any appointment. If he is to be in time he must
not pause to look at Strand-on-the-Green, that miniature village
at the water's edge, a combination of eighteenth-century elegance
and Dickensian grotesque, the last surviving relic of London according to George Bernard Shaw in the far-distant future of *Back*

to Methuselah. He must not look downstream at the boats for hire nor heed invitations to enter any of the tall, narrow Victorian houses on the Surrey side and take tea in one of the long gardens sloping down to the river. He must not linger on Kew Green, which is a steel engraving straight out of a picture book about a village which was already old a hundred years ago. Above all, he must not go into Kew Gardens, for here he may meet Virginia Woolf, and Fanny Burney and mad King George III, and William Cobbett as a gardener's boy, and Queen Victoria as a child among bluebells and laurel bushes, not to mention the innumerable floral and architectural distractions. He had better take a bus ride between the prim, grim, gray stone villas and the high, forbidding brick walls of the Gardens, broken only by great iron gates, proud with royal insignia in red and gold, until he finds himself safe at Richmond station or among the shops of Richmond town.

Here again he must be strong-minded and resist more invitations to take tea or at least step into a pastry cook's and buy some of the delicious little tarts known as Maids of Honor. He must be firm, or he will find himself hiring a punt or a skiff at Richmond Bridge, or walking along the towpath, looking back into Kew Gardens across an intervening ditch. He should postpone until a later visit the long pull uphill. He will not see the Sweet Lass herself, but many a waitress dressed up to look like her, all dimity and sweet simplicity, with cap and apron and full skirts and buckled shoes, all ready for a performance of *She Stoops to Conquer* or to serve him with toasted scones. Near the top of the hill he will see one of the most beautiful views of the Thames far below. It is a neat, well-arranged view; over a steep descent of terraced gardens, with walks and benches, flowers, bushes, grass; a tree-covered island in just the right position for the camera, flat water meadows beyond. It is all very Sunday-afternoonish, very English, extremely well done. Nature has been extremely obliging at this spot; and the courtesy is much appreciated and thoroughly enjoyed.

At the top of the hill are more great royal gates, for this is Richmond Park. Ignoring for the moment the huge Star and Garter Hotel (no longer a fashionable rendezvous for suppers and balls, its magnificent view reserved for the hopelessly maimed soldier victims of the 1914-1918 war), one enters a different world — a wilder, rougher, more magical world. Far away are the streets, the cottages, the villas, the teashops, the picnic pleasures of the Thames; far away the ordered exotic beauty of Kew Gardens, with its glittering hothouses, its pink, flat-faced palace for the Hanoverian princesses, its pretty little cottage for the pretty little Victoria; far away, too, the more solid and less inviting palace, Richmond Old Deer Park, where Queen Elizabeth I sometimes held court and allowed Sir James Harrington to demonstrate his new method of sewage disposal. Richmond Park is not pretty nor picturesque; it is, quite simply, beautiful.

In Richmond Park a free spirit may freely roam, for here are ancient trees, great glades, giant ferns. It is not for strollers only, but for walkers who do not mind an occasional stretch of rough going; not hazardous but sufficiently broken and uneven to keep the muscles moving while the mind is busy with thoughts. It does not demand sunshine and balmy airs for its appreciation, as Kew Gardens does. In rain and mist it is alluring; summer heat does not scorch its grass to extinction. There are carriage roads across it, but no great streams of traffic. There is a golf course to be avoided, unless you are a player; a small, secluded royal lodge to be skirted; and the deer do not like to be disturbed during the mating season. Not as wild as a forest nor as open as a moor, it is very far from being as tame as a well-tended park. Here one may walk for miles and hours in near solitude before reaching romantically named Robin Hood Gate, with Wimbledon Common and Putney Heath still keeping the houses at bay. "I like walking in Richmond Park," says Virginia Woolf, speaking through the mouth of Rachel Vinrace in *The Voyage Out*, "singing to myself and knowing it doesn't matter a damn to anybody. . . . I like the freedom of it — it's like being the wind or the sea."

The house which the Woolfs bought was in the town at the bottom of the hill, near the High Street. It was known as Hogarth House, otherwise No. 34 Paradise Road. There seems no particular reason for either name. The English often spatter names about with a peculiar nonchalance, but whether it is done to confuse the antiquarian or help the postman, who can say? Paradise crops up quite often in city streets without exciting any comment, a faint echo of poetry like the primroses on a steep bank hardly noticed as an express train roars by, or the last words of an old ballad caught in the challenge of a clump of London Pride struggling to sooty bloom in a pocket-sized front garden. As for Hogarth, a house with a name instead of, or as well as, a number, was thought to be a mark of gentility in Victorian times; but by 1915 nobody cared to ask why Hogarth rather than Mon Abri or something else. No. 32, next door, had a right to be called Suffield House, since it was owned by Lord Suffield. Nowadays both houses have been turned into one. There is no plaque to indicate that Leonard and Virginia Woolf once lived here and had Sidney and Beatrice Webb, and others, to dinner in the garden. The two adjoining houses are now the home of the Richmond and Barnes Conservative Association and also give appropriate shelter to lawyers and commissioners of oaths. In short, it is all very respectable and completely unromantic. No one has ever thought it worth while to accuse Virginia Woolf of being Hogarthian or Paradisal or Richmondic, though these terms could be used, regardless of their original sense, to convey disapproval as easily as Bloomsbury, given the required malicious intent.

The country house rented about this time also had a name — Asheham — which sounds as though it had not been bestowed at random but conveys a necessary link to some former family ownership instead of concealing an old joke. It stood alone, among great trees, just off the road that leads from Lewes to the sea along one bank of the river Ouse. A farmhouse, a bailiff's house, it still stands alone as a residence, though it is hidden now from the passer-by not by trees but by a large cement works which

pounds away steadily and gives off a plume of smoke to drift
across the valley.

It is not far from Lewes, the county town of Sussex, almost due
south of London, with a fast and frequent train service from the
capital, a junction for Brighton and Newhaven and many other
points along the south coast. Lewes is built on a hill, around a
castle. The remains of this old fortification now contain a neatly
kept museum. The visitor may go unchalleneged under its stone
archway without fear of being ridden down by a sudden sortie of
men in armor; he may enter the building and examine the relics
of the past centuries at leisure, or he may sit in the pleasant garden outside and see the mingling of the past and the present
spread out before him from that vantage point. It would not be
correct to say that Lewes Castle dominates the landscape, because the hill on which it stands is only one of many Downs to
the east and west, all of them with a distinctive feature to show
— a racecourse, a windmill, a "Ring" of trees — none of them im-
periously assertive; an agreeable company of old friends. What is
immediately obvious is that Lewes ties a sort of knot in the various lines of communication which meet here. The roads, the
river and the railway indicate its former strategic importance.
There is a seacoast to be watched, a hinterland to be guarded.
Encampments or stockades would have been built here ages before the Romans came or the Vikings turned their long ships into
the tidal river, on plunder or on conquest bent.

The town flows out from the castle center and trickles over the
valleys, which have been not only habitable but at peace for so
many centuries that one may still see the pleasant retreat of Anne
of Cleves, the woman whose face was her fortune because it was
so disappointingly dull that her ferocious husband, Henry VIII,
was satisfied with divorcing instead of beheading her. When
feudal barons were replaced by lords lieutenants of counties and
plumes decorated the hair of ladies rather than the helmets of
knights, there was still need to watch for mysterious lights at
sea; smugglers, perhaps, causing a diversion while their cargo

was being landed somewhere else among the marshes in the dark. Tom Paine had a brief and inglorious career as an excise man at Lewes before he went to America and used his pen far more effectively as a pamphleteer against King George III than he had ever done when he kept tally of duty paid on brandy and tobacco. During the Napoleonic Wars men stood ready on these hills to pick up signals of a victory by Nelson, or to light beacon fires of warning that the French fleet had left harbor.

That invader never came; the fires were only lit because children

> saw no reason
> Why Gunpowder treason
> Should ever be forgot,

and the safety of the House of Commons was ensured for another year every November 5 by the ritual sacrifice of burning a straw dummy of Guy Fawkes. Rockets flared and showers of colored stars fell harmlessly from a quiet sky when a queen had a jubilee or a king was crowned.

For a long, long while this downland had been a peaceful, unhaunted countryside. The hills, not cleft by glaciers, not gauntly picturesque, not relics of past convulsions of the earth, had been built up over countless centuries by countless minute cells or organisms that lived and perished and left their infinitesimal mark. Over the chalk a thin layer of earth gave roothold to grass, closely cropped by sheep to a slippery, springy gentleness, and cattle drank at dew ponds. Gorse and broom defied the wind or flaunted a golden glory in the sun. Where the earth was deep enough men planted rings of trees, like crowns, not marring the line of hill against the sky, as might be thought, but absorbed into the picture, marks of old love of the land, haunts of birds. On the upland slopes were barns and sheepfolds; in the valleys were villages and churches, stretches of woods, where beech and oak leaves pile and drift, and where the feet of men wore paths that cut below the old roots. There were roads, and then a railway, for the travelers using the daily service across the Channel, by way of Newhaven and Dieppe, inns for the farmers and shepherds coming to market or the visitors from the cities who had become addicts to the national pastime of week-end and holiday walking, modern pilgrims tramping to no particular shrine, devotees of fresh air and exercise, escaping from the confinement of urban routines and paved streets.

It is a country that displays an endless variety of scene, so subtle are its changes, from hour to hour, from hill to hill; a country that seems to offer itself seductively to the beholder and friend, and remains unchanged after his passing; that fascinates but does not excite, arousing instead a deeper emotion, less easily expressed, calling for soft words and ballads, not epics or heroics; that lies open to the sky, lets storms pass over it and then is calm, smiling, comfortable, discreet and welcoming again.

This is the countryside where Virginia and Leonard Woolf made their home; first in the lonely house called Asheham and later in a cottage in the village of Rodmell on the opposite bank of the river. She loved it deeply, but never exclusively. She was no more Sussex than she had been Cornish. She saw beauty or experienced terror, acknowledged majesty or scorned meanness, wherever they were expressed. The whole world was hers, because it was primarily the world of ideas.

Chapter V

LONDON was not a very cheerful place in 1917; nor was Paris, nor Berlin, nor any part of Europe, for that matter. It seemed as though the war would go on and on endlessly, like an incurable but not mercifully fatal disease. Russia was practically out, even before the Czar was overthrown; the United States was technically in, but months had to elapse before its mighty force could be effective on the bloody stalemate in France.

Food was scarce, lights were dim, spirits were low, casualties were enormous. Everyone grumbled and had a legal right to do so, though the results of outspoken protests against unnecessary prolongation of the conflict varied. Siegfried Sassoon wrote a striking article, "An Infantry Officer Has Done with the War," and was judged to be mentally unbalanced. Lord Lansdowne, ex-Secretary of War, ex-Foreign Secretary, ex-Viceroy of India, suggested the Allies should state the terms on which they would make peace with Germany, but even this advance toward a truce was considered untimely. Bertrand Russell, too old to be a combatant, too influential to be ignored, was fined for publishing a leaflet advocating peace and later went to prison for six months, not for anything so spectacular as sedition or treason but for a technical breach of the wartime Defense of the Realm Act (known as DORA). Conscientious objectors might be forced into uniform and threatened with court-martial, sent to work on the land, or given terms of imprisonment, according to their degree of recalcitrance or the temper of the local tribunals before which they had to state their reasons for refusing to fight.

But in spite of Zeppelin raids on moonlight nights and fine days, in spite of daily arrivals of hospital trains from the front, life went on much as usual. Young men died, but others thought themselves lucky to have week-end leave or a "blighty" wound that ensured them a pension. Theaters were crowded. No one quite knew what was happening in Ireland since the Easter Rebellion of the previous year had been suppressed, but the Irish Sweepstake continued; so did the Calcutta Sweepstake, whatever might be going on in India, or in the minds of the dark-skinned, beturbaned soldiers from that far-off land.

One day Leonard and Virginia Woolf found themselves in Farringdon Road, an unprepossessing thoroughfare which runs north and south, to the east of Bloomsbury, a continuation of the Farringdon Street which meets Fleet Street at right angles at the foot of Ludgate Hill. This whole district suffered the most devastating raids during the Second World War. During the first war it still had something of the character of a road that had once been the scene of chaffering outside an ancient gate. At one end you might buy silver communion cups and embroidered stoles; at the other end, where it joined the confusion of railway tracks at King's Cross, there were stalls selling tattered books, packets of seeds, nails and tools and treasure trove of miscellaneous variety. A fascinating street for the wanderer, though devoid of obvious charm.

Here the Woolfs had an unexpected piece of luck. In a small shop selling printer's accessories of various kinds they found for sale a complete hand-printing outfit. They bought it on the spur of the moment and arranged for it to be delivered, type and all the component parts, to their house in Richmond.

The next thing to do was to learn how to use the machine. St. Bride's Institute, headquarters of the London Society of Compositors, was clearly the best place to inquire. Here they met an obstacle that Leonard Woolf, with his knowledge of trade union organization, might have foreseen. The society was friendly but firm. It was interested in the training of apprentices to an ancient and honorable craft and in the employment of its qualified members; it did not exist for amateurs.

Leonard and Virginia understood the position very well. Rules governing the entrance to a highly skilled trade are not made for fun. They may be annoying to the enthusiastic newcomer, but they arise out of a historic need and cannot be lightly set aside. There was nothing for it but to buy a handbook and teach themselves, however laboriously, how to print. And while they were about it they would learn how to bind books, how to paste and sew and make covers. It would take a lot less time than the years of apprenticeship required by the London Society of Compositors before a man could earn a living in Fleet Street as a printer, but that was not their aim. They were both writers. Now, for a hobby, they would find out for themselves all the technicalities by which their written words became books. So the dining room of 34 Paradise Road, Richmond, became their workshop and eventually the headquarters of the Hogarth Press.

The first production which they considered came up to their exacting standards was *Two Stories,* written by them in collaboration. Only a very few copies were printed, but they were much admired. The following year they asked a friend whose work they appreciated but who was not having the success she hoped for if she would let them have one of her stories and issue it under their imprint. The friend was Katherine Mansfield; the story was one of her best, *Prelude.* This was a notable beginning, and they went on to be more ambitious and to devote more and more of their spare time to their hobby. In 1919 they produced two stories by Virginia, *Kew Gardens* and *The Mark on the Wall,* as well as *Poems* by T. S. Eliot and *The Critic in Judgment* by Middleton Murry.

The result was beyond their expectations. *The Mark on the Wall* was so well received that they had to go to another printer, the Pelican Press, to run off enough copies to meet the demand, and *Kew Gardens* received such an enthusiastic review in the *Times Literary Supplement* that they were swamped with orders.

Virginia recounts the story in her diary. "We came back from Asheham to find the hall table stacked, littered, with orders for *Kew Gardens*. They strewed the sofa and we opened them intermittently through dinner, and quarrelled, I'm sorry to say, because we were both excited, and opposite tides of excitement coursed in us. . . . All these orders come from a review in the *Lit. Sup.* presumably by Logan[1] in which as much praise was allowed me as I like to claim. And 10 days ago I was stoically facing complete failure! The pleasure of success was considerably damaged, first by our quarrel, and second by the necessity of getting some 90 copies ready, cutting covers, printing labels, glueing backs, and finally despatching, which used up all spare time and some not spare till this moment."

The ninety copies were needed immediately. To fill all the orders received from booksellers all over the country would have meant far more work than they could possibly do, since the reprint would have to be between four and five times the size of the first run, and the mechanical resources of a commercial printer were absolutely necessary. But they continued to print and stitch and glue and bind booklets, for the pleasure and satisfaction they got out of this work together. E. M. Forster's *Story of the Siren*, for instance, and Hope Mirrlees' poem *Paris* came out of the dining room at Hogarth House. But after 1920 it was no longer a case of the Woolfs' asking friends if they minded seeing what could be done by a couple of amateurs to produce an attractive little book in a distinctive format and a gay cover of board pasted over with a beautiful paper they had discovered in Italy or Czechoslovakia on their last trip abroad. Manuscripts were soon being offered to them which were too long to set up by hand and too good to be refused. The Hogarth Press was a going concern, with an increasing prestige and a steadily mounting output.

It never became a dull business routine in which they made decisions, gave orders, paid bills for wages and drew profits, while other people did all the work. When they moved back to London

[1] Logan Pearsall Smith.

and had offices as well as a home in Bloomsbury, the hand-
printing machine went with them and was set up in the basement.
Leonard Woolf used it to run off the firm's invoices and note
paper and so on, according to his own layouts. Virginia would go
downstairs at intervals to get her beautiful hands all cold and
wet and rough as she dabbled about in type, setting up pages of
verse. In Who's Who she included under "Recreation" the word
"printing."

Her letters and diaries show her active participation in the work
that was going on. She not only wrote books the press would publish, or read manuscripts submitted, or advised young authors in
need of encouragement, guidance and criticism. When the firm
had a busy publishing season ahead and circulars had to be sent
out, she was on hand, helping to address envelopes and stick on
stamps, and when they had a sudden success and a heavy load of
orders, she was with the others packing parcels for the mail or for
waiting deliverymen.

"No, I can't say I knew her," said a Bloomsbury bookseller. "All
I ever saw of her was her back as she bent down to pick up
another pile of books to be packed or walked to a desk to check
that I had what I came to call for because I had customers waiting. Days like that, she was just one of the people shoveling 'em
out. I knew who she was, of course, she was so tall, so quick, so
graceful. No mistaking her, ever, anywhere. And I'd go back to
the shop and think to myself as the customer walked off with his
copy, 'Ah-ha, you little know who handled that book last!'"

It was a very informal atmosphere. "I've been doing up parcels;
standing at a table with string and paper and hearing scraps of
interviews. Advertising touts, with tempting offers; Mr. Behrman,
Editor of Youth; Mr. Morrell, the printer. All this goes forward as
I tie (do you remember 'sweeping up leaves,' the refrain in
Hardy's poem?). My mind is all awash with various thoughts;
you; shall you take me for a drive to the sea; the cinema; and so
on; when the door opens and Dadie [G. W. Rylands, the manager]
comes in. Desultory conversation goes on, for I have to think of

what I'm doing and not close the ends of parcels for abroad —
perhaps my greatest sin as a packer. At last I say I want tea." The
bell rings and someone comes in; the telephone rings, someone
else is coming. "We all have tea together. Make toast. Room
frightfully untidy. Never mind. We all chatter hard, about music.
We compare movies and operas; I'm writing that — rather brilliant. All, to me, highly congenial, and even a little exciting, in
the spring light; hammers tapping outside; trees shaking green in
the square. Suddenly we find it's seven and all jump up." [1]

Again: "I can't manage a matinee — for one thing I always
snore; and then we're very brisk at the Press, and my services are
in demand — how I like it! Doing up parcels, please remember
open ends, Mrs. Woolf, with bagmen coming in and out and saying well goodbye all when they leave; and we all say goodbye.
And then I'm given a cup of pale lemon tea and asked to choose
what biscuit I like; and we all sit on the edge of stools and crack
jokes." [2]

She had other defects as a worker besides forgetting to leave
the ends open for parcels going abroad. She loved any new
gadget and tended to play with it. "We've bought a machine for
putting on stamps, only if you joggle it, it puts on three stamps;
has triplets, I say; (I've been doing it all the afternoon) and
Mrs. C. [a member of the staff] is shocked. The Press is very
busy; all the envelopes are going out. A genius has sent me the
most odious book, written on both sides in a crabbed hand; but
it's very good — a tour in Bohemia, by a Welshman. And we
have a vast poem and a huge novel and a monstrous memoir." [3]

Sometimes it seemed as though the work would be too much.
"We're in the midst of our worst week. It always happens — here
are all the books coming out, and our staff collapses. Last year it
was love; we abolished love, took an elderly widow instead; and
now it's measles. One little girl has measles, the other probably

---

[1] Letter to V. Sackville-West (1926).
[2] Letter to V. Sackville-West (1929).
[3] Letter to V. Sackville-West (1927).

mumps. May she go off? So we're left to deal with the bills, the parcels, the callers — a gentleman who has been to Armenia wants to write a book and discourses for an hour about Bishop Gore, Leonard thinking him to mean Ormsby Gore — hence misunderstandings. Then there's our Viola [Viola Tree] — thrown from a taxi and bruised her ribs, and must go to Brighton to recruit. Will we correct her proofs? And Lady Oxford has been at them and scribbled over every margin, 'Darling Viola, don't use the word "naturally" please — I hate it. Don't call Ribblesdale "Rib." All this is trash — ask Mrs. Woolf —' What is the printer to make of it?" [1]

A LITTLE LATER she was writing, "It's a question whether we shan't give up the Press, cut adrift, and make a bolt. Manuscripts shower; authors never cease coming. Viola's book again held up — in short the bother and the work have a little overcome us, for the moment — whether we can keep up with it I mean. But it is also great fun. If you had come in yesterday you would have seen me all strewn with little squares of paper, like a learned pig, making an index for Viola." [2]

This is what comes of taking a stroll in the hinterland of Fleet Street and buying a printing machine in Farringdon Road. The "Queen of Bloomsbury" has turned into a learned pig, and seems to like it. "Well, you may think my life a complete failure. What with one thing and another. All I say is that if it comes to giving people pleasure, I'm sure my printing Mr. Palmer's poems, as I did this summer, gave him more intense pleasure than all the *Common Readers* and *Mrs. Dalloways* I shall ever write gave the rest of the world." [3]

[1] Letter to V. Sackville-West (1926).
[2] To V. Sackville-West (1926).
[3] To V. Sackville-West (1925).

The Hogarth Press gave more than pleasure and a change of occupation to Virginia. When she had written herself into a state of near exhaustion and depression — the two states, physical and mental, were closely connected — the press gave her a comforting and healing sense of security and practical usefulness. "The point of the Press is that it entirely prevents brooding," she noted in her diary in 1924, "and gives me something solid to fall back on. Anyhow, if I can't write, I can make other people write; I can build up a business."

It also saved her the time she might have had to spend with other publishers and editors, hearing what they wanted or having her own ideas doubtfully received. "I'm the only woman in England free to write what I like," she wrote in the diary in 1925. "The others must be thinking of series and editors." She could turn down a suggestion from a publisher, "knowing that I can write a book, a better book off my own bat, for the Press, if I wish!"

All she had to contend with was the natural impatience of Leonard and Dadie urging her on to complete something she was tired of or hopeless about but would not stop revising. Although it might seem to her at the time that they were trying to "extort [a book] drop by drop, from my breast," her husband was in fact always extremely careful to see that she was not unduly pressed. He knew how her health depended on her not getting overtired or overexcited. He watched over her with the maximum of care and minimum of fuss.

He was a tremendously hard worker himself. He wrote, edited, lectured, electioneered, debated, advised, gardened, carpentered, in addition to building up the Hogarth Press from nothing to an honorable position in British publishing. The list of names now famous and ideas that have revolutionized thinking which were introduced to the English-speaking world by this press is quite dazzling.

In the early days, when their output was limited to booklets of one hundred pages or less, he collaborated with S. S.

Koteliansky in translating from the Russian Tchekhov's *Note-books* and Gorky's *Reminiscences of Tchekhov* and *Reminis-cences of Tolstoi*, little masterpieces of biography, quite new in style and still unsurpassed as revelations by one artist of the essential character of other artists with a way of life and a habit of thought entirely foreign. Ivan Bunin's story *The Gentleman from San Francisco* also dates from this time. Other countries besides Russia yielded up some of their disturbing but stimulat-ing secrets to the British public through Hogarth books. Italy was represented by that still insufficiently appreciated ironist, Svevo; Austria by the poems of Rainer Maria Rilke. The press made its largest and probably most important contribution to the spread of new ideas from the continent of Europe when it undertook the publication of the works of Sigmund Freud on behalf of the Institute of Psycho-Analysis. Poetry, fiction, poli-tics, criticism, memoirs, a steady stream of books, all noteworthy, many of them arousing controversy (not to say catcalls) at the time but later acknowledged to be modern classics. T. S. Eliot's *The Waste Land* is a case in point.

Virginia's own share in the early success of the Hogarth Press was due to the fact that her *Kew Gardens* and *The Mark on the Wall* were experimental and therefore excited interest at a time when readers were in a mood to be interested in new techniques of expression. Both these sketches are in what is loosely called the "stream of consciousness" style; that is, they are attempts to relate the inner and the outer world. But they do not consist of idle, meandering thoughts. The writer is actually in strict con-trol of the imagery, has selected and rejected material with as much care as a poet writing a sonnet.

Among the flower beds of Kew a breeze flutters, a snail crawls, butterflies hover, men and women stroll. A married couple think of the past, the man of another woman he might have married, his wife of her childhood. A snail has its problems and adventures among the leaves and stalks, while a mad old man chatters to himself about the spirit world. A pair of lovers say

one thing in words and another in thoughts, and decide to have
tea. It is hot. Couples move into the shade, with much the same
aimless and irregular movement of the flitting butterflies, the
glancing light. Everything seems to dissolve in light, like drops
of water. Voices waver into silence.

Wordless voices, breaking the silence suddenly with such depth
of contentment, such passion of desire, or, in the voices of children, such freshness of surprise; breaking the silence? But there
was no silence; all the time the motor omnibuses were turning
their wheels and changing their gear; like a vast nest of Chinese
boxes all wrought steel turning ceaselessly one within another
the city murmured; on the top of which the voices cried aloud
and the petals of myriads of flowers flashed their colors into the
air.

The sketch (or story — but if it is a story it is quite a new
kind of short story) ends as it began, with a reference to the
play of light on flowers. The effect is that of a closing chord in
music or the final line and word of a poem. The circle has been
completed; it has enclosed not chaos but a series of images
linked by a compelling inner logic.

The Mark on the Wall is different in mood and in matter,
but similar in method. The writer, sitting by the fire one wintry day, notices a mark on the wall above the mantelpiece. What
can it be? A hole showing where a nail once held up a picture
for the people who lived here before? "Very interesting people, and I think of them so often, in such queer places, because
one will never see them again, never know what happened next."
This leads back to a recollection of things lost in one lifetime
— all kinds of things: "All gone, — and jewels, too. Opals and
emeralds, they lie about the roots of turnips."

But perhaps it is not a hole made by a nail. "It may even be
caused by some round black substance, such as a small rose leaf,
left over the summer, and I, not being a very vigilant housekeeper — look at the dust on the mantelpiece, for example,
the dust which, so they say, buried Troy three times over, only

fragments of pots utterly refusing annihilation, as one can believe."

She tries to anchor her thoughts; there is something unpleasant she does not want to think about. Shakespeare, the Greeks? But this leads to generalizations, which are worthless. "The military sound of the word is enough. It recalls leading articles, cabinet ministers — a whole class of things indeed which, as a child, one thought the thing itself, the standard thing, the real thing, from which one could not depart save at the risk of nameless damnation." Which brings back memories of the time when there was a rule for everything, even for the patterns of tablecloths. What has become of those rules? What has become of *Whitaker's Almanack,* with its Table of Precedency, since the war?

To get back to that mark on the wall. It suggests now "a smooth tumulus, like those barrows on the South Downs which are, they say, either tombs or camps." And so to antiquarians, and what a pleasant life that is for retired colonels. "It gives them a feeling of importance, and the comparison of arrowheads necessitates cross-country journeys to county towns, an agreeable necessity both to them and to their elderly wives, who wish to make plum jam or to clean out the study, and have every wish for keeping that great question of the camp or the tomb in perpetual suspension." Yes, it is easy to imagine a very pleasant world — if it were not for the Table of Precedency! If it were not for the mark on the wall.

"Now that I have fixed my eyes upon it, I feel that I have grasped a plank in the sea; I feel a satisfying sense of reality." A plank brings thoughts of wood, which comes from trees, which grow, we don't know how, for years and years, through summer days and winter nights. And when the last storm comes, "Even so, life isn't done with; there are a million patient, watchful lives still for a tree, all over the world, in bedrooms, in ships, on the pavement, lining rooms, where men and women sit after tea, smoking cigarettes. It is full of peaceful thoughts,

happy thoughts, this tree. I should like to take each one separately — but something is getting in the way." Someone has
come into the room and is speaking about going out to buy a
newspaper.

"'Though it's no good buying newspapers. . . . Nothing ever
happens. Curse this war; God damn this war! . . . All the same,
I don't see why we should have a snail on our wall.'

"Ah, the mark on the wall! It was a snail."

This analysis shows Virginia Woolf's basic method. The
thoughts are connected, the words simple, the images clear.
The effect is profound. With the words, "Curse this war," everything falls into place. Now the reader knows what was the
thought that had to be avoided and that kept thrusting itself
forward, bringing to mind people one will never see again, lost
possessions, dust that buried cities, the safe world of childhood
gone forever, generals and colonels, camps and tombs. The
drumbeat has been sounded again and again; it is heard in the
final crash.

But is this a death march we have been hearing? No. There
are cymbals and flutes and violins in the orchestra, too, signify-
ing life, which persists and triumphs over death. Women make
jam and dust rooms; the arrowheads are in a museum; the old
order of precedency has gone but one can have a new sort of
tablecloth without fear of damnation; bones are buried, but
jewels are dug up with turnips; the sap rises in trees. That mark
on the wall? Inexplicable how it got there, that snail. But, all
the same, why should we have a snail on our wall?

Further readings will reveal other harmonies, other meanings.
One does not have to probe for them; they come to the surface.
These early sketches provide clues to more than her writing
method, for in them she asks questions to which she went on
seeking an answer all her life, large, unanswerable questions
about the nature of reality, the limits of human knowledge, the
possibilities of understanding ourselves and other living creatures. Here are images which will recur again and again in her

writing, turns of phrase which will later be recognized as characteristic, like familiar gestures or favorite colors. She refined upon the method, cutting out more and more extraneous detail, but the object of that method remained fundamentally simple; it was an attempt to get ever closer to what she desired to express. She wanted not only to see a vision but to share it.

For a woman who gained a reputation of being aloof, who was far too honest and sensible ever to pretend that she was exactly like everybody else, and who sometimes baffled even her most intimate friends by the complexity of her nature, she had a curious power of conveying the illusion that admission to her private thoughts was free. She was proud and yet humble, sophisticated but simple. Her writing, even at its most lyrical and allusive, remained somehow conversational, so that the reader gets a feeling of having established personal contact. She did not preach but was willing, indeed anxious, to explain. She did not demand agreement, but she did want attention, and by assuming that she was being heard she also implied that she was ready to listen.

It was this eminently civilized attitude which won such a warm response for her work. Here was something new and exciting, strange but not inexplicable, calling for active participation on the part of the reader, bringing a rich reward.

Chapter VI

HER PREVIOUSLY published work had been mainly anonymous, consisting for the most part of reviews in the *Times Literary Supplement* — "the Major Journal," as she and Leonard called it. When the editor telephoned from Printing House Square to her at Richmond, it was like receiving a summons from a high priest to take part in the weekly sacrifice on the altar of English letters. A reverential public would be duly impressed by the stately ritual, but the performers would be enveloped in robes. Any tendency on the part of choirboys to giggle or incense burners to sneeze had to be suppressed. The congregation would be permitted to comment afterwards if a soloist sang flat or a rose strewer ran short of blossoms, but not allowed to ask questions about the identity of a participant in the ceremony. Behind the scenes, of course, this reverential atmosphere did not prevail.

Virginia Woolf's name was not quite unknown to the public. It had appeared when her first novel, *The Voyage Out,* was offered as a contribution to culture in 1915. This was the book she had taken seven years to write. It fell almost flat. In the second year of the war the country had more serious business to attend to than welcoming new writers. Novel readers wanted more of the sort of thing they expected from established favorites, or something that was relevant to the problems of the civilian in wartime, such as H. G. Wells's *Mr. Britling Sees It Through.*

She said good-by thankfully to this first of her books in 1913 and only brought herself to look at it again when her second was published and she was at work on her third in 1920. She had a horror of reading her own writings, did it "always with a kind of guilty intensity" — almost as though she were spying on a dead self. Any issue of a magazine in which a contribution of hers appeared was ruined for her, and thoughts about a finished book were usually painful, reviving memories of the drudgery involved or the agonies of creation or the periods of doubt whether she would ever capture the vision as it first came to her.

She reread *The Voyage Out* because she was genuinely puzzled by the contradictory comparisons which her friends made between it and her second novel, *Night and Day*. Clive Bell was enthusiastic about the second, having been critical of the first. E. M. Forster preferred the first. She herself thought that *Night and Day* was "much more mature and finished and satisfactory"; and had reason to be. She had actually enjoyed writing the last half, and no part of it had taxed her as *The Voyage Out* had done. But when the reviewers, as well as people whose opinion she valued because she understood their standards, gave reasons for liking the first book better, she nerved herself to look at it again, not without wondering, "Is the time coming when I can endure to read my own writing in print without blushing — shivering and wishing to take cover?"

Authors are usually the least reliable critics of their own work. They know what they were aiming at, they can say what they like best. Apart from that, it is wisest, as a rule, not to ask them to express an opinion. They are apt to behave like parents who cherish a weakling because he has been hard to rear, while underrating a sturdy youngster who has never given them a moment's anxiety. Show an author a series of portraits of himself in his books and he is more likely than not to ignore a passably accurate picture, to smile indulgently at a sentimental one, and to reject vehemently one that reveals him as a strong and admirable, if rugged, character.

Virginia Woolf, faced with a picture of herself as she had been seven years previously, showed quite remarkable detachment. "What a harlequinade," she said of *The Voyage Out,* "such an assortment of patches — here simple and severe — here frivolous and shallow — here like God's truth — here strong and free flowing as I could wish. What to make of it, Heaven knows." The failures made her blush; but "my word, what a gift for pen and ink." She could understand how people "find it a more gallant and inspiring spectacle" than *Night and Day.* "On the whole," she concluded, "I like the young woman's mind considerably."

She was right, on all points. If the book had not been published in the second year of the war, its originality and power would have attracted more attention. If she had never written anything else, she would be "discovered" at intervals; she would be seen as a forerunner; her unfulfilled promise would be deplored. But as she went on to write much better books, this first novel is regarded as something of a curiosity. For it is a hotchpotch, a ragbag into which she crammed to bursting all kinds of glittering oddments. Some have faded, only recalling a memory; others still keep their luster and can be used with striking effect.

What Virginia Woolf did not note in her diary when she reread *The Voyage Out* was the weakness of its construction. The plot has a broken back and asymmetrical limbs. In later books the strength springs from the spine and is felt at the tips of delicately probing fingers. This first one is like a doll that a child has loved too much and too long. To an unsympathetic adult it is a deplorable object, no doubt. To a more understanding eye the fact that the arm by which it was lugged about hangs by a thread, that the dye from its wig has stained its painted face, and that it has lost a foot are details revealing how it was cherished, on how many imaginary adventures and actual journeys it accompanied its small owner.

The Voyage Out begins as though it were a mystery story.

Down from the Strand to the Embankment one darkening October afternoon stride a tall, eccentric couple, oblivious of their surroundings, the man lost in thought, the woman in sorrow. They pause by the river while the man recites verses aloud and the woman weeps. What is this dreadful grief that afflicts her, what doom ahead? As a matter of fact, Helen Ambrose is upset because she has just said good-by to her children for a few months in order to accompany her husband, Ridley Ambrose, on a journey for the sake of his health. The children are mentioned once or twice again, very casually. We never learn their names or anything about them; they play no part in the story, except to establish the fact that Helen is a mother. But she is primarily a wife. She loves her children dearly, but her husband is her first charge, her spoiled darling. She is an adumbration of Julia Stephen. Ridley Ambrose recalls Leslie Stephen. Rachel Vinrace, the heroine of the book, is largely Virginia herself. The author of this novel is following one of the first rules for fiction, writing about what she knows best.

But before the reader meets Virginia Stephen in the person of Rachel Vinrace he will find indications that Virginia Woolf has passed this way. Sometimes they are as faint as the marks left by the feet of a bird hopping on crusted snow; as when Helen sees the lights of the West End of London like a "small golden tassel on the edge of a vast black cloak." This tassel is an image that will recur; it is the symbol for Jinny on the first page of *The Waves*. Cloaks also are important, though their significance is hard to assess; they are mentioned time and again in various books.

Sometimes the footprints are deeper. Helen and Ridley make their way eastward along the riverside from Waterloo Bridge to Tower Bridge, through ever narrower, dirtier, noisier, more smelly streets, to where the obsolete cannons gape their empty mouths, like Chinese dragons, guarding the dead but not in the least degree terrifying the little boys who play on the cobblestones of the terrace at high tide or in the mud below when the tide is out. This was one of Virginia's favorite spots. She disliked the Tower of London, because of its gruesome history as a prison and place of execution, but she liked to find her way there on foot, when she was in London, enjoying the very names of the old city streets, Bread Street, Camomile Street, Seething Lane, and the churches, All Hallows, St. Olave's.

Here, where they can walk no farther and can see their ship anchored in midstream, they hail an ancient waterman to row them out to her. He has very few passengers these days, he tells them. "He seemed to recall an age when his boat, moored among rushes, carried delicate feet across to lawns at Rother-hithe." This is the voice of Virginia Woolf the reviewer, who can read the most ponderous volumes of memoirs and letters and find some glint of poetry in them, flashing her light into a lead mine and extracting a jewel, convincing the reader that there is not a dull book nor an uninteresting person in the world.

Helen Ambrose's beauty is frequently mentioned in *The Voyage Out*. To her niece Rachel, who is already aboard the *Euphrosyne*, she is "tall, large-eyed, draped in purple shawls, romantic and beautiful; not perhaps sympathetic, for her eyes looked straight and considered what they saw." Later in the book a man admires "not so much her beauty, but her largeness and simplicity, which made her stand out from the rest like a great stone woman." Further on still we see her as she embroiders (as Virginia did): "With one foot raised on the rung of the chair, and her elbow out in the attitude for sewing, her figure possessed the sublimity of a woman's of the early world, spinning the thread of fate."

There is a great deal more about Helen Ambrose in this book. She is revealed as shrewd, capable, humorous, active. She dances (although at forty she fears it is rather unsuitable for an elderly woman). She teases her husband out of his ill-humor or melancholy and skillfully covers up the embarrassment he often causes by saying aloud exactly what he thinks. She peeps in at

lighted hotel windows, like a schoolgirl. She manages grumbling
servants. She is excellent in a sickroom. She has strong views
about education and religion, and can express them pointedly
without being aggressive. As a character she is not completely
realized, being too many-sided and complex. Though one does
not get to know her intimately, she walks and talks and laughs,
has flesh on her bones and blood in her veins. But somehow all
the details that show her in action concern a woman who is
quite unrelated to the spectral, symbolical figure that haunts
these pages, strangely compounded of stone and shadow, the
unhuman being whose eyes look straight ahead, and who does
not come when called.

Ridley Ambrose is more sharply alive. He is not important
to the story, but he has many idiosyncrasies that remind the
reader of Virginia's father. Wherever he travels he carries his
books with him. Even on board ship he has to continue working
on his translations or editing. Life has always to revolve around
the room in which he sits "hour after hour among white-leaved
books, alone like an idol in an empty church" while his chair
becomes more and more deeply circled by the volumes he has
consulted and dumped on the floor. He objects to women's
smoking. He is quite unmusical and devoid of a sense of humor
unless a fellow scholar and he can exchange reminiscences about
events and persons quite unknown to the rest of the company;
then, even at the height of a storm at sea he is "quite oblivious of
all tumult . . . in Cambridge . . . probably about the year
1875."

Above all, he enjoys being a martyr. If the slightest thing
interferes with his routine he convinces himself that it has occurred because someone has taken pains to torment him, but
he will face it like a man. A delay in receiving an expected letter is apt to plunge him in despair. He is sure he is already forgotten and ignored by the entire civilized world. Then he will
"gaze into the depths of the looking glass, compressing his face
into the likeness of a commander surveying a field of battle, or

a martyr watching the flames lick his toes, rather than that of a secluded Professor."

It is a caricature, but not a cruel one. And his wife, dealing with these recurrent crises, is not a stone woman.

As for Rachel Vinrace being Virginia Stephen, all Virginia Woolf's books are, to quote Elizabeth Bowen, "transmuted autobiography." All fiction is, for that matter. Even the deliberate distortion or manipulation of the bare facts serves to reveal the personality of the writer. In *The Voyage Out* the attempt at self-portraiture is obvious. Rachel has to express the thoughts that troubled the young Virginia, find the answers she was seeking. Some of the questions asked in this first novel are those Virginia was to go on asking all her life. What is truth? What is reality? Can one human being ever fully know another? Not by a recital of literal facts, Rachel is sure, and Virginia will explain; for precise account ignores what is basic, one's feelings. And how can one express one's feelings in any truthful sense, particularly if one has led the sheltered life of a delicate girl of the English middle class in the early twentieth century?

There were other questions, too, more immediate and personal, confronting Rachel Vinrace and Virginia Stephen at the time this novel was written. The relations between the sexes, love and marriage, presented problems that demanded attention.

Rachel is a young woman of twenty-four, very intelligent but so immature that she seems to Helen to have in some respects the mental age of about six. An only child, motherless since she was eleven years old, she has been brought up by elderly aunts in Richmond, surrounded always by "excessive care, which as a child was for her health; as a girl and young woman for what it seems almost crude to call her morals. Until quite lately she had been completely ignorant that for women such things existed. She groped for knowledge in old books, and found it in repulsive chunks."

The seclusion at Richmond was varied by seclusion at sea, when she accompanied her father, a burly, capable man, owner of a small fleet of cargo ships that occasionally carried passengers. Her education had been of the casual kind thought appropriate for well-to-do girls at the end of the nineteenth century. She had acquired the rudiments of about ten different branches of knowledge, but had never been forced, by school discipline or competition with others, to master any subject thoroughly. "Her mind was in the state of an intelligent man's in the beginning of the reign of Queen Elizabeth; she would believe practically anything she was told, invent reasons for anything she said." The only thing she really knew anything about was music. "If this definite gift was surrounded by dreams and ideas of the most extravagant and foolish description, no one was any the wiser."

She is extremely shy, awkward, and unable to express herself. Dreamy and indolent, except as regards music, she occasionally blazes into anger against her own impotence and what she senses to be the hypocrisy of those who so kindly block her way to genuine freedom. Her frustration expresses the protest which Virginia wished to make against the system which rendered so many young women of her class and time unfit to be anything but ladies in the genteel Victorian sense, instead of healthy, useful women of the twentieth century.

The *Euphrosyne* sails out of the Thames and the voyage is uneventful. At the first port of call, Lisbon, two more passengers come aboard, Mr. and Mrs. Richard Dalloway. They come from another world altogether from that inhabited by the scholarly Ridley, the artistic Helen or the ignorant Rachel. Theirs is the world of politics and fashion.

Richard Dalloway is an ex-Member of Parliament temporarily without a seat, making use of a period of leisure to catch up on foreign affairs and to refresh himself for the task of giving Britain better, wiser and more humane laws when he returns to Westminster. He calls himself a Conservative, but that is only for convenience, he explains. He is prouder of having reduced the working day by one hour than he would be if he had written all the poetry of Shelley and Keats. And though he is prepared to work himself to an early death, if necessary, on behalf of factory girls and elderly widows, "May I be in my grave before a woman has the right to vote in England!" His pompous conversation fascinates Rachel, and he, having nothing else to do, is not averse to showing himself off to her. For he and his wife, though deeply attached to one another, are both natural-born flirts.

Clarissa Dalloway is beautiful and fashionable. She has all the social gifts and can no more help exerting an easy charm than a butterfly can conceal its brilliant colors. Her inner self is as unguessed as the chrysalis past of a butterfly is forgotten on a sunny day. She chatters endlessly and amusingly to everyone; to a sailor about ships, to Ridley about Greek, to Helen about children, to Rachel about music. And then, having bemused and flattered everyone by this show of interest in what interests them, she writes chatty letters to her friends describing the weird set of cranks she finds herself amongst. "They talk about art, and think us such poops for dressing in the evening. However, I can't help that." Helen is dismissed because she "dresses in a potato sack and wears her hair like a Liberty shopgirl's." Rachel is "a nice, shy girl — poor thing . . . only, of course, she'll get funny too. We ought to start a society for broadening the minds of the young — much more useful than missionaries!"

In her careless way she does contribute to Rachel's education. So does Richard, by a quite unexpected kiss. The revelation of her own mixed feelings, no less than the man's impulsive action, are profoundly disturbing to the girl. Something wonderful, but at the same time terrifying, has happened. She has a dreadful nightmare, in which she finds herself trapped in a tunnel and vault, "alone with a little deformed man who squatted on the floor, gibbering, with long nails." Even after she wakes she cannot shake off the horror. "All night long barbarian men harassed the ship; they came scuffling down the passages, and stopped to snuffle at her door."

Next morning the ship calls at another port, and the Dalloways depart. In this book the author has no further use for them. When the reader meets them again Clarissa will be seen as quite a different woman, though still charming, worldly and the wife of an ambitious politician; for Virginia Woolf's attitude and way of presenting a character will have changed by the time *Mrs. Dalloway* comes to be written.

The voyage continues. Helen notices there is something wrong with Rachel, and induces her to talk about it. As a result the barrier between the two women is broken and they are able to become friends; not close friends, but at least contact is established. Helen decides that when she and Ridley land at their South American destination, she will ask Rachel to stay with them instead of accompanying her father up the Amazon.

With the departure of the Dalloways, the author, seeking to come to grips with her subject, loses control of her plot. The book really does become a harlequinade; hilarious slapstick alternating with tragic symbolism, miscellaneous characters in fancy dress wandering on and off stage more or less at random, against a backcloth of the sketchiest kind.

The scene of action is now called, for convenience, Santa Marina. But all attempts to locate it on a map of South America would be useless. Actually it exists nowhere on earth — it is a little bit of Hyde Park Gate, Bloomsbury, Cambridge and Richmond transported overseas and summarily dumped. There is a house, just outside a village, for Helen, Ridley and Rachel, but it has a completely English interior and the domestic work is carried on by vaguely "native" servants who appear to know to the last detail what the British middle class expect in the way of punctuality, cleanliness and cooking. There is a hotel which might just as well be at Brighton or Hastings. The author occasionally remembers that she is supposed to provide an exotic background, but for the most part cannot be bothered.

Among the visitors at the hotel are two young men, straight out of Cambridge, clearly friends of Virginia's brothers. It is a waste of time to attempt to identify them more exactly, for all the characters are sketched from life as Virginia knew it, their names in an address book serving the same humdrum purpose as in the novel. The sketches are brilliant, but they are not finished portraits. These people exist in the story to help pull together what is left of the plot to accompany Rachel on her voyage of discovery. They also provide incidental pointers to Virginia's attitudes.

One of the young men, Terence Hewet, arranges a fantastic — and quite English — picnic, on top of a pasteboard mountain, and is strolling with Rachel when they come upon another couple, Susan and Arthur, who have just declared their love and are rapturously embracing. "I don't like that," says Rachel. Later, when he asks her what she is thinking about so deeply, she answers, "Human beings." She is aware not only of her own ignorance but of the difficulty of acquiring knowledge, whether about herself or about others, and in particular about the relationship between the sexes.

There is a dance one night at the hotel. Terence comes upon Rachel in a state of great agitation, but she finds it impossible to explain to him why his clever friend's unconscious assumption of male superiority has seemed to her not only galling but terrible, as though a door to friendship and understanding had suddenly been slammed in her face. To Terence, however, the incident seems ludicrous, and he induces Rachel to laugh.

The experienced novel reader knows that Terence and Rachel are falling in love; but they both resist the idea. Terence is the first to admit it to himself. He imagines himself speaking to Rachel. What would she answer if he said to her, "I worship you, but I loathe marriage, I hate its smugness, its safety, its compromise, and the thought of you interfering in my work, hindering me"? Uncertain of her response, he suddenly exults at the thought of her, "Oh, you're free! And I'd keep you free. We'd be free together. We'd share everything together. No happiness would be like ours. No lives would compare with ours."

It is when they are wandering in the forest while on an expedition up the Amazon that the revelation comes. They like being together, they are happy together, very happy. "'We love each other,' Terence said. 'We love each other,' she repeated." It is wonderful, but it is also terrible. She needs to be reassured. "Is it true, or is it a dream?" she asks. "It's true, it's true," he answers.

But will it last? How will it work out in practice? They are so different, so separate. She does not listen when he talks about the books he is going to write. He interrupts her when she is playing the piano. "The hopelessness of their position overcame them both. They were impotent; they could never love each other sufficiently to overcome all these barriers." He suggests "risking" an immediate marriage. She suggests breaking the engagement. "The words did more to unite them than any amount of argument. As if they stood on the edge of a precipice they clung together. They knew that they could not separate; painful and terrible it might be, but they were joined for ever."

And then, when they have reached an equilibrium, when they are planning what they will do together in a few weeks' time in London, when the future seems safe and certain, Rachel has a headache, has to go to bed, develops a fever, and, after several days of delirium, dies.

For her the voyage of exploration has ended on the farthest shore. Life goes on as usual in the hotel. Only Terence and Helen are numb with the sense of loss, appalled by the senselessness of blind fate, face the tragic mask that hides an unknowable reality.

In this first novel, so gay, so witty, so amusing, so lit by beauty and decorated with such bright fancies, Virginia asks the final,

unanswerable questions, and displays the hidden melancholy of
her mind no less than the relentless pride and stubborn courage
with which she fought it.

It was inevitable that all her friends should be awaiting the
publication of her second novel, *Night and Day,* with the liveli-
est curiosity, for so much had happened in the intervening four
years. She had in her own life solved the problem which caused
Rachel and Terence such anguish, how a husband and wife can
share everything together and be free together. She had shown
her quality as a critic in the columns of the *Times Literary Supplement* (the anonymity imposed in public was not, of course,
preserved in private), and displayed her astonishing virtuosity
and originality in *Kew Gardens* and *The Mark on the Wall.*
Her friends knew they had a fabulous bird in their midst — a
swan, perhaps even a phoenix. What kind of egg would it hatch
next?

Even her husband did not know until a few days before she
had the final typescript ready to submit to her half brother
Gerald Duckworth for publication by his firm. Her sister and
the others still had to wait a few months until the book was
ready. This was normal procedure. Virginia Woolf had a room
of her own, such as Helen Ambrose had provided for Rachel
Vinrace in the house at Santa Marina: "a room cut off from
the rest of the house . . . in which she could read, think, defy
the world, a fortress as well as a sanctuary." Leonard Woolf
never asked an author about work in progress, and read
his wife's manuscripts with the same critical detachment he accorded to other writers. At least, this is what they both hoped,
though when the verdict was favorable she was inclined to dis-
count it, and he cannot have been unaware that she was in misery until she heard what he had to say.

He devoted two mornings and two evenings to reading *Night and Day,* and then announced his approval, though he did find its philosophy very melancholy. Virginia was not prepared to dispute this. "Yet, if one is to deal with people on a large scale, how can one avoid melancholy? I don't admit to being hopeless, though: only the spectacle is a profoundly strange one," she noted in her diary, "and as the current answers don't do, one has to grope for a new one, and the process of discarding the old, when one is by no means certain what to put in their place, is a sad one. Still, if you think of it, what answers do Arnold Bennett or Thackeray, for instance, suggest? Happy ones — satisfactory solutions — answers one would accept, if one had the least respect for one's soul?"

The reader expecting something entirely revolutionary will be disappointed. What he is offered in *Night and Day* is basically the mixture as before. Again one of the main themes is how to find the right partner, how to be happy and self-respecting though married, how to be quite sure that love is not just a mischief-maker.

The form is conventional, too. One gets the impression that Virginia Woolf has been listening to advice on how to write a novel, and she is determined to get it right this time. It has been sound, solid advice, the sort of thing any good literary agent, publisher's reader or professor of English in a college would tell an aspirant. Stick to what you know; don't let your imagination run away with you; remember that the reader likes to have details, color of hair, eyes, etc; each chapter should have a curtain; don't forget your plot; don't leave any loose ends — tell what happened and when; work to a climax; end with a snap. And so on.

The result is that whenever these simple rules for beginners are heeded the book shows signs of constraint. The characters become puppets dancing on a string; incidents are contrived; the talk is witty but superficial; details are handed out like tickets of admission to a free show. It is only when the author stops being a good little girl and doing as she is told that the novel stimulates the imagination and holds the reader's attention.

The fact is that Virginia Woolf could only follow the laws of her own nature. She was both foursquare and high-flown. She could say bluntly exactly what she meant, but, once having taken her stand, her thoughts had to be allowed to go spiraling away. What she would bring down from the upper air might be the merest thistledown or a ray from a dark star. What it is no use expecting her to provide is a regular weekly menu of three meals a day. A home from home, yes; but the traveler must really have left his own home before resting at her inn.

Even before one reads the first page of a novel that has, it must be freely admitted, considerable dull and unconvincing stretches and is the least successful of her novels, the reader is caught and held by a goassamer thread. The dedication runs: "To Vanessa Bell. But, looking for a phrase, I found none to stand beside your name." What could be more simple, more revealing of the deepest love between sisters? It is so light one fears a breath might blur its perfection. It is as solid as if carved on rock.

In the opening scene of *Night and Day* we are briskly introduced to Katherine Hilbery and Ralph Denham. She is dispensing tea in her parents' drawing room, and he, a newcomer, is one of the callers, a contributor to the review edited by her father. Almost immediately there springs up an antagonism between them. She is polite but bored; he is ill at ease and provokingly rude. Each of them displays what Virginia Woolf called "angularities." This antagonism is part of the plot. It is intended to bring out the difference between their two worlds. He is a young lawyer, struggling to support a mother and large family of brothers and sisters in Highgate. She is a rich girl, of very distinguished family, living in Chelsea surrounded by living celebrities and relics of an illustrious past. But more is revealed than that Katherine is discontented and Ralph is ambitious, and that they are bound to fall in love and get married in due novelistic course. What is immediately obvious is that the author is working against the grain. Fundamentally she does not care about either of these people, but she has set herself the task of writing a novel which shall be better than her first.

Although Katherine Hilbery is said to live at Cheyne Walk, Chelsea, she appears against the background of Virginia Stephen's home at Hyde Park Gate. But Virginia Woolf had really finished with that world. She enjoyed satirizing it, but to do it justice, as it deserved, was another matter.

Katherine, like Rachel Vinrace, was an only child. Like Rachel, too, she had a secret passion. It was not for music but for mathematics; which, for a young woman of her time, might be called a guilty secret. No one was allowed to guess anything so unlikely, so discreditable, so opposed to the tradition of her family. It was known that she managed the household and was helping her mother to write the biography of Mrs. Hilbery's father, a poet, who had been so eminent and in addition such a "good and great man" that he was buried in Westminster Abbey.

Katherine's share in this work mainly consisted in trying to keep her mother to the point, to stick to a schedule that would eventually get the job finished. But after ten years, in spite of all Katherine's efforts at organization and discipline, the book was no nearer completion; and no one knew that Katherine "infinitely preferred the exactitude, the star-like impersonality, of figures to the confusion, agitation, and vagueness of the finest prose." Unlike Rachel, Katherine was sick of talking or writing about feelings; she wanted facts; she wanted action. Like Virginia, she needed a wider world than a comfortable home, a better equipment for facing life than a private education.

By following the twists and turns of the narrative of *Night and Day* we learn how Katherine first gets herself engaged, then disengaged, then re-engaged to a foolish, fretful, boring young man of her own class and background, William Rodney; how the right girl for him turns up in the nick of time; how Katherine arranges to pair them off; how Ralph Denham nearly marries another woman, Mary Datchet, who sincerely loves him but has enough sense and pride not to accept him; and how Katherine's mother, incompetent and fluttering though she is, rounds up the exasperated but infatuated Ralph and delivers him safely to her incomprehensible but beloved daughter. Two couples are triumphantly steered towards marriage with suitable partners, and Mary Datchet forswears romance and devotes herself to her life work for the emancipation of women.

THIS summary of the plot is misleading and unfair to *Night and Day* as a whole, for of course it has more than plot; it has ideas. But they are ideas which the author has expressed before, and will deal with again, much more effectively. The need to keep her characters moving in a prescribed pattern to a foreseen end interrupts the thought, and the thought impedes the action. It is as though the dancers in a minuet try to carry on a serious conversation as they bow and curtsy, advance and retreat, exchange partners and get back to places, without becoming entangled in their elaborate clothes. Jitterbuggers in jeans have more opportunities to express what is really in their minds than the ladies and gentlemen who have to pick their steps so carefully. In neither case is there any time to pause for reflection or argument about what to do next. *The Voyage Out* was more like a slow one-step on a crowded floor, during which quite a lot can be said, or otherwise expressed.

Lytton Strachey praised *Night and Day* because it was formal and classic. Virginia valued his approval, without ever being sure in advance what his opinion of her work would be, since their tastes in literature were often diametrically opposed, he preferring restrained elegance while she appreciated robustness. Clive Bell, who upheld his own interpretation of the Greek ideal and wanted to see it expressed in modern life, was enthusiastic. So was Vanessa Bell, to whom the background of Katherine Hilbery's home life was, of course, familiar, and who undoubtedly recognized all those fantastic aunts who troop in and out of the story, giving their well-meant and unwanted advice on decorum. There is a good deal of her own character in Katherine, too; her capacity for being silent and then coming out with some forceful remark, very much to the point; her impatience with endless dissections of feelings when to her, as a painter, there were other relations so much more important to be considered.

E. M. Forster shared Lytton Strachey's view that *Night and Day* had a strictly classical form, but did not care for it because he found none of the characters lovable. There is a great deal of truth in this. If one is to write about love the author must convey to the reader a strong feeling that it is very important what happens in the end. Virginia recognized that Forster had put his finger on the novel's weak spot. "Morgan has the artist's mind," she wrote in her diary. "He says the simple things that clever people don't say; I find him the best of critics for that reason. Suddenly out comes the obvious thing that one has overlooked." He himself was at this time "in trouble with a novel of his own, fingering the keys but only producing discords so far." This novel was *Passage to India,* which took him so many years to write and which, he confessed many years later, he might never have finished without Leonard Woolf's encouragement. He was probably talking as much to himself as to Virginia that day at Richmond in 1919, when he explained to her what he felt about digesting one's own experiences so that a story based on fact is sufficiently impersonal to convey a general idea and sufficiently personal to carry over to the reader the author's own feelings about his characters and their fate.

Night and Day gives little information that is new about Virginia herself, except that she had largely overcome her extreme shyness and that she had endeavored to interest herslf in the women's suffrage movement. There are several examples of the unconscious masculine attitude of superiority, which she continued to notice and to resent; but now they are shown to be ludicrous, not felt to be crushing. She had learned how to answer back any attempt at patronizing women with mockery rather than by subsiding into misery.

She had found out what women were trying to do in a practical way to get the vote. Mary Datchet is one of the most strongly realized figures in this book. She is a woman of clear insight and considerable ability, unsentimental, but with deep natural feelings. In her office in Russell Square and in her attic somewhere off the Strand, Katherine gains a notion of how campaigns are planned, leaflets drafted, finances accounted for, statistics and arguments marshaled, committees steered, halls hired, debates arranged, letters to editors written. But Mary is not an automaton. It is through her that Katherine comes to understand that she does not love the man she has promised to marry, whereas Mary does love the man who attracts and irritates Katherine. Mary's other self, quite apart from her sex life, found satisfaction in the realm of politics. It was to her what mathematics were to Katherine, what music was to Rachel, what writing was to Virginia.

So Virginia, visiting the office of the Women's Co-operative Guild after the Manchester conference, could admire the devotion of women who worked there, could believe in every ideal at which they aimed, but knew she could not share their labors. She would be no good at it, and no amount of struggling along these lines would lead her to an understanding of the inner lives of other people.

British women got the vote in 1918. It made very little difference. The heavens did not open, nor did they fall. Mary Datchet went on working, Virginia Woolf went on writing.

THE CRITICS disagreed, as usual, about *Night and Day.* The author decided, as she always did, to go on in her own way. She learned something from every book she wrote. When she was planning *The Years,* a novel that has something in common with *Night and Day,* she noted in her diary: "I can take liberties with the representational form which I could not dare when I wrote *Night and Day* — a book that taught me much, bad though it may be."

The key word here is "dare." It was because she could not let herself go at this time that *Night and Day* is so disappointing and baffling. Reading it is like walking over a beautiful carpet that has unexpectedly worn patches; suddenly one nearly trips over a hole. A very small hole, but none the less disconcerting.

One cannot even be sure of the period, except that it is definitely pre-World War I. Presumably it is Edwardian, but sometimes seems Georgian, sometimes Victorian. Mrs. Hilbery speaks of young men "always going up in aeroplanes." On the other hand, she is driven about London and in the country in a carriage. But one cannot judge anything by Mrs. Hilbery, who was "beautifully adapted for life in another planet," but had "a natural insight which saw deep when it saw at all," so that she had a "way of seeming the wisest person in the room." Still, it is odd that there is no indication of the existence of automobiles.

The telephone is mysterious, too. It seems invariably to be hidden away somewhere. Even in Mary's efficiently run office answering the telephone necessitates getting up and going into another room, but perhaps that is because the author wanted to interrupt a conversation and get her characters moving about again. In Katherine's home the telephone is a sort of little idol, perched on a shelf in an "alcove on the stairs, screened by a curtain of purple velvet." But there are so many curtains in that house, behind which people can hide and emerge melodramatically at the right moment, exclaiming, "I have heard all!"

Ideas about manners and morals are curiously mixed. Young men are concerned lest "people talk" about their being seen with young women in the streets of London late at night, but one of Katherine's cousins lives in sin and has illegitimate children on principle. Katherine can tell her mother that she and Ralph don't want to get married but are thinking of staying together in a country cottage, and this does not bring a vehement protest. In fact, Mrs. Hilbery, trying to discover what the hesitations are all about, thinks they may have something to do with an objection to a church service, involving a homily on the procreation of children and the wife's vow to love, honor and obey the husband. This is not actually what is troubling them, however; it is the same problem that perplexed Rachel and Terence in *The Voyage Out* — how to live together in the completest union and yet still be free to roam unquestioned in their separate worlds of thought. So far as ceremony is concerned, when Mrs. Hilbery characteristically asks Ralph, "You would marry her in Westminster Abbey if the worst came to the worst?", he replies, "I would marry her in St. Paul's Cathedral." Now, is this comedy à la George Meredith, or is it what might be considered a typical Bloomsbury exchange? One thing it is certainly not — the kind of down-to-earth discussion that Anthony Trollope would have given us about the fact that Katherine is rich and Ralph is poor.

And then there are the baffling references to clothes. There is a magnificent description of a visit to a music hall:

. . . an entertainment where Polar bears follow directly upon ladies in full evening dress, and the stage is alternately a garden of mystery, a milliner's band-box, and a fried-fish shop in the

Mile End Road. . . . The hall resounded with brass and strings, alternately of enormous pomp and majesty, and then of sweetest lamentation. The reds and creams of the background, the lyres and harps and urns and skulls, the protuberances of plaster, the fringes of scarlet plush, the sinking and blazing of innumerable lights, could scarcely have been surpassed for decorative effect by any craftsman of the ancient or modern world. Then there was the audience itself, bare-shouldered, tufted and garlanded in the stalls, decorous but festive in the balconies, and frankly fit for daylight and street life in the galleries.

But, one asks, was evening dress worn in music halls? Is not the author thinking of the Opera at Covent Garden, or a performance by the Russian Ballet at the Coliseum?

Every now and then the description of women's clothes raises doubts of whether this is a strictly realistic novel or not. Were there really so many cloaks and veils and flying draperies for daytime wear in those days, or is the author trying to convey an impression of romantic vagueness about the appearance of women, seen advancing from a distance, in contrast to the tightness of the men who carry sticks in town and pay calls on Sundays in tail coats? When Katherine is so frantic to see Ralph and clear up one of their misunderstandings that she rushes out of the house in the middle of tea still holding a piece of bread and butter, how did she manage to put on her cloak and pin on her hat without finding this morsel of food a nuisance?

Night and Day is dated and yet one cannot fix the date with any exactitude, within ten, twenty or thirty years. It is when it is timeless that it is memorable and convincing. No detail about Katherine's appearance or dress, such as an improbable line of fur on the hem of a skirt, brings her so clearly before our eyes as the description of her in a Lincolnshire garden one wintry night, seeing "nothing in the universe save stars and the light of stars; as she looked up the pupils of her eyes so dilated with starlight that the whole of her seemed dissolved in silver and spilt over the ledges of the stars for ever and ever indefinitely through space." She is most real when Ralph, seeing her again after an absence, hesitates

. . . in order to prevent too painful a collision between what he dreamt of her and what she was. And in five minutes she had filled the shell of the old dream with the flesh of life; looked with fire out of phantom eyes. He glanced about him with bewilderment at finding himself among chairs and tables. . . . He summoned all the faculties of his spirit to seize what the minutes had to give him; and from the depths of his mind there rose unchecked a joyful recognition of the truth that human nature surpasses in its beauty, all that our wildest dreams bring us hints of.

When Virginia Woolf forgets that she has harnessed herself to a conventional plot, when she rides freely the whirlwind of passion in this way, we recognize, even in a book that is a step backward in her progress, a writer of genius.

Chapter VII

THE GROUP of friends who began to assemble in Bloomsbury in the nineteen twenties were different from the pioneers who had begun to attract attention in 1910. There were newcomers, such as Stephen Tomlin, the sculptor, and Raymond Mortimer, the critic, Oxford men who broke the rule that the only entry to Bloomsbury was by way of Cambridge; David Garnett and Francis Birrell, who not only wrote but sold books in their shop, just as Roger Fry sold furniture and ceramics made at the Omega Workshops, thus disposing of the notion that a true Bloomsberry was an aesthete and nothing more.

The essential difference was that the original members of the group had substantial achievements to their credit, which means that they had not only reputations but critics who attacked them and — far more damaging — imitators.

Lytton Strachey is a case in point. His *Eminent Victorians* appeared in 1918, and *Queen Victoria* in 1921. Both books were immensely successful and deservedly so. When he wrote a biography he did not exhume a corpse, parade it lugubriously and then rebury it under a tombstone engraved with a moral and misleading epitaph. He lacked reverence, could not be intimidated, was not a death worshipper. Instead he had immense curiosity, patience, gaiety, wit and a lucid style. The lives of great men did not remind him that he could make his life sublime, but that human nature was infinitely variable, the turn of events supremely unpredictable. A survey of the past might be edifying, but the purpose of a biographer was not to force it to be so; it could be entertaining as well as truthful.

The trouble about Lytton Strachey was that the precision and ease of his writing lured so many people who lacked his sense of the past, his standard of values, and his erudition into thinking he could be copied. They imagined that all one had to do was to replace sentimentality by malice, to knock a statue off its pedestal and jibber among the fragments. The result of such antics was the production of so many inferior and false biographies that the public soon tired of the ghoulish game of romping around the Victorian graveyard. Where are they now, these imitators? They are among the great unnamed who cannot be called to account when those who were a part of Bloomsbury in its glory ask those who use the word carelessly or with contemptuous intent, "What exactly do you mean?"

Lytton Strachey's reputation is dimmed now because he is part of a past so like our own that we cannot yet recapture it. There is a roseate glow over the Victorian and Edwardian times because two devastating wars separate us from them. He worked in the brief dawn of a day that seemed bright with hope, when the need was to shake off the horrors of a nightmare and to forget yesterday's mishaps. We are in a similar period, subject to the same fears that there will be a drenching downpour to spoil the excursion we have planned.

Clive Bell was another original member of the Bloomsbury Group who explored the past and planned for the future, whose writings on aesthetics provided entertainment as well as commanded respect while stimulating discussion. Leonard Woolf examined the British Empire and imperialism in general, and went on working to build a new world based on reasonable hopes that might well have been considered shattered forever when the old International fell apart in 1914. Maynard Keynes was still another who refused to be daunted, even when his work at the Paris Peace Conference showed the danger that what the old men wanted was not at all what the young men had died for and the children of the future had a right to expect. All of these men were serious, but none of them was solemn or had any desire to live apart.

One by-product of the growing fame of Maynard Keynes was that he was indirectly the means of introducing the work of Bloomsbury writers to the United States. Their books would have crossed the Atlantic sooner or later in any case, but they traveled more quickly than they might have because word got around in New York that there was an extremely brilliant young man from the British Treasury at the Paris Conference who was writing a book on *The Economic Consequences of the Peace* which included some remarkable portraits of Wilson, Clemenceau and Lloyd George, among others. An enterprising young publisher, Alfred Harcourt, was so much impressed by the reports that he wanted to secure the book for his newly founded firm.

He took an early opportunity to go to London to see Keynes about it, and while there he caught sight of a very peculiar-looking individual who, he was told, was Lytton Strachey, said to be working on a forthcoming life of Queen Victoria and doing it so thoroughly, the story ran, that he was lodging near the Albert Memorial to keep in the right mood. The young man from New York immediately tried to buy the American rights for this book too, but Strachey's British publisher was not even amused by the suggestion. Such haste and such levity were not, at that time, considered quite the thing.

Maynard Keynes, on the other hand, was so much impressed by the American way of doing business, so pleased by the welcome given to his book in the United States and by the expert and vigorous handling of its sales when a second edition was called for because the first was an immediate sellout, that he later ventured to suggest, in his polite, tentative, British way, that possibly the American publisher might be interested in a forthcoming book by his friend Lytton Strachey.

The result of this hint and this introduction was a direct approach to Lytton Strachey, followed by the resounding success of

Queen Victoria under the imprint of Harcourt, Brace & Company in 1920.

Further introductions and further direct approaches followed, and soon the names of Virginia and Leonard Woolf, E. M. Forster, Roger Fry and Clive Bell were appearing on the same publisher's list. It was all very pleasant and profitable. At a time when the Bloomsbury Group was being accused in London of being either too austere or too frivolous, the American publisher found them all very charming, intelligent and straightforward people. Far from being snubbed by these allegedly haughty and reserved British intellectuals, Don Brace thoroughly enjoyed going to Sunday breakfast with Mr. and Mrs. Maynard Keynes in Gordon Square. His hostess, the lovely, the incomparable ballet dancer Lydia Lopokova, cooked for them on the kitchen range.

The theory that they lived behind some kind of barbed-wire or electric fence to keep out intruders was, in fact, all nonsense. They simply exercised the normal right to choose their own company, to open and close their doors like anyone else. No one could, of course, challenge this, but the legend that grew up about their extreme exclusiveness was helped by their never seeking publicity nor providing a spectacle.

They had gay parties in one another's houses, at which they dressed up and acted charades or danced — there was one memorable occasion when Duncan Grant, trying to execute an impromptu *pas de deux* with the Russian ballerina Lydia Lopokova, landed ignominiously on his back. Sometimes they just sat on the floor and talked. But they did not give recitals of their poems, as the Sitwells did. There were no large parties that would cause the neighbors or any curious passer-by to wonder what was going on and why there was such a collection of cars parked in the square or linger to see if any recognizable celebrity might be glimpsed going in or out. There was at the time no columnist to note that so-and-so had been seen dining at the Café Royal, to hint at a new romance or to start a rumor about another book that would shake the foundations of society.

They were not fashionable, neither were they Bohemian. Bloomsbury as a district never became a part of London where the tourist could be sure of seeing the English version of Montmartre or Greenwich Village in its heyday. It was possible to live in Bloomsbury all one's life and not be aware of having either famous or notorious neighbors. A Bloomsbury resident, asked for her recollections of the Bloomsbury Circle, replied, "Which one? It was as full of circles as Dante's Inferno. If you mean the intellectuals of the twenties, I knew about them, of course, without caring in the least where they lived. They struck me as being human and omnipotent, imagining themselves as Lucifer, with Lucifer's pride but without his unfortunate fall, forever a thorn in the side of God, so to speak."

This, while admittedly the purely personal reaction of a woman who read and wrote and lived in Bloomsbury without liking it or feeling herself to be part of it, is fairly typical, and indicates how difficult it is to be precise about the Bloomsbury Circle. Something was stirring; that was evident to any sensitive person. But it was something in the air rather than in any particular spot. It might prove to be a big wheel moving by the grace of God; it seemed unlikely that it was an ordinary merry-go-round.

Although the outward calm of Bloomsbury's streets and squares was not disturbed by the comings and goings of Virginia's friends, the parties were not always exactly decorous. In a letter which she said was written "by the glare of the snow, sitting up in bed, in precisely ten minutes, for the cook to post when she goes to buy a dish of meat," she described a party at which she had not been present, being sick at the time. "The party went off. Lady Oxford was refused admittance. . . . I like the barbarous incivility and independence of Bloomsbury manners. Wm. Courtauld was also outed. So they kept themselves to themselves; and got tipsy." [1]

But one has to beware of taking literally everything that Vir-

[1] Letter to V. Sackville-West (1926).

ginia wrote in her letters, which were dashed off, like her diary entries, at top speed, rather faster than the fastest typewriting, she claimed. They were meant to be read by those who knew the sound of her voice and her habit of making jokes and launching into extravagant exaggerations; and even so, she sometimes felt she might be forced to use colored inks to convey her shades of meaning, or put in some kind of mark to indicate, "Smile here." Her notion of getting tipsy was her own, for with her a very little wine went a very long way. She liked the idea that a little alcohol released one into a world where foolishness was allowable.

"I have drunk a bottle of wine for dinner," she wrote in a letter from the south of France, "and the world goes gently up and down in my head. Suppose one had wine every day, at every meal — what an enchanted world." [1]

Her puritan upbringing made the thought of being rather silly and rather rude at times extremely inviting. One may be quite certain that what she called "barbarous incivility" would hardly pass for the real thing in less polite circles, and equally certain that none of her friends ever slammed a door in a woman's face or threw a man downstairs. There was a tigress in her which dreamed of freedom but had grown used to captivity, and knew it could produce quite an impressive effect merely by yawning and retiring to its little black hole, beyond the sight of visitors to the zoo.

There were less inhibited characters than hers living in Bloomsbury, who cared nothing about appearances and indeed seemed willing to flaunt their eccentricities, if they were ever aware that they might appear to be rather odd. Lady Ottoline Morrell was one who never felt the need to conform to current fashion. If the fancy took her to wear a crinoline, to carry a shepherdess's crook garlanded with brightly colored ribbons and to walk her Pekingese dogs through the streets of Bloomsbury in some striking but outmoded array, she did so. But then she

[1] Letter to V. Sackville-West (1928).

was an aristocrat, a niece of the Duke of Portland, born to command, immune to criticism. Moreover, she was tall and had what used to be known as a presence, which even conventional costume and hair less obviously dyed a ferocious red would have failed to disguise. In New York her appearance would have provoked curiosity about what she might be advertising; in Paris there would have been raised eyebrows and suggestions for a style more suitable to her figure and for make-up more skillfully applied; in London both the curiosity and the desire to improve on that picture would fade almost at once into the conclusion that she must be a great lady, otherwise she would never dare go around looking like a figure of fun.

She was not an artist herself, unless being a hostess is regarded as an art, but she had excellent and catholic taste in the arts and both discernment and benevolence in her appraisal of human beings. At her beautiful old manor at Garsington, near Oxford, or at her London home in Gower Street, one could be sure of meeting interesting and intelligent people, young or old, already eminent or giving promise of making their mark.

Virginia liked and admired her, recognizing the genuine character behind the eccentricities, and knew her well enough to be amused by and critical of her on occasion. "Ottoline turned up the other night, dropping powder, and protesting about women who make up," she wrote in a letter; and again: "Ottoline took me motoring one midnight in London; and the effect was stupendous — St. Paul's, Tower Bridge, moonlight, river, Ottoline in full dress and paint, white and gaudy as a painted tombstone, erect on Tower Bridge in the midst of all the hoppers and bargees coming home drunk on Bank Holiday." [1]

Lady Ottoline Morrell cared so little whether her friends thought her either comical or stupendous that when Virginia was thinking of writing some short biographies of living people, she suggested herself as a subject. Nothing came of this idea,

[1] Letter to V. Sackville-West.

however. Perhaps it was just as well, for Virginia could be censorious and Ottoline often irritated her by asking too many awkward questions instead of accepting a simple excuse, even if it was a patent evasion.

Both women, in fact, were great questioners, though in different styles. "Ott" went straight ahead, asking exactly what she wanted to know, without the slightest idea of giving offense by being too personal. As she received the required information she appeared to make a mental note of it, so that a young man meeting her for the first time might wonder whether she was filing his name for future references as a possible footman or deciding whether he should be brought to the attention of the Prime Minister or would interest W. B. Yeats.

Virginia's approach was more oblique and more bewildering. In order to get people talking about themselves she would often pretend she knew where they had just come from and what they were going to do next, and so would playfully trick them into protesting that their lives were not like that at all. Then, having lured them into a false security, she would be capable of suddenly slipping in a very serious and personal question, such as, "Do you believe in God?" or "Have you ever been in love?" If the witness on the stand had sufficient presence of mind to realize that this was part of the teasing-testing technique, he would give a straightforward and truthful answer, and the basis for friendship was laid. But if he equivocated or showed signs of resenting such treatment, she lost interest. To be accepted into Bloomsbury society the newcomer had to be sufficiently sure of himself not to be intimidated or overawed, whether by Lady Ottoline Morrell's drawl, Lytton Strachey's glassy glare or Virginia Woolf's glancing wit.

Lord David Cecil was one of those who first met Virginia at Lady Ottoline Morrell's house at Garsington, then again at the Chelsea home of another remarkable woman, Ethel Sands, the painter, who was born in America but had lived most of her life in England and France. Having cleared these two hurdles safely, he was invited to tea at Tavistock Square, where the Woolfs lived after leaving Richmond.

Surprisingly solid teas, they were too, he remembers, with plenty of good cake, and muffins with honey. Virginia herself did not eat much, but appreciated good food. "Tea" with her was not just a euphemism for a cocktail, to be swallowed quickly in a crowded room to the sound of aimless chatter. It marked a definite pause in the day's activities. The guests were comparatively few but sure to be interesting, and the talk would be equally worth while.

Virginia was a good talker, but never attempted to dominate the conversation. Her manner was natural and unaffected. When she asked a question, you felt that she really expected an answer because she was genuinely interested, though she remained detached. Even if it was a teasing question, interjected to get a sharp reaction, you felt that, critical and formidable as she might be, her real purpose was to understand people who were different from her, living outside her world, which was necessarily limited by her poor health and strict upbringing. Many of her friends were rigid anticonventionalists and felt the need to shock those who did not share their particular point of view. She herself was more tolerant; she respected attitudes and beliefs quite different from her own.

Only on one subject was she passionate, and that was literature. Nothing would make her deviate from her standard of what was good or bad in writing. About religion and politics she was ready enough to admit people might genuinely hold opinions she thought mistaken, but she knew and cared about books, and would uphold her own view against all comers. She would listen, but her convictions could not be shaken. She might decide to read further in the work of an author whose intentions she did not fathom or whose style did not appeal to her — James Joyce, for instance — but she would not join a cult either of adoration or denunciation. Tastes might differ, yes. Understanding might be extended, yes. But that critical standards should be lowered, emphatically no.

There was one point on which she and all her friends were agreed. That was the importance of frankness on all subjects under discussion. This often resulted in their conversation's being, as Lord David Cecil described it, decidedly bleak. Her own talk was not, because it was so lit by her whimsical humor and vivid phrasing. She was appreciative of physical beauty in either sex or any age and could sum up a character in a few apt words: "a great grey moth" or "she has a dusty soul."

The usual group greeting to a stranger was a blank stare, sometimes the sketchy offer of two fingers at shoulder height, and a drawled "How do you do?" These mannerisms, of course, lent themselves to parody and were, in fact, imitated by those who thought such antics would enable them to pass as genuine Bloomsburyites. But, whether the accent and manner was real or assumed, the candidate for initiation might be overcome with awe or might equally be rendered helpless with suppressed laughter.

One begins to understand how it was that the Bloomsbury Group achieved two reputations so contrary that it is now impossible to disentangle them. Here were people who behaved with gay impudence, doing serious work, and protecting their privacy and freedom behind a façade of hauteur. They were unmummifying the Victorian age, taking art for an airing, blowing the dust off economics, expressing the youthful awakening from the nightmare of the war; and because one of their number, Lytton Strachey, had a high voice, weak eyesight, a limp manner and a preference for eighteenth-century primness — which might be outward and visible signs of an inward and spiritual grace but could also be copied by any comedian — they were regarded in many quarters as being thoroughly affected and false. What was the truth, asked the serious and baffled observer? They had to be labeled somehow, and Bloomsbury became the chosen tag.

Looking back at them now one is reminded of the youthful Pip in *Great Expectations*, swaggering in his new glory down the street and meeting the irrepressible Trabb's boy. "Deeming that a serene and unconscious contemplation of him would best beseem me, and would be most likely to quell his evil mind, I advanced with that expression of countenance." Devoted Dickensians will remember the startling effect this produced on Trabb's boy, ending with that outrageous urchin "attended by a company of delighted young friends, to whom he from time to time exclaimed, with a wave of his hand, 'Don't know yah!' Passing abreast of me, he pulled up his shirt-collar, twined his sidehair, stuck an arm akimbo, and smirked extravagantly by, wriggling his elbows and body, and drawling to his attendants, 'Don't know yah, don't know yah, 'pon my soul, don't know yah!'"

Do the Bloomsbury Group represent Pip, or Trabb's boy, or both?

Virginia did not adopt the highly stylized group manner of acknowledging an introduction. We have Lord David Cecil's word for it that she always smiled when greeting a stranger, and others confirm the graciousness and ease of her manners, which were without a trace of condescension. Sir Hugh Walpole, who was so shy that he positively invited embarrassing situations to befall him, who was admittedly put through his paces before becoming an intimate of the group, and who was frankly terrified of meeting her for the first time, has recorded his appreciation of her "delicate hostess care, her courtesies and dignities," and has described how her combination of reserve and aloofness with a human, living and inquisitive quality induced him to talk to her as he was never able to talk to any other human being.

Everyone who knew her personally speaks in much the same way. It did not matter very much whether you were a man or a woman, whether you approached her with awe or with determination not to be taken in by any kind of humbug; you came away feeling that, unless you held on hard to what was left of your critical faculties, you would find yourself helplessly doomed to love her.

It is curious to note how friends behave when asked questions about her. They try hard to be exact and impersonal. Obviously she was not perfect, because no one can be. She must have had faults, and one should try to remember them in order to give a correct impression. So they search their minds for something disagreeable to say, something that will give depth to their picture, prevent it from being too glowing and idealized and possibly sentimental. And all they bring up from the past are pleasant memories. They speak of her kindness and generosity and warmth, and it makes them feel kind and generous — they want to give the listener all that they have to offer about her over the years.

They remember how she tormented herself and others if she thought she was being underrated or ignored and inferior writers were preferred to her. But instead of this being stated, as it could very well be, as "She was very vain and jealous, often stupidly so. There were times when you wanted to shake her and tell her not to be silly, she's been all through this before and she knew perfectly well it would all be forgotten tomorrow," it comes out in some such phrase as, "She was very responsive to admiration and criticism, could not ignore either." The interviewer senses that the speaker feels again the old impulse to shelter her when she was sad, the old pleasure in seeing her when she was naïvely boastful and flirtatious and gay. They speak of her smile, and they smile too. They speak of her beauty; and then they are lost. The struggle is over; the old charm has reasserted itself.

At the end of nearly two hours' talk about her, Lord David Cecil made a final effort to be judicious and to give a verdict in accordance with the evidence and one befitting his position as a writer and a professor at Oxford. "The group was like nothing else that preceded it," he said. "Nothing like it will probably ever occur again. She, too, was a flower that blooms only once."

Chapter VIII

APART from what she was as a person, what was she doing to arouse such admiration?

In spite of ill-health, which often restricted her writing to one hour a day for weeks at a stretch, she was at work on a novel, producing reviews and critical essays, and polishing the stories or sketches which were published from Hogarth House in 1921 under the title of *Monday or Tuesday*. This small volume is now out of print, but its contents, which included *Kew Gardens* and *The Mark on the Wall*, are to be found in the posthumous collection of her stories, *A Haunted House*.

Two items she did not wish to preserve. One, entitled *Blue and Green*, is very short, a fragmentary, impressionistic and not entirely successful experiment in new hieroglyphics. The second, called *A Society*, is much longer and quite different in method and tone. It is a humorously satiric account of a meeting at which young women report on what they have found out about the world in the preceding five years. One investigator reads a paper on "Honor" and tells how the Royal Navy took its revenge on the perpetrators of the *Dreadnought* hoax. This is very funny, but Adrian Stephen's little book, which sticks to the facts, is even more amusing. Another member of the society gives a report about literature and truth, based on her experiences when, dressed as a man, she worked as a reviewer. It is vivacious but inconclusive; and since the subject of reviewing was one on which Virginia Woolf felt very strongly and expressed herself from time to time, in speech and in writing, with much more vigor and cogency than in this early ironical sketch of the situation in the twenties, little is lost by its not being reprinted.

Of the remaining items, *Monday or Tuesday* is a bravura exercise in atmospheric writing. Its significance lies in the title, which was one of Virginia's private shorthand phrases to convey the idea that a literal fact seldom reveals an essential truth. *A Haunted House* is slight; the ghosts of two lovers revisit the scene of past happiness; a sleeper, aroused by the faint sound of their steps and their whispered words, wakes fully to cry, "Oh, is this *your* buried treasure? The light in the heart." Virginia was doubtful about this story, fearing it was sentimental. It is, but remains of interest because it foreshadows her later and much more masterly handling of a similar theme in the middle section of *To the Lighthouse.*

The String Quartet describes the chatter in a concert hall before a performance starts, then tries to capture the images and emotions aroused by the music, and concludes with the farewells of the listeners. Lytton Strachey thought it was "marvellous," and this praise so elated Virginia when her husband told her of it one dreary day after she had been to Scotland Yard about a lost purse (she was always losing things) that she walked over Hungerford Bridge, that hideous iron structure across which trains thunder, "twanging and vibrating" — and forgot to buy coffee. (She often forgot the errand she had set out on, and recorded these lapses quite gaily. She was not proud of being absent-minded, never dramatized herself as eccentric. But her scale of values allowed her to be tolerant of and amused by her own failings in practical matters, while her artistic conscience demanded the sternest discipline and the closest attention to detail.)

The longest story in the volume is *An Unwritten Novel.* An unhappy-looking woman seen in a railway carriage excites the writer's interest. She tries to reconstruct her story from the few hints dropped. But when the journey ends, she finds she has

been entirely mistaken. The lonely, frustrated heroine of the
novel is met at the station by an unimagined character, and goes
on her way happily with her son. It is a simple enough idea. But
Virginia Woolf is not content with the simple enough conclusion that, try as one may, one can never be sure one has guessed
the truth. She adds a characteristic coda:

And yet the last look of them . . . brims me with wonder,
floods me anew. Mysterious figures! Mother and son. Who are
you? . . . Wherever I go, mysterious figures, I see you, turning
the corner, mothers and sons; you, you, you. I hasten, I follow. . . . If I fall on my knees, if I go through the ritual, the
ancient antics, it's you, unknown figures, you I adore; if I open
my arms, it's you I embrace, you I draw to me — adorable world!

This is more than a trick of technique, an instance of her
planning a story as though it were a musical composition, with
definite movements, changes of tempo, transpositions into different keys, introducing new themes or repeating old ones
with variations, giving the dominant melody now to one instrument, now to another, and summing up in a finale and a flourish.

It is the statement of a creed. "I believe in truth. I believe in
people. I believe that I must tell the truth as I see it, in so far as
in me lies. I know that I must do it my own way. So help me
God." And since a confession of faith reached by inner questioning not learned by rote without understanding is a revelation of character, one salutes here the real woman.

She had already flung down her challenge to the older, established, time-honored authors of her day in the essay *Modern
Fiction,* published in 1919 (see *The Common Reader,* Vol. I),
which concludes:

There is no limit to the horizon. . . . Nothing — no "method,"
no experiment, even of the wildest — is forbidden, but only falsity
and pretence. "The proper stuff of fiction" does not exist; everything is the proper stuff of fiction; every quality of brain and spirit

is drawn upon; no perception comes amiss. And if we can imagine the art of fiction come alive and standing in our midst, she would undoubtedly bid us break her and bully her, as well as honour and love her, for so her youth is renewed and her sovereignty assured.

In *Night and Day* she had faithfully followed the old rules. Now she was going to set up her own. She saw, dimly enough at first, the possibility of writing a book in which *The Mark on the Wall, Kew Gardens* and *An Unwritten Novel* would "take hands and dance in unity."

The idea came to her in 1920, when she was thirty-eight and feeling much happier than she had been at twenty-eight. She planned this new kind of novel as she sat looking at the fire at Hogarth House in January. It was to have "no scaffolding; scarcely a brick to be seen; all crepuscular, but the heart, the passion, humour, everything as bright as fire in the mist."

By April it had a name, *Jacob's Room*, and actually kept that title. Most of her books changed and developed so much as she wrote that they might have two or three different titles before they were completed. This time, she felt, the shadowy idea was being firmly realized, though she knew that when she was ready to begin writing it regularly she would have to brace herself against the inevitable slackening of the creative power after an exhilarating start. But she promised herself that she would write nothing in this book that she did not enjoy writing.

In August she found that each day's work was "like a fence which I have to ride at, my heart in my mouth till it's over, and I've cleared, or knocked the bar out." In September she had an attack of discouragement; James Joyce was probably doing the same sort of thing but very much better. She was so much inferior to Leonard in every way — a hateful idea, not in itself but because it might mean she was obscurely and despicably jealous of her husband's superiority. For forgetting to buy coffee or losing her purse she could be forgiven, but for allowing herself to be discomposed by mean thoughts, never.

Whatever the reason for the sudden check — and in all likelihood it was because she had driven herself too hard and was tired — the kettle had gone off the boil. It was not until November of the following year that the last words of *Jacob's Room* were written. Then followed the usual revisions, rewriting, retyping, accompanied by the usual disillusionment and fears of failure; the usual surprise when in July 1922 Leonard read it and accepted it for publication; the usual seesaw of dread and elation about the opinions of the critics and the public when it appeared in October. But by that time she was hard at work on two other books, a new novel and a collection of essays, and could hardly be bothered about an old dream. In 1926 she could look back on it and describe it as a battle.

The reading public, forewarned by *Monday or Tuesday* and the essay on modern fiction, was not forearmed against the shock and delight of *Jacob's Room*. Opinions differed violently. A daily newspaper attacked it as the work of an "elderly sensualist"; which made her laugh — she was forty, and as for being a sensualist, that is obviously one of those words that come in handy when one is overcome by an impulse to heave half a brick at something one dislikes and fears. Sir Hugh Walpole, writing nearly twenty years later, recalled the electric effect the book had on him when he first picked it up while relaxing in a Turkish bath. He sat up, his wrappings fell off, and he knew that he had found one of the books of his life.

Between these two extremes were calmer judgments, though some of them were expressed in the somber warnings of the prophets of doom. There were critics, Middleton Murry among them, who meditated on Proust and James Joyce and Virginia Woolf, and decided that the novel, as an art form, had gone about as far as it could go. After *Jacob's Room* the deluge! Farewell our old contents. No more novels after this one. What the Russians, chiefly Dostoevski, had so recklessly begun, the Frenchman and the Irishman had carried on, the Englishwoman had now completed. Poor old, battered, glorious English literature would have to start all over again; somewhere in T. S. Eliot's *Waste Land*, too.

Less austere and exalted people, unprofessional critics, common readers, were in the meantime reading the book and talking about it, enjoying it and enjoying talking about it. The reason for the talk was that it differed so much from other novels that many readers found it difficult; so dazzling as to be obscure. It was the Postimpressionist Exhibition all over again. It was exciting, but what did it mean?

For such newcomers three readings, one after another, are recommended, not as a duty but as a way to pleasure. A first, rapid reading for general effect is like going to a party and finding a room full of strangers. A second, slower reading, in order to get the story straight, is like greeting your hostess, being introduced, catching a few names, recognizing a few faces, finding a seat and joining in the conversation. The third reading will probably be very slow indeed; you will find yourself lingering, reluctant to leave, for you have made friends, met people you promise yourself you must see again, get to know better and better. You will thank your hostess for a delightful evening, hoping she means it when she says, "You must come again soon," so that you can resume an old argument that somehow went astray because you suddenly found yourself not only listening but talking, not merely enjoying but sharing.

THE STORY is basically simple. Jacob Flanders is a child, then a boy, then a young man; finally, abruptly we have his room but not his company. To sum up in this way is like saying that a sermon is against sin, a romance is about love, an opera is a drama set to music.

The novel is, indeed, operatic. The opening pages, like the first bars of an overture, make a direct assault upon the attention. The curtain goes up. Scene follows scene, character after character steps to the footlights, recitative leads into aria, there are duets, quartets or massed choruses, action is delayed or carried surging forward; sometimes the singer and sometimes the music predominates; there is diversity and there is unity. Comment between the acts and immediately after the performance may seem strangely superficial, but what the memory has stored away may be just as strangely profound.

Jacob is the center of this musical drama. The author keeps him firmly there. It is the observer who continually changes position, sees him through other eyes, in different places, at varying times; hears voices that are not his. For Jacob himself seldom speaks, almost never listens. He is not seen moving, but as having moved; that is to say, the scene has changed. The globe has been twirled; where it stops, that the author describes.

We first glimpse him as a child playing on a beach in Cornwall, while his mother, a widow, writes a letter and wonders vaguely where he can have wandered now. His brother calls to him, but he is somewhere alone, unheeding, discovering a rock pool, a live crab, a sheep's skull, a rock that looked like his nurse from a distance, a man and woman asleep in the sun. He is rounded up, scolded, lugged home. A hurricane rages that night. Jacob sleeps securely, while the wind roars and the waves crash, and the crab tries to struggle out of the tin bucket and the precious skull lies at the foot of the child's bed. His mother, his brother, the beach, the sunset, the walk home to the lodgings, the garden at night, two women bending over a baby's cot like conspirators — all these are presented in turn while Jacob sleeps, the treasures of the day on or by his bed, the story of his adventures locked in his brain.

This is the method followed throughout the book. There is the outer world of sharp, physical reality, where circumstances alter cases, cause is linked to effect, decisions are made, events occur; there is the other world of thought and imagination and desire, not to be described, only guessed at, explored in silence, where the distance traveled is measured by what is left behind, what is ahead cannot be known. There are the cities where the pavements ring under the feet, villages where the neighbors notice the visitors who come to call on a widow; and there are the seas on which one voyages alone.

Jacob lives at Scarborough and collects butterflies. He goes to school at Rugby, and then to Cambridge. We see him in the train on his way to the university, through the eyes of a nervous lady:

> She was fifty years of age, and had a son at college. Nevertheless, it is a fact that men are dangerous. . . . Taking note of socks (loose), of tie (shabby), she once more reached his face. She dwelt upon his mouth. The lips were shut. The eyes bent down, since he was reading. All was firm, yet youthful, indifferent, unconscious — as for knocking one down! No, no, no! . . . He had not realized her presence, she thought. Yet it was none of *her* fault that this was not a smoking carriage — if that was what he meant.
>
> Nobody sees any one as he is, let alone an elderly lady sitting opposite a strange young man in a railway carriage. They see a whole — they see all sorts of things — they see themselves. . . . It is no use trying to sum people up. One must follow hints, not exactly what is said, nor yet entirely what is done.

But in the course of a page and a half we see three people, the dreaming, handsome, indifferent young man, the fluttery matron, who when she arrives safely at Cambridge (which swarms with similar young men), forgets him completely "as the crooked pin dropped by a child into the wishing-well twirls in the water and disappears for ever": and Virginia Woolf, the unseen observer, reading, looking at the landscape, pondering on the mysteries of life, making up stories about the real though hidden life of her silent companions. The compact security of an English railway carriage was a favorite framework for many of her pictures. She traveled a good deal — between London and Lewes, from here to eternity.

Volumes and volumes have been written about the lives of

young men at Cambridge and other universities. Virginia Woolf
compresses them all into about twenty pages of *Jacob's Room*.
She knew Cambridge well, having visited it frequently when her
brothers were students there. She respected it, perforce, as a
home of learning, but her descriptions of it show more than a
touch of irreverence. In spite of her feeling for history, the
traces of its monastic past irritated her. Does the light of Cambridge burn not only into the night but into the day? she asks.
She sees the professors under this light, "how priestly they look!
How like a suburb where you go to see a view and eat a special
cake!"

Again, while admitting Cambridge is loved and remembered,
she gets impatient with all the "talking, talking, talking — as if
everything could be talked — the soul itself slipped through the
lips in thin silver disks which dissolve in young men's minds like
moonlight." A time would come when a man would grow old,
"when the silver disks would tinkle hollow, the inscription read
a little too simple, and the old stamp look too pure, and the
impress always the same — a Greek boy's head. But he would
respect still. A woman, divining the priest, would, involuntarily,
despise."

The religious observances do not impress her. "Look, as they
pass into service, how airily the gowns blow out, as though nothing dense and corporeal were within. What sculptured faces,
what certainty, authority controlled by piety, although great
boots march under the gowns." But why allow women to take
part in these services, since the presence of women distracts the
mind, even women vouched for by the theology, mathematics,
Latin and Greek of their husbands? Jacob's mind wanders; he
"looked extraordinarily vacant, his head thrown back, his hymn-
book open at the wrong place. . . . He caught Timmy Durrant's eye; looked very sternly at him; and then, very solemnly,
winked."

She questions even more than the reality of the Christian
faith celebrated so regularly and with such outward devotion.

Virgil is intoned, but "what if the poet strode in? 'This my image?' he might ask, pointing to the chubby man, whose brain is, after all, Virgil's representative among us." And then, remembering no doubt her aunts Katherine and Caroline Stephen, she shows us old Miss Umphelby, whose lectures are not half as well attended as those of the chubby man, but who also sings Virgil as she saunters along the Backs, "melodiously enough, accurately too, though she is always brought up by this question as she reaches Clare Bridge: 'But if I met him, what should I wear?' "

So does Virginia Woolf take her mocking revenge upon the ancient institution where she was never able to study.

Jacob is among his fellow undergraduates, reading, arguing, roaring with laughter, eating cherries out of a paper bag, betting on the boat races, never getting quite enough to eat in his lodgings, thinking about poetry and other countries and that there was "too much brick and building for a May night. . . . He stood smoking his pipe while the last stroke of the clock purred softly round him. . . . He looked satisfied; indeed masterly; the sound of the clock conveying to him (it may be) a sense of old buildings and time; and himself the inheritor; and then tomorrow; and friends; at the thought of whom, in sheer confidence and pleasure, it seemed, he yawned and stretched himself."

He walks home and, "being the only man who walked at that moment back to his rooms, his footsteps rang out, his figure loomed large. Back from the Chapel, back from the Hall, back from the Library, came the sound of his footsteps, as if the old stone echoed with magisterial authority: 'The young man — the young man — the young man — back to his rooms.' "

The author is not mocking here. She loves these proud, silly, serious, laughing young men, the confident inheritors of a mysterious tomorrow. But she has introduced into the gay music of their progress a note of warning. It is heard several times in this chapter on Cambridge, the clocks, the footsteps, or something that is either not explained, or explained too easily. "The young

men were now back in their rooms. Heaven knows what they
were doing. What was it that could *drop* like that?" "Now and
then there was a thud, as if some heavy piece of furniture had
fallen, unexpectedly, of its own accord, not in the general stir of
life after dinner." There is a curious interjection in the passage
about the service. "Gravely sounded the voices; wisely the organ
replied, as if buttressing human faith with the assent of the elements." But, suppose the chapel were a forest, where a lantern
burns and insects gather, senselessly, knocking their heads against
the glass. "Ah, but what's that? A terrifying volley of pistol-shots
rings out — cracks sharply; ripples spread — silence laps smooth
over sound. A tree — a tree has fallen, a sort of death in the
forest. After that, the wind in the trees sounds melancholy."

This mysterious warning is sounded at irregular intervals
throughout the book. There is so much else to notice and think
about that the reader pays it as little heed as do the different
characters who appear, play their parts, and then are gone as the
author gives her globe another spin and their country has its
allotted night. But the note is registered in the memory. It will
be heard again, when its true meaning will be given.

Meanwhile Jacob and his friend, Timmy Durrant, sail around
Land's End and the Scilly Isles, ending their vacation at the
Durrant summer home at St. Ives. This is not the St. Ives of
Jacob's childhood in the opening chapter, nor the Talland
House of Virginia's childhood as she was later to write about it
in *To the Lighthouse*. The imperious Mrs. Durrant is certainly
not Virginia's mother; there is perhaps a touch or two of Lady
Ottoline Morrell in the brief sketch of her giving advice and
orders to impassive cottagers, driving about those Phoenician-
haunted moors in her smart pony carriage, setting off so quickly
after a pause that the boy Curnow, whose only function is to sit
bolt upright on the back seat, has only just time to swing himself up by the toe of his boot. The sudden flick this emphatic
lady gives to her sleek ponies is like the swift movement with
which one can imagine the author opening an album at just the

right page to show an old, amusing but perhaps irrelevant photograph.

It is idle to speculate on the identity of Mrs. Durrant. Any one of a half-dozen sitters may have provided various features for a composite picture. What is more important is to note, in passing, the skill of the writer and the quality of her observation. Earlier writers, and Virginia Woolf herself in her earlier books, would have felt it necessary to describe the boy Curnow and his social background more fully, to relate how he jumped down, helped the lady dismount, opened the cottage gate, and held the horses' heads while Mrs. Durrant was laying down the law about potato blight and the importance of proper medical attention for an ailment known in patent medicine advertisements as "Bad Legs." Here Virginia has reached that stage of easy hospitality where she can invite the reader to help himself to anything he fancies. As a result the boy Curnow is caught forever by the toe of his boot and by his saying nothing.

The Durrant house at St. Ives is full of young people and children. Jacob is a success, one gathers. He is parentally approved of as a friend for Timothy and a possible future husband for Clara Durrant. But he has to make his way in the world first, and Clara is shy. The romance is stillborn, buried under the leaves with which she covers the bunches of grapes she cuts in the greenhouse.

Another twirl of the globe and we are in London. Jacob is working somewhere in an office, living in Bloomsbury, studying at the British Museum, having a good time at gay parties with his friends, paying his respects to his mother's friends at more formal gatherings. Nothing particular about him, except that old ladies like him and young women fall in love with him.

Virginia Woolf's feelings about London were different from her feelings about Cambridge. London might be loved or hated, feared or enjoyed; it could not be mocked, for she was a part of its surging life. She lived in one of those Bloomsbury houses where "long ago great people lived, and coming back from

Court past midnight stood, huddling their satin skirts, under the carved door-posts while the footman roused himself from his mattress on the floor, hurriedly fastened the lower buttons of his waistcoat, and let them in." She knew the Bloomsbury rooms that "are shapely, the ceilings high; over the doorway a rose, or a ram's skull, is carved in the wood. The eighteenth century has its distinction. Even the panels, painted in raspberry-colored paint, have their distinction."

Sometimes there is a figure in the passing crowds who might well be Virginia herself: "Bright yet vague. She is perhaps twenty-two. She is shabby. She crosses the road and looks at the daffodils and the red tulips in the florist's window. She hesitates, and makes off in the direction of Temple Bar. She walks fast, and yet anything distracts her. Now she seems to see, and now to notice nothing."

Jacob is glimpsed in the hurly-burly. At a gay party he may look "quiet, not indifferent, but like some one on a beach, watching." But walking home, from Hammersmith to Holborn between two and three in the morning, it all seems to him a "magnificent world, a live, sane, vigorous world. . . . A young man has nothing to fear. On the contrary, though he may not have said anything brilliant, he feels pretty confident he can hold his own." He has enjoyed the party, met ten or eleven people he had not known when he set out, including a poet and an actress, "a line of light perpetually beneath her. It was only 'My dear' that she said, but her voice went jodelling between Alpine passes. And down she tumbled on the floor, and sang, since there was nothing to be said, round ah's and oh's." Jacob "liked them all; he liked that sort of thing. In short all the drums and trumpets were sounding."

But not always. He meets Florinda (who has no surname but "now and again is a Princess, but chiefly when drunk") at a Guy Fawkes bonfire on Hampstead Heath one November night, followed by a dance at a hotel at which, since he would not dance, his head was wreathed with paper flowers, he was seated on a white and gilt chair, and glass grapes were hung on his shoulders, "until he looked like the figure-head of a wrecked ship." He walks home with Timmy Durrant between four and five in the morning, down Haverstock Hill, triumphant, boastful, shouting Greek, convinced that he and Timmy "had read every book in the world; known every sin, passion and joy." He thinks of Florinda. "She had called him Jacob without asking his leave. She had sat upon his knee. Thus did all good women in the days of the Greeks. At this moment there shook out into the air a wavering, quavering, doleful lamentation which seemed to lack strength to unfold itself, and yet flagged on; at the sound of which doors in back streets burst sullenly open; workmen stumped forth."

Florinda is sick, Florinda is stupid, but Florinda, he convinces himself, really loves him, and for her sake his mother's letters lie unopened until it is more convenient to read them. And then one night he sees her upon another man's arm.

The light from the arc lamp drenched him from head to toe. You could see the pattern on his trousers; the old thorns on his stick; his shoe laces; bare hands; and face.

It was as if a stone were ground to dust; as if white sparks flew from a livid whetstone, which was his spine; as if the switchback railway, having swooped to the depths, fell, fell, fell. This was in his face.

It is an unforgettable picture. No one could write this who did not know everything about jealous fury. The desolation that follows is described in one short paragraph. The sounds of the city, the barrel organ playing "like an obscene nightingale beneath wet leaves . . . the words the poor shout across the street at each other (so outright, so lusty)" reach him as he sits alone in his room while the clocks strike ten — an hour at which nobody can go to bed — and tries to distract himself.

Other women with whom he might have been happy, even if only for a time, fall romantically in love with him, but he remains indifferent or unaware. He goes with Fanny Elmer, a model from the Slade School, to the Chelsea Arts Ball or to the ballet at the Empire. He takes Clara Durrant to the opera at Covent Garden or visits her in her fashionable home; "A virgin chained to a rock (somewhere off Lowndes Square) eternally pouring out tea for old men in white waistcoats." He reads Plato or Marlowe in the British Museum, quite unmoved by the difficulties of the elderly lady on one side whose books overbalance and the anger of the feminist on the other side who groans as she waits for the library attendant to bring her volumes because no room has been left on the circle of gilt names round the dome for any woman writer.

He wanders in and out of St. Paul's Cathedral, where "if a boot creaks, it's awful" and where "Sweet and holy are the angelic choristers. And for ever round the marble shoulders, in and out of the folded fingers, go the thin high sounds of voice and organ," and where Mrs. Lidgett, tired with scrubbing the steps of the Prudential Society's office, rests her old bones by the tomb of Wellington, the great Duke, "whose victories mean nothing to her, whose name she knows not, though she never fails to greet the little angels opposite, wishing the like on her own tomb."

As he reads, writes, argues, works, plays, the life of London surges round him, and he is a part of it. The Bloomsbury intellectual is lost in the crowds that stream incessantly across the bridges. Impelled by reason, hurrying to catch the nonstop trains to the suburbs? No, says Jacob — or is it Virginia? — "It seems as if we marched to the sound of music; perhaps the wind and the river; perhaps these same drums and trumpets (*heard before*) — the ecstasy and hubbub of the soul."

Open any of these pages and you will catch the gleam of a jewel; or, it could be, the eyes of a wild animal in the jungle.

The observer is choked with observations; but help yourself, says the author, it is all yours, take what you like. Listen to the sound of drums and trumpets, or to the voice of the drunken woman who beats on a closed door and cries all night, "Let me in." Stride with the young men, who know all about the Greeks,

and the laughing girls, hatless but triumphant; or shuffle with
the old man who has been, it seems, crossing from the Surrey
side of the river to the Strand these six hundred years or more.
The glory and the squalor, these are London, these are life. Ask
for anything you wish, except long words and pretended emotions.

AFTER London comes Europe. Jacob goes to Paris, to Milan,
and on to Athens. Virginia Woolf had visited all these cities, but
never lived in them; here her touch is less sure. Sandra Went-
worth Williams, the married woman with whom Jacob falls in
love, is less sympathetically drawn than Fanny Elmer or Florinda
or Clara Durrant. He himself falters and wavers. He must return to England to be real. Now the globe must turn the other
way.

Now the agitation of the air uncovered a racing star. Now it
was dark. Now one after another lights were extinguished. Now
great   towns — Paris-Constantinople-London — were   black   as
strewn rocks. . . . The wind was rolling the darkness through the
streets of Athens. . . . At length the columns and the Temples
whiten, yellow, turn rose; and the Pyramids and St. Peter's arise,
and at last sluggish St. Paul's looms up.

Thomas Hardy roamed the heavens this way in *The Dynasts*,
faster, more majestically than in any space ship of today.
And now the sounds are increasing.

The steamers, resounding like gigantic tuning-forks, state the
old old fact — how there is a sea coldly, greenly, swaying outside. But nowadays it is the thin voice of duty, piping in a white
thread from the top of a funnel, that collects the largest multitude,
and night is nothing but a long-drawn sigh between hammer-
strokes, a deep breath — you can hear it from an open window
even in the heart of London. . . . People still murmur over the

last word said on the staircase or strain, all through their dreams, for the voice of the alarm clock.

The bright day dawns, the summer's day

which has long since vanquished chaos; which has dried the melancholy mediaeval mists; drained the swamp and stood stone and glass upon it; and equipped our brains and bodies with such an armoury of weapons that merely to see the flash and thrust of limbs engaged in the conduct of daily life is better than the old pageant of armies drawn out in battle array upon the plain.

There are processions along Whitehall. The wires of the Admiralty shiver with communications. Prime Ministers are speaking. The Kaiser is receiving somebody or other in audience. In Athens the ships in the Piraeus fire their guns.

The sound spread itself flat and then went tunnelling its way with fitful explosions among the channels of the islands. Darkness drops like a knife over Greece.

Mrs. Flanders hears the guns. And then she goes with a friend of Jacob's to clear up the hopeless confusion in which he left everything just as it was in the distinguished eighteenth-century rooms to which he will never return.

For what we have been reading is a war novel. Now we know the meaning of all those mysterious sounds. Some years later Thomas Mann would give us a similar jolt when he showed Hans Castorp in his *Magic Mountain,* dreaming and debating and then suddenly hurling his life away in battle; and even more years would pass before Erich Maria Remarque wrote of the actual fighting in *All Quiet on the Western Front,* breaking the dam that held back the flood of war reminiscences. During the war men such as Henri Barbusse and Siegfried Sassoon had cried aloud in agony and fierce protest. Then came the interval when numbness and silence fell, when one could not bear to remember, when life demanded that one should look ahead and rebuild for the future. It was Virginia Woolf who first had the courage to say, "Life could be splendid. But is it?" This was the challenge, not only in literary method but in living content, which she issued.

AGAIN it is obvious that a brief analysis does not reveal all. Little has been said about Mrs. Flanders and the way her life story in Scarborough is contrapuntally interwoven with the life of her son in Cambridge and London, though this is a theme that is well worth tracing. And the literary critic can complain that the author intrudes herself too much, is too conversational with the reader, letting an unexplained "I" or "We" climb on the stage now and then, with disconcerting effect on the illusion — as though the conductor of the opera had drawn attention to himself rather than to the music. It is a legitimate complaint, as the author would have conceded, for she felt she might have tightened the book up here and there. But she could have gone on to plead justification, since Fielding, Thackeray, Dickens, Scott, even Shakespeare did it; and Mozart and Beethoven can frequently be heard saying "Now, watch this" or "I *ask* you!"

From the point of view of Virginia Woolf's own life story, it is more worth noting that there is in this book no father to be fought, no yearning for a mother, no searching by a young woman for the right husband. This is a young man's book. A fortunate, privileged, talented young man. The stored treasures of civilization were his, from ancient Greece to Edwardian England. Where is he now? What became of all those dreams?

They were gay parties in Bloomsbury; but the Bloomsberries were not mere triflers.

Chapter IX

IN 1919 THE WOOLFS had to leave their country retreat, Asheham, as the house and land on which it stood were required for other purposes. The house, still hidden from the road, is now part of a large cement works. A plume of smoke rises when the furnaces are in full blast; the chimneys, whitened by dust, have a purposeful, structural dignity, so that this reminder of industrialization in the midst of farming country has become a landmark instead of an eyesore. The noise of the machines pulverizing the stone and the smell of the smoke are carried on the wind, and could be an intolerable nuisance; but by a curious piece of luck something in the configuration of the hills prevents their troubling the inhabitants of the little village of Rodmell on the opposite bank of the river Ouse.

It was here that the Woolfs made their new home, in a cottage known as Monk's House. The name and the situation, hard by the church, suggest that the place has a history, not sensational so much as representative, but Leonard and Virginia were far less concerned with resurrecting the past than with making their house progressively more weatherproof, comfortable and beautiful. It had been neglected by the previous tenant, a half-crazy old man who had lived there alone for some years. The roof leaked, doors and windows did not fit, the chimneys were choked, modern sanitation was lacking, the garden was a wilderness, containing a pigsty, a collapsing hen house, overgrown paths leading to a small, untidy orchard.

All this had to be changed, but gradually, as money and time

could be spared; both were closely budgeted and carefully expended. Virginia's husband, who describes himself in *Who's
Who* as having two recreations, printing and gardening, worked
tirelessly, in all weathers, on the half acre or so of land. Gales
and floods and teeming rain, which were sometimes enough to
prevent her from taking her daily walk, could not keep him indoors if there was an urgent job to be done. Virginia herself
liked to pretend that all such strenuous, almost heroic, activity
was not only outside her department but beyond her understanding, particularly if she was talking or writing to a friend
who was a gardener. "Leonard is grafting or pruning — which
is it? — perhaps neither." "I should get it all wrong if I told
you about the primulas and the perigoneums, and how the
peach has put out three inches of bud since we were last in
Sussex — last weekend, that is." "The snowdrops are out and
the w.c. has broken and Leonard and Percy Bartholomew [a village neighbor] are stamping about the garden in waterproofs
and I'm sitting in the Lodge feeling rather cold." "The week
after next we go to Ireland . . . I may be windswept into the
sea. But what would you care? 'No,' you'd say, 'we had *Petu-
laneum Ridentis* in that bed last year. We'll try the *Scrofulotum
Penneum* there this.' So you'd bury me under." Occasionally she
would admit that she did something practical and unskilled in
the garden, with poor results, such as contracting lead poisoning
from painting a greenhouse. But as a rule she was an on-
looker, a benefactor and a beneficiary. "We've made another
pond, too. At first the water slanted up one way, down another.
And now where can I buy pots, Italian, and a statue? That's
my contribution to the garden." [1]

All this sounds very magnificent and exotic, but actually was
on a small and quite manageable scale. The two ponds (*not*
swimming pools) are scarcely larger than the portable rubber
contrivances which now appear on suburban lawns for children
to splash in during the hot weather. The Lodge is simply a

[1] Letters to V. Sackville-West.

small wooden shack where she retired every morning, even when there were week-end visitors, to do her writing. At first it was fairly close to the house, but later was moved as far away as possible, to a more sheltered and sunnier position beyond the orchard, and a brick-paved path was laid through the garden so that she could go to work or return for meals and company in a matter of seconds without being drenched to the skin by rain or swept off her feet by the winds that tear through the gap in the downs at Lewes or sweep in from the sea at Newhaven. The statues and pots, which are strategically placed so that a Renaissance boy can be glimpsed from a window, looking as though he had just strayed in and lingered in a dream among the fruit trees, or a nineteenth-century version of a Greek caryatid gravely gives back stare for stare to anyone re-entering the house from the garden, were extravagances acquired in a period of prosperity. They are not only beautiful in themselves, they recall the beauty of other days, record memories of other scenes, and incidentally express what Virginia meant when she wrote in defense of highbrows: "We all have to earn our livings nowadays. . . . But when we have earned enough to live on, then we live" (see "Middlebrow" in *The Death of the Moth*).

Virginia Woolf wrote because she had to. There was an inner compulsion from which there was no escape; indeed, no thought of trying to escape. She also wrote for money, but money was never the primary consideration. The income she inherited had shrunk to rather less than half its original value, owing to increasing prices and rising taxation, but fortunately her books sold, the Hogarth Press prospered and the rates she could command for articles rose. Nevertheless the family fortunes varied considerably. She and her husband took stock regularly of their resources and prospects, and planned expenditures accordingly. Sometimes her weekly allowance of pocket money would rise by a shilling or two, and sometimes she would take a cut. If she had been in good health and finished a book on schedule and earned extra money by articles and stories and the press had done well, then Monk's House could have a bathroom and a hot water system or a paved terrace. But if income had been slight and expenses heavy, then such comforts and improvements would have to wait until they could be afforded. The cost of new sheets, a comfortable sofa, an extra bedroom, might have to be weighed in the balance against acquiring a meadow adjoining the orchard on which someone might build a house and cut off access to the river.

The Woolfs were not rich and never aimed to be, since the pursuit of money for its own sake is a particularly irksome form of slavery, and they wanted money to buy freedom — freedom to travel and to work at what interested them. Wealth could not prevent them from working like demons at anything they wanted to do, nor could it buy friendship and the respect of neighbors. Financially they were better off than most of the people they lived amongst in Rodmell, and they knew that this, together with their more fastidious tastes and wider range of interests and experiences, tended to set them apart. This realization could be a source of acute discomfort to Virginia, who wanted to enter imaginatively if not actually into any kind of life different from her own. It had two other effects; it made her meticulous about money matters, proud to be independent and to show that she too could watch the pennies and repay small debts; and it prevented any ostentatious display in improving Monk's House.

From the road it looks like any other cottage. The front door, at which a grandmother might sit and shell peas on a fine day, or two men might seal a bargain about a horse or a load of hay by drinking a mug of beer together, is no longer used. But this is not enough to excite the attention of the passer-by, since the entry to many a cottage is by a humbler back door. Only the non-utilitarian character of the garden and the interior of the house show what changes have been made.

The first impression is that the house and garden are one; the flowers have crept into the house; the order of the house has imposed itself on the garden. The second impression is that both are bathed in light.

The average farmer or farm laborer is not concerned with light; he has enough of it, working from dawn to dark in all seasons of the year. He looks at the sky to read the weather signals and all they mean in terms of work connected with his crops and livestock. What he and his wife appreciate indoors is the warmth and security of four walls, night and storms shut out. So cottage rooms are usually small and dark. The windows are curtained and partially blocked by some evidence — a sewing machine, a family Bible, an evergreen plant in a painted pot — to indicate to the curious that the house is clean and well-kept and the children have been taught to mind their manners, whatever malicious gossip in the village may whisper to the contrary.

But city folk suffer perpetually from never having enough space and light. They knock down walls and expose rafters and paint their walls cream. Brick floors don't remind them of work to be done in the dairy or washhouse. Furniture of unstained or lightly stained wood does not speak to them of kitchen tables and chopping blocks. A roaring fire is their answer to cold, regardless of who has to cut logs or bring them to the hearth. They seem to have no feeling that a staircase, pointing the way to bedrooms, ought to be decently hidden. Books are all over the place, even in corners that might be conveniently used to secrete a pile of darning waiting to be done. The consolations or warnings of religion, in the form of texts, are not displayed, and there are no family portraits, enlarged and tinted photographs, hung on the walls. In fact, people from town seem to the older generation of villagers to have very peculiar notions of what constitutes a proper sitting room.

The younger generation, many of whom work in the towns now that light industry has invaded the agricultural south of England, or who go there more frequently and with more cash in their pockets than their elders used to handle, will miss at Monk's House the overstuffed armchairs, the spindle-shanked tables and the Laocoön lamps for sale "on easy terms" in the modern furniture stores. More sophisticated migrants from the city to the country will wonder what has become of the cocktail bar, the sporting prints, the iron trivets, the copper warming pans, the Toby jugs, the storm lanterns, the brass door knockers and similar paraphernalia.

Such period pieces, whether hopefully or heartlessly acquired, have not been hidden in an attic or cellar or sent on yet another round of auction sales, for they never found a place in Virginia's rooms. No interior decorator was ever called upon to advise her what was correct or fashionable. She and her husband furnished their homes to suit themselves; that is quite obvious. They exercised a highly cultivated and individual taste, not fantastically eccentric because their standards of judgment were sound. Is this beautiful? Do we need it? Can we use it? Shall we go on liking it? Not: is this valuable or impressive, suitable or shocking, ancient or modern?

The result is both harmonious and exhilarating. A variety of objects, brought back from their travels or acquired on their doorstep, have settled down together. Pictures by Duncan Grant, embroideries by Virginia from designs by Vanessa Bell, vases by Roger Fry, cups painted by Graham Sutherland have without any difficulty made their peace with rugs of traditional pattern from the Balkans, plates from Italy, mirrors from Holland, drapes from Spain, bookshelves made in the village. A friend from China was delighted to recognize in 1953 objects which she had helped Virginia's nephew Julian Bell to buy at a fair in a temple in Peking in 1936. And out of all this, which sounds as though it could be a mere jumble of incongruous elements, comes an overall impression of England in the 1920s. Everything seems to relate to that point in Virginia's life when she realized it was possible to have tablecloths of different patterns

without risking "nameless damnation . . . leaving us all with
an intoxicating sense of illegitimate freedom," as she described
in *The Mark on the Wall.*

There is a sort of innocent, determined gaiety about it — a
gaiety that is defiance, laughter that is a shout. It is all inex-
orably clean, not with the corrosion of antiseptic but with the
sweep of wind. There is resilience and resistance; nothing mum-
bles, creeps, hides in corners. The colors have faded into the
fabrics, sunk into the floors. There is a fierce fastidiousness, as
though the impatience of youth still fought the encroachment
of age. The rooms do not show the elegance of forethought, the
kind of talent some beautiful personalities have for providing
themselves wherever they go with a suitable and expres-
sive background; instead they bespeak, as Lord David Cecil
put it, "the rooms of a schoolgirl — but a very nice schoolgirl."

The garden seems sedate, after the house, which has been so
triumphantly invaded by light. The flowers, having their last
fling in autumn abandon, preparing to settle down until next
spring or waiting to be rescued in the nick of time before the
first frost, are less riotous than the flower paintings indoors.
Faint traces of where the pigsty once stood are still discernible.
They have an archaeological interest that has no connection
with the length of time since that small victory over unsightli-
ness was achieved; who knows what may not be beneath — old
ploughmarks, a Roman pavement, fragments of a British canoe,
a bracelet from a Viking arm, the footprint of a mammoth?
Time is telescoped; the years and the centuries are lost, only
the moment remains.

Past the trimmed hedge, along the paved walk, one approaches the wooden studio, glimpses the squat-towered, conical-
steepled, sturdy stone church. The orchard is a storehouse of
sunshine, which has filtered through the leaves, fallen with the
blossom or been packed with the fruit these many years. There
is a sudden view of empty meadows, with cattle on a rising slope

beyond. Further away and higher are the hills; and then the white sky. The effect is intoxicating.

It was here, in Rodmell, that Virginia found for many summers that she had "entered into a sanctuary; a nunnery; had a religious retreat; of great agony once; and always some terror; so afraid one is of loneliness; of seeing to the bottom of the vessel . . . and got then to a consciousness of what I call 'reality'; a thing I see before me: something abstract; but residing in the downs or sky; besides which nothing matters; in which I shall rest and continue to exist." [1]

A leaden portrait bust of her has been cemented onto a fragment of brick wall that marks where the garden ends and the orchard begins. It has not yet had time to sink into the scene. Perhaps it never will for those who knew her personally or feel they know her through her books and so have an image of her that cannot be expressed in metal or stone or on a canvas. The sculptor, Stephen Tomlin, has caught something of the agony and terror. But the "reality" she sought remains inexpressible. The great eyes are blind. To show us what the artist saw, as he strove with intractable material to capture that reality, the portrait needs to be exposed to the elements until it fears

> no more the heat of the sun
> Nor the furious winter's rages

but has by natural magic become part of "that fading and rising of the light which so enraptures me in the Downs; which I am always comparing to the light beneath an alabaster bowl." [1]

It was in 1924 that the Woolfs moved their town home, leaving Richmond and returning to Bloomsbury. She had had

[1] *A Writer's Diary.*

little grumbles now and then about being cut off from friends at Richmond: "Out here no one comes in to waste time pleasantly. If they do I'm cross. The labour of going to London is too great. Nessa's children grow up, and I can't have them in to tea, or go to the Zoo."[1] But she knew that these were mere excuses for ill-humor because she was not writing freely. When the words began to flow again, then it did not matter much where she lived.

A more practical inconvenience was that the Hogarth Press was growing by leaps and bounds. She felt obliged to apologize when she invited anyone to dine: "We don't dine so much as picnic, as the Press has got into the larder and into the dining room." It was no longer a question of a printing machine and trays of type; there were the ever-growing piles of manuscripts, books, correspondence. Printing would continue to be their hobby, but they needed adequate space and a central location for their business as publishers.

THE PROBLEM was solved by renting a house at number 52 Tavistock Square. Leonard and Virginia lived on the two top floors, two floors below were occupied by a law firm, and below that came the offices and storerooms of the Hogarth Press. These had once been kitchen and servants' quarters in the Victorian days of large families. Anyone who has ever lived in a semibasement flat in one of these old houses knows that even the most drastic conversion to modern use leaves them full of mysterious cupboards and corners and dark holes and unexpected doors and other signs that not so very long ago every household was a sort of fortress planned to stand a siege, inhabited in its lower regions by retainers constantly occupied in repairing the ravages of dirt and time and hearty appetites.

[1] *A Writer's Diary.*

Such premises are commodious enough but not exactly comfortable.

The office staff worked in the front; the manager had to be tracked down to his lair in what had once been a pantry; room was found in a former scullery or washhouse for the old printing machine, which was still used for hand setting of type, though the books were commercially printed and bound elsewhere. No space was required for a board room, nor was it thought necessary to provide an elegant reception room to impress salesmen and quell authors. And yet everyone who ever worked for the Hogarth Press enjoyed the informal atmosphere and made light of any discomforts and disadvantages, which were equally shared, or ignored, by the Woolfs themselves.

At the rear, built over what had once been the back yard, was a large stock room lit by a skylight, which Virginia used as her study. Here she would write steadily for the allotted number of hours every morning, oblivious of her surroundings, uninterruptable when deep in thought, but ready enough, when the watch propped beside the inkpot showed that she had done her stint for the day, to take part if required in the bustle of activity going on outside.

The move, in spite of careful planning, seems to have been rather chaotic, for though it took place in January she had to warn her friend Vita Sackville-West, when inviting her to lunch one day in mid-March: "Prepare for a complete picnic, among the ruins of books and legs of tables, dirt and dust and only fragments of food."

At first the workroom seemed wonderfully spacious. "Come and see my bare studio in the basement," she wrote in May, "very nice to sit in this hot weather, with one chair, one table, one bed, one bookcase." But all this changed as time went on. What happened to the bed, whether it was moved or simply snowed under, is unknown. Anything that was not wanted immediately or could not be found room for elsewhere was stacked here — pictures by Vanessa Bell and other artists as well as books, manuscripts, packages of unbound volumes, old records and files.

Virginia did not mind, so long as her own writing table was inviolate and no one touched her ever-growing pile of notebooks, rough drafts, time sheets, manuscripts in various stages of revision. She might mislay all sorts of personal belongings or forget some small domestic errand, but she could always select just the book or paper she needed for her own work from the midst of apparent confusion, just as a blacksmith or a garage mechanic knows where to find in some dark corner just the right nail or tool or spare part saved, from yesterday or from years back, for eventual use.

John Lehmann, the poet, has described the studio as a forest or the holiest part of the house. To Winifred Holtby, the novelist, it was a submarine cave in which one moved among books and papers as among the rocks and ledges of that underwater world which so fascinated Virginia's imagination. "The light penetrates wanly down between the high buildings overhead, as through deep waters, and noises from the outside world enter only in a subdued murmur, as from very far away." To Virginia the narrow passage through the basement at Tavistock Square was like the path through the garden and orchard at Monk's House; both led to where she hoped to find the kind of reality and truth she sought.

Upstairs was another sort of reality, that which is to be found in friendship and laughter and the interchange of ideas. Here, in a room rather similar to the one at Gordon Square and decorated like those in the country home with the pictures and objects she and her husband chose because they really liked them, she welcomed her intimates, relaxed over tea, listened to gossip or to politics, gave or received criticism about books and art.

After tea she would try to snatch half an hour for her diary or slip out for a quick call on a friend before dinner, or just wander about the streets and squares. London stimulated her, when she was in a receptive mood and did not find it too exhausting, distracting and noisy. "It takes up the private life and carries it on, without any effort," she wrote in her diary. "Faces passing lift up my mind; prevent it from settling, as it does in the stillness at Rodmell." From the thousands of impressions she received she would try to note down a few, something to be stored away which later might be made to yield its essence. The magpie part of her mind could not resist picking up details that might turn out to be treasures, telling her more than was immediately revealed.

Always searching, seldom bored, enjoying almost everything, infinitely variable in mood, she could soar from dejection to ecstasy, and rest in content after a moment of vision. Walking in Russell Square she might see mountains in the sky and the moon rising over Persia, might doubt the reality of her own existence as a separate personality walking this strange earth, and then bump against some exact fact and feel refreshed and invigorated, ready to continue the search for the unknown, to trudge through the desert until again the mountain snows gleamed amid the clouds. She had no formal religion in which to express these mystical experiences. The agnosticism in which she had been reared forbade her to say that what she sought, and sometimes found, was the peace of God that passeth all understanding, but she knew that, walking in Bloomsbury, she might "turn but a stone and start a wing" and see "The traffic of Jacob's Ladder pitched between Heaven and Charing Cross."

Chapter X

THE YEAR 1924 was, she reflected at its close, a satisfactory one, on the whole. The change of houses had not been as "catclys-mic" as she had feared. "After all, one doesn't change body or brain," she wrote, in one of her few lapses into sententiousness. Even if it did make her "oscillate for days," that was life, that was wholesome. "And if we didn't live venturously, plucking the wild goat by the beard, and trembling over precipices, we should never be depressed, I've no doubt; but already should be faded, fatalistic and aged."

The underlying reasons for this feeling of satisfaction were that she had almost finished two books, done a great deal of other writing, and gained a new friend. This was Vita Sackville-West, to call her by the name she still uses for her poems, novels and weekly gardening column, although to be correct she was an Honorable, as the daughter of a peer (Lord Sackville); a Mrs., by virtue of her marriage to the Honorable Harold Nic-olson (himself a member of a noble family, an ex-diplomat, former M. P., and a critic, biographer, novelist and editor); and is now Lady Nicolson since her husband was created a Knight Commander of the Victorian Order in 1953.

The friendship began in 1922 with Mrs. Woolf admiring Mrs. Nicolson's poems, wanting to read her book about her family history and the great house of Knole, which the first Queen Elizabeth had given to her Lord Treasurer, Thomas Sackville. It continued through 1923 with Mrs. Nicolson dining with Mrs. Woolf at Richmond or at Gordon Square, where Mrs.

Clive Bell had an interesting collection of photographs of eminent Victorians ("No party, and please don't dress"). Gradually the formalities were dropped ("I wish you could be induced to call me Virginia"); and the two women were exchanging jokes and criticisms and discussing everything under the sun, from poetry to face powder.

Virginia wrote from Spain: "I am sitting in a café with a band, ten million Spaniards playing dominoes, and old men trying to sell lottery tickets. . . . We've had a splendid time up in the Sierra Nevada, staying with a mad Englishman who does nothing but read French and eat grapes." Or from Rodmell, asking if there was any chance that the Hogarth Press could have a Sackville-West book. They could, and it would be ready in July of 1924. That was good news; was it a poem or a story? "Oh how I envy you, finishing books straight off." It was a story, and when it appeared in October (Vita being as good as her word about when it would be ready), Virginia wrote: "*Seducers in Ecuador* looks very pretty, rather like a ladybird. The title, however, slightly alarms the old gentleman in Bumpus's" (the famous bookshop in Oxford Street).

On receiving the manuscript from the author, Virginia had mixed shrewd criticism with warm praise of the book. It was the sort of thing she would have liked to write herself. "It is not, of course, altogether thrust through: I think it could be tightened up, and aimed straighter; but there is nothing to spoil it in this. I like its texture — the sense of all the fine things you have dropped in to it, so that it is full of beauty in itself when nothing is happening — nevertheless such interesting things do happen, so suddenly, barely, too; and I like its objectivity so that one can play about with it — interpret it in different ways. . . . I am very glad we are going to publish it, and extremely proud and indeed touched, with my childlike dazzled affection for you, that you should dedicate it to me . . . (I'm now shy — and so will cease)."

So it went on, the friendship gradually and naturally ripening. The Woolfs visited the Nicolsons at their house, Long Barn, near Vita's childhood home. "I was enchanted and made envious by my visit," wrote Virginia. "Knole almost crushed me — for I detest being unable to express anything of what I feel, and certainly couldn't. Then there was the Barn, which has led us to think of rebuilding our own cottage. So you see, I was thoroughly happy and very miserable." Would Vita come to see her at Rodmell? "We would offer you what Leonard says I must confess to be the most uncomfortable bed in the smallest room in Sussex." And this could easily not have been one of Virginia's characteristic exaggerations, at that time when every improvement of, or addition to, Monk's House had to be carefully planned.

But real intimacy was achieved only after the two women had wrangled their way through a misunderstanding. "I enjoyed your intimate letter from the Dolomites," wrote Virginia. "It gave me a great deal of pain — which is, I've no doubt, the first stage of intimacy — no friends, no heart, only an indifferent head. Never mind; I enjoyed your abuse very much." Vita protested she never wrote any such thing. To which Virginia replied, "But really and truly you did say — I can't remember exactly what, but to the effect that I made copy out of all my friends and cared with the head, not with the heart. As I say, I forget: and so we'll consider it cancelled." On returning to London from Rodmell she found the actual passage which had upset her. "We are just back; what did I find on the drawing room table but a letter from which (to justify myself and utterly shame you) I make this quotation: 'Look on it, if you like, as copy — as I believe you look upon everything, human relationships included. Oh yes, you like people through the brain, better than through the heart,' etc. So there; come and be forgiven."

A small incident, interesting only because of the light it throws on Virginia's character; her sensitivity and her toughness, her desire for affection and her willingness to accept criticism. There was a difference of ten years in age, but the older woman listened to the younger woman, took her advice on all sorts of practical matters, and reported back when she had done as she was told. If Vita said she ought to widen her circle, she would try to do so. "I have met Mr. Thomas Hardy, Charlotte Mew (the greatest living poetess), Siegfried Sassoon, Nancy Cunard, and rather expect in the course of the next ten days to meet Percy Lubbock. So you see I'm exploring our profession thoroughly."

She could give advice, too. What she really deeply appreciated in a relationship, on any level, was a frank give-and-take, a kind of resistance which paved the way to more understanding. This approach to intimacy, she felt, could be achieved by her with women but seldom with men. It took a long, long time before she could outgrow the feeling that men secretly, almost unconsciously, distrusted and despised women. Even an old, dearly loved friend, like E. M. Forster, could make her wonder if he was not actually shrinking from her, "as a woman, a clever woman, an up to date woman," or even send her into a paroxysm of fury similar to that which made Terence Hewet burst out laughing at Rachel Vinrace when St. John Hirst had appeared to patronize her in *The Voyage Out*.

This regression to the fears of her early womanhood sometimes occurred long after she reached maturity. But with women it was different; one could be silly with them, or wise with them; could occasionally achieve with them "a relationship so secret and private compared with relations with men." It was this feeling which caused her to write in *Jacob's Room*, in one of those odd intrusions of herself which have been noted: "Who shall deny that this blankness of mind, when combined with profusion, mother wit, old wives' tales, haphazard ways, and sentimentality — who shall deny that in these respects every woman is nicer than any man?"

Some people would deny it, but few would trouble to affirm it. Like a discussion on which do you prefer, cats or dogs? the answers reveal more than the speaker knows. Virginia forgave women their faults, because she felt at her slippered ease with them. She could not excuse men for their virtues, because they made her feel she had to strain toward some impossible ideal. Her indulgence toward feminine softness and her severity toward masculine sternness had an emotional origin, revealing the kind of woman she would have liked to be. It was not her fault that she was clever, and no one had any right to blame her for it. It was her fault if she was vague or careless or forgetful, but these were minor matters which she would deal with herself; whereas a suggestion that she was essentially coldhearted, faithless to feelings because she sacrificed the heart to the brain, this was outrageous. It brought her face to face with an image of herself as she desired not to be.

Moreover, if the accusation was true, what became of *Mr. Bennett and Mrs. Brown?* This was the title for a paper Virginia read to the Heretics Club in Cambridge in 1924. The Hogarth Press issued it as a pamphlet in the same year, and it is included in the later volume of collected essays, *The Captain's Death Bed.*

It was her spirited reply to the critics (including Arnold Bennett) who said that she failed to create characters in *Jacob's Room.* She did not claim that she had done so, but explained that she did not intend to persevere in the attempt by continuing to use the methods of Arnold Bennett, H. G. Wells or John Galsworthy. She admired these writers, she said, and enjoyed their books. She entirely agreed that it was the business of the novelist to express characters. But so far as she was concerned these three major Edwardians were out of date; as models for the new Georgian writers, they were stultifying.

To illustrate her point she used one of her favorite devices. She told her audience a story about something that was supposed to have happened to her in a railway carriage. As in the case of *An Unwritten Novel,* she sat opposite a small, elderly, unhappy woman, observed her and tried to understand her, sympathetically, imaginatively. Later she considered how differently any English novelist would write about this woman (whom she called Mrs. Brown) as compared with any French or Russian writer. She went on to ask how Wells, Galsworthy or Bennett would have presented Mrs. Brown to the reader. Wells might have seized upon the evidences of poverty and then gone on to write about her as though she were a citizen of his coming Utopia. Galsworthy, burning with the same kind of indignation against the evils of the times, would have seen her as something used, broken, thrown away. Bennett, "alone of the Edwardians, would keep his eyes in the carriage." But would he, for all his careful noting of detail, be any more successful in capturing the spirit of Mrs. Brown? Her background, her family circumstances, the house she lived in, yes; the sort of woman she really was, no.

Virginia Woolf freely admitted that, following the popular conventions and using the great Edwardians' methods of accurately noting details, she too had failed to transmit the impression Mrs. Brown made on her. It would be easier to write a three-volume novel, in the sedate, leisurely Victorian manner, about Mrs. Brown's family and their adventures, than to convey exactly what she meant. The best she could do, at the moment, was to "say, despairingly, that all sorts of scenes rushed into my mind, to proceed to tumble them out pell-mell, and to describe this vivid, this overmastering impression by likening it to a draught or a smell of burning."

It was an appalling predicament to be in, but she served notice here, as she had previously done in the essay on modern fiction, that as the older writers showed her no way out of it, she and her contemporaries and friends, D. H. Lawrence, T. S. Eliot, E. M. Forster, James Joyce, Lytton Strachey (to name only a few of the pioneers and exponents of the new methods) would have to do the best they could do to put the "Mrs. Brown who is eternal, who is human nature, who changes only on the surface," before the understanding reader.

For the modern reader is in the railway carriage too; he is

bewildered by the complexity of his feelings, overwhelmed by the disorder of the thousands of impressions received. Why does he humbly let the realists tell him everything about Mrs. Brown except what she is really like? He is asked to co-operate, not merely to be patient until the postwar writers had perfected their new methods; to insist that they tell the truth, to resist all substitutes and evasions, to join with them in the determination never, never to desert Mrs. Brown.

This attitude to the reader and to the writer's subject matter is a very important element in Virginia Woolf's criticism. She does not write down to the reader; she talks to him, assuming, with a natural politeness, that he is as intelligent and appreciative as she is, that he would not be visiting her picture gallery unless he really wanted to see what was there, and that he might enjoy talking about what he saw, either with the custodian or with his friends afterwards. Sometimes the talk is serious, raising the question of the joint responsibility of reader and writer; sometimes witty and humorous, admitting that this or that is what the important people say, but privately, you know, I think it is all a lot of stuff and nonsense. But the comment is never superficial or sentimental, always honest, to the point, and admirably illustrated.

It is because she managed to convey this impression of easy intimacy, without condescension or flippancy, that her essays have such an appeal. When she published almost at the same time in 1925 two very different books, there began the argument which still continues — at which did she excel, at critical or at creative writing? If all the poets and novelists who admire her claimed her as theirs, and all the critics asserted the opposite, or if the critics praised her novels and the novelists praised her criticism, it might be possible to reach a conclusion. But, alas for those who wish everyone to fit neatly into a slot and remain there, this is not so. One still has to pay one's penny and take one's choice.

She herself would have been glad if only people would make

up their minds. "Ha ha!" she wrote to Vita Sackville-West, "I thought you wouldn't like *Mrs. Dalloway*. On the other hand, I thought you might like the *Common Reader,* and I'm very glad that you do — all the more that it's just been conveyed to me that Logan Pearsall Smith thinks it very disappointing. But oh, how one's friends bewilder one! Partly, I suppose, the result of bringing out two books at the same time. I'm trying to bury my head in the sand, or play a game of racing my novel against my criticism according to the opinions of my friends. Sometimes Mrs. D. gets ahead, sometimes the C. R."

She got deeper satisfaction out of her novels; they cost her prolonged agony, but they exercised her faculties more fully. To write the essays she had to bend her mind to an uncomfortable angle, but sometimes she turned to them for refreshment, drawing new vigor from attacking new problems. "I have to write a lecture for school girls; 'How Should One Read a Book?' and this, by a merciful dispensation, seems to me a matter of dazzling importance and breathless excitement."

There were two reasons for this feeling, a physical and a mental cause. She had been ill for some weeks, with annoying relapses just when she was convinced she was better. "Owing to standing or sitting three minutes too long in the Press I am put back to bed — all the blame now falling on the Hogarth Press. But this is nothing very bad — I feel as if a vulture sat on a bough above my head, threatening to descend and kick at my spine, but by blandishments I turn him into a kind of red cock." But at last she was getting better, reaching a stage when even the doctor and Leonard would have to admit that she was in "robust health." Anyway, she was sitting up, had no pain and no temperature, and was anxious to get back to work. The second reason was that she could envisage her audience; the angularity of attitude did not afflict her when she knew to whom she was talking. Some of the girls might be restless and inattentive, but mostly they would be curious and not in the least awe-struck. It would be like talking to friends.

She liked young people and had, says her niece Ann (daughter of her brother Adrian), a great gift of putting them at their ease and in this way bringing out the best in them. "The great thing about meeting Leonard and Virginia was that there was never any condescension about them. If one disagreed one said so and they never appeared to assume that they must be right because they were older and more experienced and persons of intellectual and artistic understanding. We, on the other hand, never assumed that they disagreed with us because they were fossilized old fogies who could not understand the needs and aspirations of the younger generation. Indeed I have never met people who were less of fossilized old fogies. I always felt I was a clever, attractive and amusing person when I was with her or even when writing to her, though I was not at all so sure of it at other times. I don't want to give the idea that conversation with Virginia was always on the highest plane and that her company somehow transformed one into a prodigy of wit and intellect. As often as not it was of the more nonsensical sort, make-believe and speculation as to the goings on of people we didn't know, the sort of games one plays as a child, but much more fun when played with her because she was so good at it, especially when it involved deflating pompous or publicized people. When she was being a child she could do it better than any of us and when she was being a grown up we could do it nearly as well as she could."

So her lectures to schoolgirls or to older people at Cambridge or Oxford, and the essays collected in *The Common Reader* and other volumes resembled very much the kind of conversation she had with her friends in the Bloomsbury house. Trabb's boy would have found nothing for derision in them. People who are old, tired, mentally wary, tend to regard her as in some obscure way a threat and to keep alive the idea of a Bloomsbury Group that was intent on being exclusive. But those who have remained young, active, free and adventurous in spirit cannot be bothered with any of this rubbish. They go straight to her books and get what they want from them; that is, from her. And it is invariably something very positive, gay, stimulating and provocative.

The importance of criticism, as compared with reviewing, was a topic often discussed in Tavistock Square. Current books, Virginia felt, needed criticism; young writers needed help. The illustrious dead were studied in schools and universities, in courses that might effectively destroy any love of literature but enable the student to get a degree or diploma by writing three hundred solemn pages about the evolution of the Elizabethan sonnet. At other schools one could learn the tricks of writing for money. In the daily press and the literary-cum-political weeklies the harassed reviewer of too many books did his hasty best to tell the public what new volumes would serve to pass an idle hour. But uninspired teaching and superficial comment could not help a young writer to know whether or not the breath of life was in his work.

Virginia often talked about the possibility of producing some kind of mimeographed sheet, perhaps for private circulation, where books would be seriously analyzed and judged, not for the amusement of the public but for the benefit of the author and his fellow writers. Nothing ever came of this scheme, nor of a similar idea of setting up a sort of literary tribunal where authors could meet one another and review each other's work face to face.

This was the practice among her friends, with results that she found very salutary. Some of the nonwriting members of the Bloomsbury Group felt that justice, not mercy, was too often the rule, and wondered why that poor baby in Forster's *Howard's End* was laughed at as though it were the squalling bundle the Ugly Duchess threw at Alice when she was having her strange adventures in Wonderland. But Virginia knew the value of honest criticism, was ready to defend herself if attacked, and gave as good as she got.

Her comments on books by her friends were impersonal but

helpful, truthful and often extremely vivid. "In some passages you are in danger of being too clever," she once told Elizabeth Bowen. "You are trying to throw a lasso with a knotted rope." A remark of this kind was worth more than a column of praise from a reviewer who had no understanding of what the writer was trying to achieve and so was unable to suggest why the result was not entirely satisfactory.

In accordance with her theory that "abuse" was one approach to intimacy, Virginia was also capable of being quite philosophical about adverse criticism, even from dear friends, often discounting it in advance. "Lord, how you're going to hate this book," she would write gleefully, when busily at work on something that pleased her. Frankness was never allowed to interfere with friendship. Only when she thought she detected in another's work qualities that revealed something cheap and dishonest in a personality did she fly into a fury of disgust, as though the literary lapse from a state of grace had been a personal affront; and then the affection and respect would return, she would review her feelings and conclude that perhaps she had been jealous.

This was the case with Katherine Mansfield. The Hogarth Press had been proud to publish her story *Prelude,* when she was unknown and struggling. Leonard and Virginia believed in her when others did not, and proved it practically. But when *Bliss,* one of Katherine Mansfield's most frequently reprinted and reread stories, first appeared, Virginia flew into a rage. A poor story, badly written, and revealing the author's callousness and hardness as a human being, she considered. "I don't see how much faith in her as a woman or a writer can survive that sort of story," she noted in her diary. "I shall read it again, but I don't suppose I shall change."

She did change, not about the story but about the writer. "Her hard composure is much on the surface," she decided. Then again she doubted. In 1926, writing from a sickbed, she told Vita Sackville-West, "I've been reading Katherine Mansfield with a mixture of sentiment and horror. What odd friends I've had." In 1931 she once more examined her thoughts and feelings, and in the course of a long letter to Vita summed them up in this way:

"As for Katherine Mansfield, I think I've got it nearly right. We did not ever coalesce; but I was fascinated and she respectful; only I thought her cheap and she thought me priggish; and yet we were both compelled to meet simply in order to talk about writing. This we did by the hour. Only then she came out with a swarm of little stories, and I was jealous, no doubt; because they were so praised; but gave up reading them not on that account, but because of their cheap, sharp sentimentality, which was all the worse I thought, because she had, as you say, the zest and the resonance — I mean she could permeate one with her quality. . . . Also, she was for ever possessed by her dying; and had to press on through pages that should have taken years in ten minutes — so that our relationship became unreal also. . . . But the fact remains that she had a quality I adored, and needed: I think her sharpness and reality — her having knocked about with prostitutes and so on, whereas I had always been respectable — was the thing I wanted then. I dream of her often — and with some odd reality too."

This jealousy, to which Virginia freely confessed whenever she detected it in herself, seldom had a personal origin, though it might flare up if someone who had been highly praised to her had the misfortune not to come up to expectations. This was the case with Elinor Wylie, whom she met in 1925. The occasion was disastrous, as Virginia described it to Vita, writing to ask for the loan of *The Venetian Glass Nephew.* "Oh, what an evening. I expected a ravishing and diaphanous dragonfly; a siren; a green and sweet-voiced nymph — that was what I expected, and come on tiptoe into the room to find — a solid hunk. . . . All the evening she declaimed unimpeachable truths; and discussed our sales: hers are three times better than mine, naturally. . . . But I must read her book."

A second meeting was no more successful. "I quail before the Venetian nephew. Another meeting with that arid desert has sickened me. The only curiosity is — how does she do it — Francis Birrell, Aldous Huxley at her feet, and she no better than a stark, staring, naked maypole." No wonder that Edmund Wilson, in *The Shores of Light,* wrote that the meeting "though Elinor may have distorted a little — had sounded rather disagreeable." According to Elinor Wylie, Virginia had wanted to know why she wrote in literary English instead of something more natively American, in the line of Ring Lardner, for instance. Whatever the exact truth, the two women might admire one another's work but could not establish a personal friendship.

And yet, where one might expect some element of rivalry it did not occur. Virginia's references to Dame Edith Sitwell are uniformly admiring. Considering the powerful, electric personalities of both women, one might have expected sparks to fly when they met. But the two queens of English literary society seem never to have found themselves, as they so easily might have, in any position of rivalry.

They were both at a Bloomsbury party when Virginia, who had been out of sorts, "with glass between me and everybody," saw "as through a telescope (she looked so remote and washed up on a rock) Edith Sitwell in her brocade dress, sitting silent." Evidently they both felt the same way about that evening's festivities.

Later Virginia wrote to Vita about a visit from Edith Sitwell, "whom I like. I like her appearance — in red cotton, many flounced, though it was blowing a gale. She has hands that shut up in one's own hands like fans — far more beautiful than mine" (Virginia was proud of her own beautiful hands, and with good reason). "She is like a clean hare's bone that one finds on a moor, with emeralds stuck about it. She is infinitely tapering and distinguished. She told me awful Brontë stories about being cursed by her mother as a child and made to kill bluebottles in a hot room. I like talking to her about her poetry. She flutters about like a sea-bird, crying so dismally."

Later that year Edith Sitwell adversely criticized Vita Sackville-West. As a rule anyone who dared do this (apart from herself) brought the sharpest condemnation from Virginia, but this time she was eminently fair. "I like her (Edith)," she wrote. "She's a character. I don't think you probably realise how hard it is for the natural innovator, as she is, to be fair to the natural traditionalist, as you are. It's much easier for you to see her good points than for her to see yours."

Soon after, when Vita was still feeling sore from the attack, Virginia wrote with intent to soothe, to remind Vita that she too had her troubles. "Pity poor Virginia, dragged off to meet Arnold Bennett, who abused me for a column in last night's *Evening Standard;* and Shanks [the poet], your brother in the Hawthornden [most coveted of literary prizes in England, which Vita had just won] calls me a 'dishonest writer' — so you see, if you have Edith, I have Shanks."

Actually the meeting with Arnold Bennett went off well, although, according to her own account in her diary, Virginia behaved very badly, teasing and baiting that fundamentally shy, stammering panjandrum of contemporary English letters. He did not mind, because everyone else present stopped talking to listen to their conversation. He may have thought it was a case of Dignity and Impudence, he being the larger and more imposing of those two dogs in the popular Landseer picture, well aware that each kind of animal or human being must act according to its own nature, so that hard feelings are a waste of time and energy. When he died she wrote a very just appraisal of him as a man and as a writer.

Nor did H. G. Wells resent Virginia's attack on him in *Mr. Bennett and Mrs. Brown,* which is rather more surprising, because he was apt to take offense and could easily have been in conflict with Leonard Woolf on some political issue. But they remained friendly. "Wells —" she suddenly interjects into one

of her bubbling, chattering notes to Vita, "but no: I won't repeat any more great men's compliments (of course I shall;
dozens of times over). . . . You think I'm so damned vain I
can be trusted to blabber everything — well, it's true." But precisely what H. G. Wells said remains unrecorded.

One thing is clear. The major literary stars remained untroubled in their courses; it was their satellites who were perturbed
by any new arrival in the sky.

She was as much aware of the inherent falsity of cults and
"schools" in literature as she was uncomfortable about extremes
of fashion in clothes. Some people were so constituted that they
could find satisfaction in either of these two types of formalism;
she could not be bothered. A bare minimum of attention to
such matters, enough to escape the trap of idle eccentricity,
would suffice. Thereafter one must be free. One of the pieces of
sound advice she gave to young writers is to be found in her
Letter to a Young Poet. Writers "dress themselves up. They
act their parts. One leads; the other follows. One is romantic,
the other realist. There is no harm in it, so long as you take it
as a joke, but once you believe in it, once you begin to take
yourself seriously as a leader, or as a follower, as a modern or
as a conservative, then you become a self-conscious, biting, and
scratching little animal whose work is not of the slightest value
or importance to anybody." The real leaders, those who had
found their own paths and continued to follow them, would
agree. It was the less original and independent writers and critics, the cultists, who felt insecure and so took to biting and
scratching.

She was also ready to give advice on matters with which she
was much less qualified to deal. When Vita told her that she had
an idea for a poem telling the history of a Kentish village, Virginia was enthusiastic. This was how she thought it could be
done: "Plan it out roughly on a great sheet: let each little note
branch and blossom in the night, or when you're waking (the
beauty of this subject is that everything will come in —

cabbages, moon, church steeple): occasionally open some old history, or life of some unknown man, but not to read carefully — to dream over. So in a week — no, three or four days, the whole poem will be booming and bubbling in your head; meals seem but a temporary contrivance barring the way." If only it were as simple as that.

In her own work, of course, she knew there was a vast difference between having an idea in one's head and writing down something that approached expressing that idea. This was as true of criticism as it was of fiction. For example, she met George Moore at a party in 1926, and recorded in her diary what he looked like and some of the things he said. Her only comment was that, "save for the usual shyness about powder, paint, shoes and stockings, I was happy, owing to the supremacy of literature. This keeps us sweet and sane. George Moore — me, I mean."

A few days later she wrote Vita a fuller report of what she had been doing and whom she had been seeing. "Then I met Rose Macaulay and George Moore (d'you remember scolding me for not meeting writers?). What I say about writers is that they are the salt of the earth (even if to say it I must say something of my rapture for the middle classes — the huntresses, the stockbrokers). With both of these people, Rose and George, one can tell the truth — a great advantage. Never did anyone talk such nonsense as George. 'Do not tell me you admire Hardy, Mrs. Woolf? My good friend, tell me if he has written a single sentence well? Not one'. . . . Whatever I said, he poohpoohed . . . he attacked Conrad and Henry James and Anatole France; but I can't tell you how urbane and sprightly the old poll parrot was; and (this is what I think using the brain does for one) not a pocket, not a crevice of pomp, humbug, respectability in him; he was fresh as a daisy."

Then compare this galloping comment with the measured tread of her criticism of George Moore in the essay on him in *The Death of the Moth*. It is a restatement of the same central

idea; that he was sweet and sane, but silly; capricious and posing, but faithful to himself. Reading his memoirs, shocking as
he tries to make them, so that "by his own confession he ought
to be excluded from every drawing-room in South Kensington,"
nevertheless "we explore from start to finish, from those earliest
days in Ireland to these latest in London, the habitation of his
soul." She sums up by saying that "No one so inveterately literary is among the great writers; literature had wound itself about
him like a veil, forbidding him the free use of his limbs; the
phrase comes to him before the emotion." But he is a "born
writer, a man who detests meals, servants, ease, respectability or
anything else that gets between him and his art . . . has taught
himself an accent, a cadence, indeed a language . . . which,
though they are not English but Irish, will give him his place
among the lesser immortals of his tongue."

It is interesting to note, too, that there is not a word in this
essay to indicate that she ever met him personally. This scrap
of information is not suppressed, but quietly dismissed as irrelevant. Every page, every paragraph bears her hallmark, but she
does not obtrude between the reader and what she wishes to
show him. Her attitude is not standoffish, but it has its stateliness and dignity.

No one could guess from reading "The Enchanted Organ" in
The Moment and Other Essays that the woman whose selected
letters she was reviewing had been not only Miss Thackeray,
Mrs. Richmond Ritchie and Lady Ritchie but also Aunt Annie.
Her younger sister Minnie had been Virginia's father's first wife;
she had lived with them after the marriage and for a short time
after Minnie's death had ruled Leslie Stephen's household, driving him nearly to distraction because her exuberance could
never fit in with his sobriety of character, despite mutual affection. Virginia's father had been even more frantic when she announced her engagement to Richmond Ritchie, and it took the
calm common sense of a neighbor to whom he went for sympathy in his agitation to make him realize that his objections to

the match were not founded upon morality but upon jealousy. This wise friend, who gently and tactfully laughed him out of his tantrum, later married him and became Virginia's mother. Aunt Annie was a familiar figure at Hyde Park Gate, and continued to be affectionately regarded and visited by the young Stephens until her death at a great age in 1919.

The same reticence is to be seen in *Victorian Photographs of Famous Men and Fair Women,* by Julia Cameron, published by the Hogarth Press in 1926. Both Roger Fry and Virginia Woolf wrote introductions to this volume, he discussing the aesthetic merit of the portraits, she telling the story of the photographer's life. He analyzed, amongst others, three pictures, pointing out how the lighting brings out the architectural strength and symmetry of the bony structure of the head, though the hands are too much cut up and some small, sharp accents on the folds of the dress and a pendant break the continuity of the design. They were photographs of Mrs. Herbert Duckworth. There is no mention of the fact that Mrs. Duckworth became Mrs. Leslie Stephen and the mother of Mrs. Woolf.

It is obvious, once you know, for there is something haunting about these pictures, a strange feeling that you have seen this woman somewhere else. You have, in portraits of Virginia Woolf. The resemblance to her mother is quite striking. The outlines are softer, the nose is different, more purely Greek, the attitude more relaxed and passive — Julia Jackson Duckworth Stephen was inured to the ways of portrait painters since early childhood, whereas Virginia seems to have faced a camera as though it were a firing squad. But here are the same long, nervous hands, the same soft, straight hair, the same shape of skull and brow, the same dreaming eyes and responsive mouth. In the jeweled, cloaked and shadowed figure of the Victorian photograph one is aware of seeing only one aspect of the real woman, receives an impression of latent power, of hidden reserves, of a serenity that may mask deep inner conflicts.

Virginia's own contribution to the book is an extremely racy

portrait of the portraitist. She was one of seven sisters born in
India, all beautiful, spirited, distinguished and more or less eccentric in varying ways. She was a friend of Tennyson's; she
married a quiet clergyman of infinite patience and considerable
renown. Her father was reputed to have been "the biggest liar
in India." He crowned a scandalous life with an unedifying
death and even his corpse refused decent burial, according to
stories told by Dame Ethel Smyth's father. Her mother was the
daughter of the Chevalier Antoine de l'Etang, who had been
a page to Marie Antoinette and who carried a miniature of that
queen all his life and into his grave. All this, and scores of other
details, are related without one hint that the stories are part of
a family chronicle which Virginia heard in her childhood; for
Julia Pattle Cameron had been one of her mother's aunts.

The introduction reads as though it were written at top
speed, but there is evidence that she expended her usual care in
checking her facts and in selecting and assembling her material.
She wrote to Vita Sackville-West, enclosing a copy of a coronet,
enquiring, "Is this real or a sham? I'm trying to prove my Great-
Aunt's descent from a Neapolitan adventurer and a French
Marquis. But I have no time." A few days later she wrote
thanking Vita: "You are an angel, but I didn't mean you to
take so much trouble. God knows about the Marquis. Probably
the whole thing is different in France — he may have been the
son or the nephew of a marquis (I think that was the legend),
and anyhow I suppose I can say, vaguely, 'aristocratic,' and
leave it. I want to prove her base and noble — it fits in with her
oddities. I might spend half a lifetime over her." She could
have asked one of her half brothers, but finally decided to let
it go as not sufficiently important.

Nevertheless the idea of having a romantic French ancestry
continued to amuse her. She was very shy about speaking
French, though she read it easily. Vita tells the story of how she
overheard her asking a sailor on a cross-Channel boat, *"Est-ce
que la mer est brusque?"* Naturally this way of inquiring

whether the sea was rough became a standing joke, and she was mercilessly teased about it. She did not mind, but retorted when she could. "Did you know that I talk French very well? That is with great fluency, some inaccuracies, and a good many words not in use since Saint-Simon? This is the report of my French teacher. I have lessons. It is the greatest fun. I am thinking of learning Spanish, Italian and Russian, not for the languages, but for the life histories of the professors. I only want you to know the fact: that I do talk French, because you will never hear me; and then I get a little more even with you in real-womanliness. All real women talk French, and powder their noses." So she wrote in 1928. A few days later she returned to the same point. "Did I tell you how well I speak French? 'Madame, you must have French blood in you!' 'Yes, sir, my great-grandmother was a French marquise.' Ah, but I think I told you of the exquisite joy that gives me. And you'll never hear me — that's what's so tantalising for you: the great-grand-daughter of the French marquise."

It is pleasant to be able to record when critical writing afforded her diversion and refreshment, because she often complained that it was hard work, yielding little satisfaction since it exercised only one part of her brain. "To write criticism now is like keeping my hand clenched, so much do I want to stretch and write fiction," she wrote to Vita in 1929, when she was gradually shaking off a headache that had kept her "amphibious" for a month, and was in the stage of arguing with the doctor about how much work she might do and how she should arrange her life in the future so as to avoid crossing that hairbreadth line between a slight tiredness and complete exhaustion. She must take things more easily, the doctor was saying. But "These illnesses are such a bore — four weeks clean out of my life." She proposed telling the doctor that what she was suffering from was "suppressed imagination." Let her get up and let her write fiction, and she would be well again.

One is tempted to diagnose suppressed anxiety as one underlying cause for the discomfort she felt when forced to limit herself to shorter compositions. Her father had been a critic and a biographer, and his figure still loomed in the background of her mind. Whether she was competing with him in either of these two fields of writing or whether she was begging for his approval is a question for the psychologists; but clearly there is an association of ideas. It was near enough to the surface of her consciousness for her to realize that if he had lived on she would have written no books; that is, she would have had no real life of her own. He did not write fiction; therefore when she was at work on a novel she was free of the necessity of fighting or fearing him. This was the room of her own, which he entered only with her permission and at his own peril, for there she would deal with his phantom as roundly as she had dealt with the Angel in the House, who had to be dispatched before she could write at all.

Yet none of these "angularities" appear in her finished critical essays. One of their most outstanding features is their urbanity. They have an easy flow that lures the reader on even when he does not share her taste, agree with her estimate, or accept her conclusion. There is no sign of all the hard work given to preparing for the party. And when the guests are comfortably settled, the children of the house — a large family — are brought in for inspection and prompted to do their little best. The hostess is privately very proud of them, though of course it would not be polite to say so, and it is best to appear slightly deprecatory. Such an attitude will serve to mask any slight nervousness about how the little brats are going to behave. So she smooths a hair ribbon here, tugs a jacket there, pushes a shy one forward, holds an eager one back, with the lightest of touches; and goes on smiling, even if she is secretly afraid that Christina Rossetti must be sickening for something, she's so quiet; or wonders what Sir Thomas Browne has got in his pocket now, for pity's sake; or wishes that show-off Macaulay would leave Addison alone, he's quite conceited enough already; or trembles to think what sort of mess the bathroom and playroom have been left in, toys, books, dirty clothes left all over the place, homework not finished, all kinds of rubbish brought in from the garden, she'll be bound. What a handful, all these children, so different, so incalculable, so dreadful, one has to admit; but such darlings, when all is said and done. Please like them, just a little — they are doing their best and did beg to be allowed to come in and see the company — before we have to close the book and they all disperse once more into their private worlds.

It is this attitude, compounded of genuine humility and absolute mastery of the forces at her command, which gives Virginia Woolf's books of criticism their peculiar charm and also explains why she is often underrated as a critic. She isn't serious enough, doesn't use long words or formulate any elaborate theories. She really seems to think that literature is to be enjoyed; that poetry is for singing, not merely for learning by heart and quoting correctly on suitable occasions; that the beauty of pictures is as free as a sunset, there to be looked at and appreciated. The watchful puritan who lurks in most of us in these highly competitive days tends to be alarmed by such apparent light-mindedness. Is it not dangerous doctrine that all artists, however much they think they have to express themselves or deliver a message to the world, however disdainful or aggressive they may appear to be, really wish desperately to please? Can one really be sure that one doesn't have to be edified or instructed, that one can wander at will in the palaces and gardens of beauty?

But Virginia Woolf cannot stop to answer these questions. After perhaps the eightieth attempt she has finally succeeded in "darting in to deliver the final blows" and has finished *The Common Reader*. What an undignified way to refer to a collection of essays that have appeared in the very best journals and are concerned with the illustrious dead! One would think the writer of these pieces had suddenly turned into Miss Betsey

Trotwood, snatching up a stick and chasing the donkeys out of her garden, to the great delight and admiration of little David Copperfield. Virginia Woolf laughs, brushes the dust off her hands, says over her shoulder, "Read the introduction — I've done a neat little job on Dr. Johnson there," and is off down the garden path to write the book that was demanding to be written once *Mrs. Dalloway* was finished.

Chapter XI

SHE WAS thankful when *Mrs. Dalloway* was completed, for if *Jacob's Room* had been a battle, this succeeding novel had been an agony, all but the end. So it seemed to her, looking back, although the diary reveals that it had had the usual checkered history, lacking only the rapturous start. She was distrustful of it from the beginning. In August 1922 she wrote, "I am laboriously dredging my mind for *Mrs. Dalloway* and bringing up light buckets. I don't like the feeling. I'm writing too quickly. I must press it together." But *Mrs. D.* began to take control, to "usher in a host of others, I begin to perceive."

At first she saw only one chapter, then dimly another, perhaps to be called *The Prime Minister,* perhaps to be published separately. But by October, when this second chapter was almost done, the oddest things were happening. *Mrs. Dalloway* had branched into a book; Clarissa Dalloway, recalled after the lapse of years from her gaily insincere leave-taking of Helen Ambrose and Rachel Vinrace in *The Voyage Out,* given a new personality, a different background and a leading role to play, now split into two characters.

As first planned, the book was to open with Mrs. Dalloway going out to buy flowers for a party, and to close with her suicide at the end of the party. And then a new figure began to take shape in the author's mind. "Septimus Smith? Is that a good name?" When the book was finished it was this young man, a shell-shocked soldier, who had killed himself. The news of his death reaches Mrs. Dalloway while she is entertaining her guests. She does not know him, rather resents the mention of such a disagreeable item from the evening papers; but feels mysteriously identified with this stranger who has thrown his life away as she once threw a shilling into the Serpentine.

Small wonder that, with this kind of thing going on, with a design "so queer and so masterful" shaping in her brain, Virginia should fluctuate between writing furiously and being tempted to abandon the book altogether. Sometimes she felt she had too many ideas; sometimes a whole morning's work would produce no more than fifty words, each one "distilled by a relentless clutch on my brain." She varied from feeling that the book "seems to leave me plunged in the richest strata of my mind," and wondering whether she was writing from deep emotion or merely posing when she said she wanted to criticize the whole social system, to set life and death, sanity and insanity, side by side; to deal with important, central things, even if they did not lend themselves to beautiful language. She could not stop making it up, this "most tantalising and refractory of books," nor could she find out what was the matter with it. But suppose, she asked herself, the determination to go on arose from her desire to show the Murrys that *Jacob's Room* was not a blind alley. That was an annoying, even a degrading thought, which she tried hard to dismiss. She would have to persist because the book interested her, even if she foresaw that it was going to be "the devil of a struggle" and she was always having to "wrench the substance" of her mind to fit it.

She was, in fact, writing at two different levels, and both were unpleasant. She did not really like Clarissa Dalloway; the character was based on an original who fascinated but also irked her. What was the real truth about women who moved serenely in the fashionable world of affairs and seemed to find satisfaction in giving large parties attended by prime ministers and poor relations, old friends and casual acquaintances? There was a glitter and strangeness about the lives of such women that both attracted and repelled her. She longed to understand creatures so different from herself. She could not simply condemn them out of hand — to do so would be to betray her faith as a novelist and to desert Mrs. Brown because she traveled by Rolls-Royce instead of by train — but she could not approve of them wholeheartedly while their routines seemed so senseless and empty. So she struggled to overcome her impatience and prejudice, while gratifying her curiosity.

She wrote to Vita Sackville-West about another woman, similar in kind to Clarissa Dalloway: "She is a woman of the world. To me an almost unknown type. Every value is different. Friendship, let alone intimacy, is impossible. Yet I respect, even admire. Why did she come, I kept wondering; felt so gauche, and yet utterly indifferent. This is a sign one never speaks the truth to her. She skated over everything, evaded, palliated, compromised; yet is fundamentally kind and good. It's odd for me, who have some gift for intimacy, to be nonplussed entirely." In describing one day in the life of Mrs. Dalloway she was at war with her own impatience and failure to answer the question, why did the "woman of the world" come to visit her? The result of this determination to be sympathetic was, as Lytton Strachey pointed out, that she alternately laughed at Clarissa Dalloway and covered her, "very remarkably, with myself."

Septimus Smith she did not know personally; but she knew about madness. She had felt the glory and the terror of seeing faces and hearing voices from beyond the grave. She had lived through moments when exaltation and despair were inextricably merged, when a conviction of understanding all the secrets of the universe was accompanied by the crushing weight of responsibility for all human errors, when the boundaries of personal identity disappeared and the individual was lost between prophecy and doom, when extinction was consummation, life so marvelous that death was its positive and crowning affirmation.

She knew, too, the torment of doubt when infinity receded, the awful anguish when the visions faded, the ghastly fear that the confusions might return, shutting one off from human help, closing the eyes and ears once more to the living voices and loved faces of those who remained firmly anchored in temporal reality. She experienced sympathetically the terrible unhappiness of the sane who are deserted and denied by those in delirium and whose only relief from intolerable pain lies in taking whatever practical means can be devised to recall to everyday life the tormented wanderer in nightmare land.

She realized also that one must admit that these tragic lapses from normality occur, that at present we know very little about their causes or cures, that it is no use calling them by pretty names and that to pretend to ignore them as though they were somehow shameful is in itself an abdication of reason. Previous attitudes of regarding those afflicted by mental sickness in any of its myriad forms as being inspired by God or possessed by demons had been replaced by more subtle social taboos, based on fear and ignorance. The sufferer was no longer reverenced as a prophet or treated as a criminal. But no great steps could be taken towards averting or curing mental derangement until the "curse" could be removed from it, the ban lifted from its mention.

This is so obvious today that it is hard to measure the courage required thirty years ago to write about it frankly, from the inside, as one having authority. Other writers, from the greatest to the least, have shown us madness from the outside — Lear raving, Ophelia wandering in her wits, Falstaff babbling — ghosts appear on time and do a workmanlike job of directing the traffic of a plot in the correct moral direction — observers soliloquize about noble minds being here o'erthrown. Virginia Woolf takes us into a world of confusions, where beauty itself betrays, where punishment awaits unknown crimes, where apparitions are all the more terrifying because their message cannot be understood.

The distraught Septimus Smith, glaring at nothing and talking to himself in Regent's Park one sunny June day, excites only a vague sense of unease in passers-by, while his unhappy wife, Lucrezia, feels stricken because the arm she takes to lead him across a road is merely a bone, because the real man whom she loves and for whose sake she has left her friends and home in Italy is lost to her. The great, powerful, all-knowing doctors who have been consulted about him are a million miles from understanding his desperate plight; indeed, it is their clumsy attempt to coerce him into a cure that precipitates his final, frenzied defiance. Only Clarissa Dalloway, fighting in herself the fear that her own life has been frittered away in lies and chatter, can understand how the brute power exercised by such men (one is a guest at her party) can be felt by the helpless as "obscurely evil, without sex or lust . . . capable of some indescribable outrage — forcing your soul, that was it — they make life intolerable, men like that."

With such an intractable theme struggling for expression, it can easily be understood that Virginia Woolf was at times nearly desperate. "The mad part tries me so much," she wrote in her diary, "makes my mind squirt so badly that I can hardly face spending the next weeks at it." She was uncertain, too, about Clarissa Dalloway. In spite of what she called her tunneling process, digging out caves behind her characters, had she succeeded in giving any depth to the portrait? she asked herself. Or did she remain "tinselly"? Did some lingering dislike of the original obscure her vision, or was it not a fact that one should be able to dislike people in art without its mattering? Maybe some characters had the faculty of detracting from the importance of what happened to them, as though they remained treeless islands in a shallow lake?

The posing of such questions gives a clue to Virginia's own character. Some writers are only happy — and convincing — when writing about types of people they dislike; they have to get rid of their spleen, to express a deep distrust of themselves in a lively hatred of all humankind. Virginia Woolf was not among these minor satirists who flaunt all their lives the awkwardness of adolescence.

She could tease and jeer and be spiteful in life, but not in her writing, because she did not think these were admirable traits. She noted with great pleasure when an old friend said she resembled her mother, who looked like a Madonna but sometimes had a glint in her eye that was, there was no other word for it, vicious. Lord David Cecil caught that same glint, and described her as a "mocking Madonna." But there was, she knew, more to her mother and to herself than this ability to show their claws on occasion; there must be more to every human being than sardonic humor, however entertaining and indeed refreshing, can reveal.

Virginia enjoyed but was at the same time ashamed of her own fierceness. In particular she disliked being peevish. She wanted, she admitted, to appear good to herself. Her own "angularities" pricked her. She desired to be able to give more love, show more gentleness. She feared her own coldness, and expressed this fear explicitly in her diary, when she mentions the dilemma of the writer who is forced, in the same instant, both to feel and to observe his feelings. This fear is shown in *Mrs. Dalloway*. Septimus thinks human nature condemned him for his crime of indifference; Clarissa sees her life corrupted by caution and compromise.

It might be expected that, with such a difficult double theme, the book would be somber, lumpy, dense. Actually it is luminous and fluid.

Consider Mrs. Dalloway's name. One thinks of a flower, a daffodil cool and stately. The daffodil becomes a daffadowndilly, bringing to mind old rhymes, a sound of tinkling bells, the light movement of butterflies and fairies. Yes, Mrs. Dalloway is a fairy. The critics are right who say she is no more than a wraith, a mist on a mirror, having glitter without substance. But she is not the kind of fairy who is the playmate and protector of children. She is a figure from adult folklore, a green woman, a *belle dame sans merci* to steal the soul away; she is Undine, too, searching for a soul but unable to steal it, grateful to those who helped her to be what she wanted, gentle, generous-hearted.

She even wears a green dress. Here she is, in her moment of triumph, as she "escorted her Prime Minister down the room, prancing, sparkling, with the stateliness of her gray hair. She wore ear-rings and a silver-green mermaid's dress. Lolloping on the waves and braiding her tresses she seemed, having that gift still; to be; to exist; to sum it all up in the moment as she passed; turned, caught her scarf in some other woman's dress, unhitched it, laughed, all with the most perfect ease and air of a creature floating in its element . . . as if she wished the whole world well, and must now, being on the verge and rim of things, take her leave."

Virginia did not intend her to be a changeling sprite. She wanted her to have blood, not ichor, in her veins. She tried hard to invest her with corporal reality. She gave her a home in Westminster, and little practical jobs to do about the house — to buy her own flowers, mend her own dress, remember to send love and compliments to the cook for an excellent dinner. But the "house was as cool as a vault. . . . She felt like a nun who has left the world and feels fold round her the familiar veils and the response to old devotions." The cook is real enough. Her name is Mrs. Walker, and she is Irish and whistles all day long. When the maid brings her the compliments and the news that the Prime Minister is expected, all she feels is, "Did it matter, did it matter in the least, one Prime Minister more or less? It made no difference at this hour of night" with the dishes piling up on top of her, it seemed, however hard they washed up in the scullery, and still supper to be laid. In a few lines the reader is given the freedom of the whole household, but Mrs. Dalloway remains obstinately insubstantial.

She has a husband, Richard. He has the same name as he bore in *The Voyage Out*, still follows the same occupation of gracing the House of Commons. But he has lost what vitality he had in that book; might as well be a hayrick in this, so little power of movement does he show. Virginia has even taken from him that kiss which so startled and alarmed Rachel Vinrace. In *Mrs. Dalloway* it is twice mentioned in flashbacks as having been forced on a girl as punishment for advocating votes for women. This rings true; one feels the author's old resentments stirring. This time the man in the case is a minor character, picked almost at random from the assortment of types Virginia disliked so thoroughly that she did not scruple to be fair to them but whom she nonetheless imbued with enough life to tread solidly on firm ground. He, too, has a suggestive name — Hugh Whitbread. He is three parts dough and one part gold lace, no doubt, but the novelist has caught him in her net.

The girl who was kissed is Sally Seton, and she also is thoroughly alive. When Virginia found in the course of her tunneling behind her characters that she had to invent Clarissa Dalloway's memories, she recalled a great many of her own, and distributed them generously. To Sally Seton she gave her remote French ancestry and the miniature of Marie Antoinette so cherished by the romantic Chevalier. It becomes, incidentally, a ruby ring which Sally has to pawn to get enough money to visit Clarissa's home when they are both girls, where she outraged her elders by smoking cigars in her bedroom or by being seen running naked along a corridor on her way to the bathroom, and delighted her contemporaries by her wild escapades, such as riding her bicycle along the top of a terrace parapet and threatening to denounce Hugh Whitbread at family prayers. She still remembers the incident of the kiss, but it has not turned her into an embittered feminist. She arrives unexpectedly at Mrs. Dalloway's party as Lady Rosseter, very rich, married to a bald man with a huge buttonhole, several cotton mills and a vast house near Manchester. She is older, happier, less lovely than Clarissa remembers her to have been, but she is still the same Sally. "I have five enormous boys," she announces immediately, and plunges right away into animated talk about the past with

Peter Walsh. Why, oh why, had not Clarissa married him instead of Richard Dalloway?

A great deal of the novel is devoted to Clarissa and Peter asking themselves the same question, remembering the summer when they had been so passionately in love and had quarreled so incessantly. Virginia Woolf employs here one of the two commonest reveries that offer escape from uncomfortable facts. Almost every child at some time or another indulges in fantasy about a marvelous life in which his "real" parentage is disclosed; and almost every child has caught a peculiar overtone in his father's or mother's voice when speaking of someone from the days before they met one another, fell in love, became engaged, got married. This idle harking back to a time when freedom of choice seemed possible may be very fleeting and a source of secret amusement, or it may reveal a suppressed fear that one's life has somewhere taken a wrong turning.

Peter Walsh and Clarissa Dalloway do not understand why it seemed so impossible, years ago, that they should marry one another; they have, on meeting again, moments of complete understanding and intimacy, and they experience the old irritations. Why is she so insincere and frivolous? he asks himself. Why can't he stop fidgeting with that pocketknife? she wants to know. Thus they continue to resuscitate and then to strangle the old love that still unites them, although they are both past fifty and imagine they have outgrown youthful follies. Actually Peter, for all his forthrightness, is more of a romantic dreamer than Clarissa. He is proud of his failures; she is getting ready to admit hers. But they must follow the separate paths they have chosen.

Clarissa has a daughter, an unformed girl in her teens, much more her father's than her mother's child. "Here's my Elizabeth!" says Clarissa, introducing her to Peter Walsh. That annoys him. "Why not 'Here's Elizabeth' simply? It was insincere. And Elizabeth didn't like it either," Peter thinks. He does not know that Clarissa spoke so possessively to hide her fear that Elizabeth is, in fact, not hers, having transferred her love and allegiance to a woman who teaches her history and talks to her about religion. Virginia could not write about a motherless child; she wrote, instead, about a childless mother.

The object of Clarissa's jealous hatred is appropriately named Kilman. She is poor, ugly, learned, devout; she has suffered for her principles, she serves good causes, she wears heavy shoes and a green mackintosh. She is a clutching monster, thinks Clarissa. She is a poor old thing, thinks Elizabeth, with the casual kindness of the young, who do not know the value of the gifts they bestow on lonely and unhappy people. Elizabeth is determined to be a doctor, even if her mother does think it silly; or else she will live in the country with her dogs, who are so much nicer than the young men who have recently begun to behave so foolishly, likening her to a poplar, a hyacinth, a river. The girl belongs to no one yet, not even to herself. She rides hither and thither on buses, untroubled, uncommitted to any course.

For her part Miss Kilman heartily reciprocates Mrs. Dalloway's feelings. Each woman would like to annihilate the other. When Miss Kilman can hardly contain her furious envy and contempt, she takes refuge in God. Clarissa's only escape from the devouring sense of guilt with which the mere sight of Miss Kilman overwhelms her is to rage against the twin tyrants, love and religion, which both seek to destroy the privacy of the soul.

Here the novelist lays on her character a burden that is too heavy. The reader is startled by the violence of the protest, astonished by the clarity with which it is expressed. Something has gone wrong with this intricate weaving of plot and a pattern. The hummingbird has become a hawk. This is no longer Mrs. Dalloway; it is Virginia Woolf who speaks.

These abrupt transitions are not intentional. They are part of the valiant attempt to tear the tinsel pretense from Clarissa Dalloway and show a real woman beneath the social hostess. They do not succeed because, in spite of the fact that Mrs. Dalloway has recently been so ill that she walks in the shadow of death, that her gaiety is like a banner courageously but uselessly upheld in the face of a rapidly advancing enemy, one cannot believe that she ever had enough solidity and strength of purpose to engage in such a fight against melancholy and despair. She has not the brains to evolve what Peter Walsh describes as "This atheist's religion of doing good for the sake of goodness," nor the courage to declare, "Those ruffians, the Gods, shan't have it all their own way."

The author has been too generous of herself, one feels; or, rather, she has not been sufficiently discriminating in scattering her gifts. She has been kind enough to Mrs. Dalloway already, letting her walk through the London streets on a fine June day in 1923 and understand and enjoy so much; giving her such a store of memories and a host of friends with whom to share golden moments from the past. She was wise to bring in minor characters to express her thoughts in their own language — a barnacled old woman in Regent's Park feeling kinship with a young girl newly arrived from Edinburgh — a nondescript man tempted to lay down his pamphlets, abandon "that plaguey spirit of truth seeking" and rest quietly awhile in St. Paul's. It was right that Peter Walsh should denounce the humbugs and also join in the song of praise to the city's pulsating life. To Septimus Smith properly belong the intolerable anguish and unbearable mystery of visions that defeat understanding. He must fall that Clarissa may arise.

But first she must face him in death whom she had never known in life, and face her own failures. "That young man had killed himself. Somehow it was her disaster — her disgrace. It was her punishment to see sink and disappear here a man, there a woman, in this profound darkness, and she forced to stand here in her evening dress."

But Virginia Woolf was determined to snatch Clarissa Dalloway back from the darkness. She lets her see, in the house opposite, an old lady going quietly to bed.

It was fascinating, with people still laughing and shouting in the drawing room, to watch that old woman, quite quietly going to bed. . . . The clock began striking. The young man had killed himself; but she did not pity him, with all this going on. There! the old lady had put out her light! the whole house was dark now with this going on, she repeated, and the words came to her, Fear no more the heat of the sun. She must go back to them. But what an extraordinary night! She felt glad that he had done it; thrown it away. The clock was striking. The leaden circles dissolved in the air. He made her feel the beauty; made her feel the fun. But she must go back. She must assemble. She must find Sally and Peter.

So she is reborn to another day. The book ends with Peter, the last of her guests, awaiting her, wondering, "What is this terror? What is this ecstasy? . . . What is it that fills me with extraordinary excitement? It is Clarissa, he said. For there she was."

Is this a love story? A ghost story? A parable of despair defeated, of inadequacy overcome, of life perpetually renewing itself?

Chapter XII

VIRGINIA WOOLF'S reputation and popularity both increased with the publication of *Mrs. Dalloway* and *The Common Reader*. Her friends and the critics might argue which was the better of the two books and give her solemn advice about the path she should follow, criticism or novel writing, but the reading public gave her an equal welcome from whichever direction she came. She was the same person whether she was inviting them to share her understanding of other writers or offering them her own work. The criticism was alight with fancy, the novel was weighted with ideas; the reader could be entertained, stimulated or deeply stirred, according to the nature and extent of his response.

Before she had even finished *Mrs. Dalloway*, the blind alley into which *Jacob's Room* had threatened to lead stretched so freely before her that she knew what her next novel was to be. "I see already the Old Man," she wrote in her diary in October 1924. The "Old Man" was her father; the book was *To the Lighthouse*. She would have to let it simmer in her mind first, not to think it out too clearly, but to add to it in leisure moments, till the time came to write it down.

By the following May she had decided it was to be short and to have in it her father's and her mother's characters, memories of St. Ives and her childhood, as well as "the usual things — life, death, etc." But her father was to be the center: "sitting in a boat, reciting. We perish, each alone; while he crushes a dying mackerel." This was the last scene and the one that, in the event, gave her the most trouble to get quite right.

Gradually the conception changed. The sea was to be heard throughout; the garden at St. Ives became more important; the sail to the lighthouse gained significance; the element of time and its flight appeared; the structure of the book, in three parts, showed itself. Sometimes she saw her theme as firmly centered on her father, while a few days later she envisaged a much wider, slower book, with more characters, emotions and ideas more generally spread. She began to wonder whether what was growing in her mind could rightly be described as a novel at all; perhaps "elegy" was more nearly correct for a prolonged poetic contemplation of past scenes.

She planned to start writing it when she went to Rodmell for the summer, but in the meantime she was deep in other projects. "I can't stop writing," she told Vita in May 1925. "I'm ashamed to think how many stories I've written this month, can hardly bear to keep my fingers off a new novel, but swear I won't start till August."

There was so much else to do first. She was "weighed down by innumerable manuscripts" submitted to the Hogarth Press: "Edith Sitwell; twenty dozen poets; one man on birth control; another on religion in Leeds; and the whole of Gertrude Stein, which I flutter with the tips of my little fingers, but don't open." And then there were the books she had to read because she was writing about their authors; De Quincey and Richardson and again De Quincey, "because I'm in the middle of writing about him, and, my God, Vita, if you happen to know, do wire what's the essential difference between prose and poetry — it cracks my poor brain to consider."

She had other problems to consider and other jobs to do. Just when she was busiest she discovered that somehow or other her wardrobe had got into a deplorable state and something urgent had to be done about the clothes situation. "I'm sitting in an old silk petticoat at the moment with a hole in it, and the top part of another dress, with a hole in it, and the wind is blowing through me." But perhaps she could manage to fit in a brief visit to Vita at Long Barn, Knole, the next week. "Having done De Quincey by then, I should be care free of prose and poetry: I should have packed the top part of my dress (what is it called?) and the skirt; my books and papers, and three petticoats which I bought yesterday, and now the Cook says they're not petticoats, she says they're chemises. I ask you, how is one to know? Answer me, shall I come on Monday night? Or will you come up [to London] on Monday and let us dine together at a new place where they have a great variety of food and drinks, and they give you roses, and there are looking-glasses which reflect the most astonishingly commonplace scenes — a fat woman gobbling — in such a way that one feels one is dangling among octopuses at the bottom of the sea, peering into caves and plucking pearls in bunches off the rocks."

The efforts of a Soho restaurateur playing decorating tricks on his customers with glass tanks and mirrors and colored lights excited her fancy but could not keep her long from her main interests. "Please tell me about your poem. I rather think I shall like it; but I am very old-fashioned in my poetry, and like reading Crabbe. What I wish is that you would deal seriously with facts. I don't want any more accurate descriptions of buttercups and how they're polished on one side and not on the other. What I want is the habit of earthworms; the diet given in the workhouse — anything exact about a matter of fact — milk, for instance. From that proceed to sunsets and transparent leaves and all the rest, which with my mind rooted upon facts, I shall then embrace with tremendous joy. Do you think there is any truth in this? Now, as you were once a farmer, surely it is all in your head ready. Tennyson, you see, was never a farmer: Crabbe was a parson, which does as well."

This fantastic prescription for a poem and provocatively casual references to farming and Tennyson and Crabbe led to an argument, a discovery and new theories about prose and poetry. "I've been fuming over your assumption that my liking for the poet Crabbe is avowed," Virginia wrote. "I assure you that I bought a copy out of my own pocket money before you were weaned. . . . I find to my surprise that Crabbe is almost wholly about people. One test of poetry — do you agree? — is that without saying things, indeed saying the opposite, it conveys things: thus I always think of fens, marshes, shingle, the East Coast, rivers with a few ships, coarse smelling weeds, men in blue jerseys catching crabs — a whole landscape, in short, as if I had read it all there; but open Crabbe and there is nothing of the sort. One word of description here and there — that is all. The rest is how Lucy got engaged to Edward Shore. So if your poem is, as you say, all about the woolly aphis, I may come away from it dreaming of the stars and the South Sea.

"I must stop: or I would now explain why it's all right for me to have visions but you must be exact. I write prose, you poetry. Now poetry, being the simpler, cruder, more elementary of the two, furnished also with an adventitious charm, in rhyme and metre, can't carry beauty as prose can. Very little goes to its head. You will say, define beauty — but no, I am going to sleep."

Corresponding with Virginia Woolf was as exciting as talking with her; it was impossible to predict what was coming next. It must have been rather like taking a very intelligent and active child for a walk in the country; one could never tell when the harum-scarum would jump into a ditch, scramble up a bank, gallop across a field, to return flushed and triumphant with a sprig of honeysuckle, a handful of berries or a rare butterfly. Small wonder that such a woman felt hopelessly lost and frustrated in a large and fashionable department store. She could consider herself insulted by employees so superrefined in manner and so carefully trained to caution and patience that many customers positively reel away from the suggestion that of course they are at least duchesses in disguise but naturally their wish to remain incognito will be respected. Virginia seems never to have got any pleasure out of playing her part in this curious game of mock gentility.

"Every time I get inside a shop," she confided to Vita, "all the dust in my soul rises and how can I write next day? Moreover, somehow my incompetence, and shopkeepers not believing in me, harasses me into a nagging harpy. . . . You must have disorganized my domesticity, so that directly you went a torrent of duties discharged themselves on top of me; you can't think how many mattresses, blankets, new sheets, pillow cases, petticoats and dustpans I have had to buy. People say one can run out to Heal's and buy a mattress. I tell you it ruins the day: two days: three days. . . . Last week I sold four mattresses and bought the cook new bedroom curtains. Now I must waste a whole afternoon and suffer sheer agony in shops again buying a hat. . . . I can't tell you how intense my unhappiness has been, starting up in the night, and clenching my hands, all over going out to dinner, and buying a hat."

She was not really incompetent and actually organized her life very well. When she or Vita were traveling, Virginia made a careful note of where each of them would be at different times so that they could keep in touch with one another by correspondence, and her long, though hastily written, letters never failed to turn up at the right address at the right time. What fretted her to distraction was any piling up of domestic duties and social obligations that interrupted her writing when the ideas were coming thick and fast and the fury of creation was upon her. Then even to meet a Frenchman who would tell her about Proust was part of "this gritty misery" that afflicted her.

The plan for a peaceful summer of hard work on the new novel was ruined by a troublesome illness, following the publication of *Mrs. Dalloway* and the first volume of *The Common Reader*. She did make a "quick and flourishing attack" on it, completing twenty-two pages in less than a fortnight, but fainted at a birthday party for her young nephew Quentin Bell at nearby Charleston, and for weeks was in bed "living that odd, amphibious life of headache." Again and again she would feel convinced that she was perfectly well But the headache persisted. "I can't talk yet without getting these infernal pains in my head, or astonishingly incongruous dreams," she confided to Vita. "Two dull people come to tea, and I dream of precipices and horrors at night, as if — can they keep horrors, and precipices concealed in them, I wonder? Then if you come, I should perhaps dream the other way about, of bumble bees and suet pudding. Read this over, you will see that a compliment is implied. I'm really better, and only waiting for Leonard to say the word to ask you once more if you can't come here."

Leonard and Vita, however, understood one another and the need Virginia had for complete rest and quiet. Vita drove across the Weald as far as Rodmell, leaving gifts and a message, and evoking this response: "Oh, you scandalous ruffian! To come as far as this house and make off! When the cook came up to me with your letter, and your flowers and your garden, with the story that a lady had stopped a little boy in the village and given him them, I was so furious I almost sprang after you in my nightgown. Ten minutes talking wouldn't have hurt me, and it would have been such fun.

"As for the garden and the flowers, words fail me: in fact I can't bear writing when I might have been talking. The garden has had a jug of water carefully poured over it and the flowers are in a broken pot. But beware how you give me things — woolwork is my passion. Another present from you, and a tea cosy worked with parrots and tulips will arrive, and what would you do then? No: write to me: or better, come and see me: but I will let Leonard decide. Did I write you — I'm afraid I must have — a dismal, complaining, downtrodden letter? There was no reason for it . . . only just as one recovers, one always curses — it is a sign of health. Here I am, very comfortable, sitting in the sun in the garden, with your fascinating creation, which reminds me of a Chinese mountain, by my side, and my woolwork, and, as you guess, masses of books."

There were always the hopeful authors to occupy her enforced leisure. "This morning the thickest manuscript you ever saw arrived from an inspired grocer's boy at Islington, who, being inspired, has not had it typed, and says he will give up grocery for literature if we encourage, or even if we don't: but read it every word, we must: while Miss Somebody from Wandsworth writes to say she divines a human heart in me, and will I tell her how, without insincerity, she can so titivate her heroine's character that it will win popularity with a large number of readers, since she has not a penny in the world, her two or three old mothers to support, and nothing will induce her to give up literature. You must admit that this passion for writing novels in the remoter suburbs is all much to their credit, and worth twenty Mrs. Dalloways at least."

This lighthearted way of referring to the unpublishable material and the requests for help that poured in almost daily to the press did not conceal the fact that Virginia read carefully everything that was offered, replied courteously to the letters, and gave much helpful advice and criticism. "The grocer had to go back — what a weight I found him to carry to the post! The Lady at Wandsworth says she must see me; has no money; feels the romance of virginity in her bones: so I've told her to write it out of them in her own proper name. Why these cloaks and disguises? The idea had never struck her that her one novel, with ten different names, is all about herself. She thinks the idea bold and fascinating. So do I. There is an odd mixture of fascination and futility about her, but she'll come, and spend an hour, and oh, how I shall squirm at the end of the time! But then, you see, Providence has so arranged it that other people's lives are romantic; and so by creating and being created one swims along, never knowing the truth about anything. It is Providence after all, that you should have illusions, I mean."

She begged Vita to go on having illusions about her. "Do keep it up — your belief that I achieve things. I assure you I have need of all your illusions after six weeks of lying in bed, drinking milk, now and then turning over and answering a letter. We go back [to London] on Friday — what have I achieved? Nothing. Hardly a word written, masses of complete trash read. The blessed headache goes — I catch a cold or argue violently and it comes back. But now it has gone longer than ever before, so if I can resist the delights of chatter, I shall be robust forever."

She planned to live a quiet winter. "I'm going to live the life of a badger, nocturnal, secretive, no dinings out, or gallivantings, but alone in my burrow at the back." The basement studio at Tavistock Square seemed like a haven where she could really work once more. One concession to society she would make; she would have one gala night a month. "The Studio will be candle lit, rows of pink, green and blue candles, and a long table laid with jugs of chocolate and buns. Everybody will be discharged into this room, unmixed, undressed, unpowdered. . . . Your cousin has lent me his piano, and I intend to break up the horror of human intercourse with music.

"It struck me on my snail's walk to the river this afternoon (I have now had tea and lit the fire, unsuccessfully) that the fear and shock and torture of meeting one's kind comes from the conditions — being clashed to each other unmitigatedly, on a sofa — pure, neat, entire (I can't think of the word I want). Now, if we could be dispersed a little — could we visit St. Paul's, or the Tower, or Ken Wood, where the scenery or the noble buildings intervene between us, then we should sail gradually and calmly into latitudes of intimacy which in drawing rooms are never reached. Do you agree? Every Wednesday I shall take a trip in an omnibus with someone to mitigate the shock of human intercourse. But I was going to write about *Hamlet*, which I read last night, but have no time. What a bore! Directly one begins a letter one has to stop. I was going to say, too, something so interesting. But anyhow, when is your poem coming? Now I feel afraid of having asked for it, as I cannot criticize poetry, only buzz outside like an old intoxicated frantic bee: whereas you go about your business calmly within. How I envy you!

"By the way, the great excitement of my life, responsibility and in a sense burden, because Leonard is furiously jealous, is your garden. The Cook shouts, 'Oh ma'am, a crocus is coming up.' Then, 'A mouse has nibbled the crocus, ma'am.' I spring up, accuse Leonard, find it's a false alarm. But you have complicated my relations for life."

Clearly the plans for a quiet life in London were quite illusory. A woman so vivaciously responsive to every stimulus, so interested in other people even when she knew that contact with them would tire her inexpressibly, would never be calm, never remain for long in any burrow.

She was ill again when she returned to London, all writing forbidden. It was nearly Christmas before she was on her feet once more. Vita's husband was being sent by the Foreign Office to Persia ("My love to Harold. Beg him not to drop me when he becomes an Ambassador"). Vita would join him ("I am very sorry for you — really — how I should hate Leonard to be in Persia. But then, in all London, you and I alone like being married"). But Vita was going to finish a book in Persia; could the Hogarth Press have it? And she must see Vita before she left. The doctor was at last persuaded that she was well enough to do some visiting, and she spent the Christmas holiday at Charleston with the Bells and then at Knole, with excellent results. "The doctor says I'm ever so much better than before Christmas. Did I have a thorough rest when I was away? So I said it was Long Barn [Knole]; early hours; lack of exciting conversation; staying with the aristocracy, in short. 'Ah, I see. Good food and no mental or physical strain.'"

But completely calm and relaxed Virginia could not have been, for in a few days she is writing, "I left a rain coat, and crystal ruler, a diary for the year 1905, a brooch and a hot water bottle somewhere — either Long Barn or Charleston — and so contemplate complete nudity by the end of the year." Packing her bag for a week-end visit must have been quite an experience.

Almost as soon as she was back in Tavistock Square she

caught influenza — well, it might have been German measles, the doctor said. Anyway: "I'm so furious: I was to begin that wretched novel today, and now bed and tea and toast and the usual insipidity. Oh, damn the body." Luckily it was a false alarm. By the end of January 1926, when already a few crocuses had shown themselves in the square, she was boasting, "I can write now, never before — an illusion which attends me always for fifty pages. But it's true. I write quick — all in a splash; then feel, thank God, that's over."

The resolution about hibernating in a burrow was forgotten. "Have I seen anyone?" she replies to Vita's query from Persia. "Yes, a great many people, by way of business mostly. Oh the grind of the Press has been rather roaring in my ears. So many manuscripts to read, poems to set up, letters to write. . . . I am going to have a little dramatic Society — I mean a flashy actress came to see me, who having had her heart blighted, completely, entirely, irretrievably, has most unexpectedly got work, and says will I come and see her behind the scenes. I like the astonishing profusion of these poor creatures — all painted, glittering and unreal; with the minds of penny whistles: all desperate, what with being out of work, or in love; some have illegitimate children, one died on Sunday, and another is ill with typhoid. They think me a grotesque, semi-human gargoyle; screwed up like a devil in a cathedral; and then we have tea in some horrid purlieus of Soho, and they think this frightfully exciting — my unscrewing my legs and talking like a book. But it won't do for long. It is a snobbery of mine, to adore every society but my own."

There was always something happening to prevent her from writing *To the Lighthouse*. She was asked to meet a Spaniard in Holloway, a Frenchman in Chelsea, and see an Italian dance in Soho; also she must buy a hat sometime. It made her feel desperate, so that she had to take a sleeping draught. Even a visit from Lytton Strachey, who came up from his retreat in Oxfordshire, did little to ease the "gritty misery," though he was enthusiastic about an article she had just written, "which, as we never praise each other's writing now, did for the moment illumine me."

Nevertheless, she continued to gad about. "I went to hear Tolstoy's daughter lecture on him and her mother. The Countess Tatiana spoke and I hated us all for being prosperous and comfortable and wished to be a working woman, and wished to be able to excuse my life to Tolstoy. Not that it was a good lecture. It was quite dull. But seeing his daughter, a shabby little black old woman, a perfect lady, with his little eyes, excited me: and made the whole world inside my head spin round, and tears come to my eyes — but this always happens to me when the disgusting and fetid story of Tolstoy's married life is told me — by their daughter too. And also, in Hill Street, Berkeley Square, to an audience which seems to have cheeks made of *pâté de foie gras* and sables on their backs and nothing, nothing left of humanity or emotion at all. 'The ladies will know what it means to nurse thirteen children,' said Tatiana: but I felt that the ladies did not even know . . ." At this point words failed her. Vita could guess the rest.

This emotional outburst is understandable. She, Virginia, a devoted daughter, was trying to write about her mother and father. It was not a "disgusting and fetid" story. Quite the contrary. But it was on her conscience that the only peace and happiness she could know was when she was recalling her childhood at St. Ives, at a time when, it seemed, everyone was prosperous and comfortable and beautiful and gay, when waves sparkled in sunshine and bees hummed among flowers and children played cricket and young people fell in love and candles were lit at the dinner table and at the end of a long day a husband and wife sat quietly side by side and without words declared their love. A serene, idyllically peaceful world. Yet the burden was on her to penetrate the reality beneath that beautiful surface, to tell the truth about how time passes and dreams fade and "we perish, each alone"; without maligning the beloved dead she had to write of anger and pride and selfishness and fear as well as laughter and loveliness and trust and understanding.

And she had to do it in a world that had changed, materially and mentally, since the war. She had to face her ghosts, to appease her artistic demon, and also to listen to unemployed miners singing in the streets for bread, and to Maynard Keynes and her husband explaining with dreadful lucidity and awful calm what deflation of currency and rationalization of industry meant in terms of national disaster and human misery. The Hogarth Press was issuing pamphlets which were widely read, although the booksellers disliked handling these cheap paperbacks on which so little profit could be made. It was a period of political tension and economic anxiety, not a time to go gaily about one's private affairs with the firm conviction that all was well everywhere. The evidence to the contrary was too grim and pressing to be ignored. And yet that "wretched novel" insisted on being written, though the heavens fell, South Wales was a devastated area, the Clyde shipyards were deserted, steel furnaces cold and mills silent in county after county, and mournful hunger marchers converged on London without ever disturbing the complacency of Berkeley Square.

"I am back again in the thick of my novel," she wrote to Vita at the beginning of February 1926, "and things are crowding into my head; millions of things I might put in — all sorts of incongruities, which I make up walking the streets, gazing onto the gas fire. Then I struggle with them from 10 to 1; then lie on the sofa and watch the sun behind the chimneys; and I think of more things; then set up a page of poetry in the basement, and so up to tea. I have shirked two parties and another Frenchman and going to tea and buying a hat; but I really can't combine all this with keeping my imaginary people going. Not that they are people; what one imagines in a novel is a world. Then, when one has imagined this world, suddenly people come in — but I don't know why one does it, or why it should alleviate the misery of life, and yet not make one exactly happy, for the strain is too great."

She wanted to have done with it all and be free. "Of course I want to see deserts and Arabia. I worried Leonard for an hour about taking a year off and seeing the world. We will go to Burma, I said; to the South Seas; we have only one life; we are growing old. And he has a passion for the East, so perhaps we shall." But it was a dream. Instead of a year abroad they had a few days of motoring through England with some of Leonard's relations, and she had a new enthusiasm.

"I promptly fell in love — with being stockbrokers, with never having read a book (except Robert Hichens), with not having heard of Roger, or Clive, or Duncan, or Lytton. Oh, this is life, I kept saying to myself; and what is Bloomsbury, or Long Barn either, but a contortion, a temporary knot; why do I pity and deride the human race, when its lot is so profoundly peaceful and happy? They [her companions] have nothing to wish for. They are entirely simple and sane. She has her big dog. They turn on the Loud Speaker. When they take a holiday they go to the spring of the Thames where it is as big as a man's arm, not big enough for a boat; and they carry their boat until they can put it in, and then scull all the way down to Marlow. Sometimes, she said, the river is level with the banks and it is perfectly deserted. Then she said to me suddenly as we were looking down at the wood from her window, 'That's where the poet Shelley wrote *Islam*. He tied his boat to the tree there. My grandfather had a walking stick cut from that tree.' You always run up against poetry in England; and I like the dumb poetry; and wish I could be like that. She will live to be a hundred: she knows exactly what she enjoys; her life seems to me incredibly happy. She is entirely unvexed, unambitious; and, I believe, entirely right."

This sudden passion for "the living, unconcerned, contented, indifferent middle classes of England" persisted for a while. "Talk of the romance, the experience and upset and devastation of Persia! I've lived in Persia half my life" (in her imagination, she meant) "but never been among the stockbrokers till this Spring. They are entirely direct, on the top of every object without a single inhibition or hesitation." There was nothing in her life, she felt, that equaled one day in theirs. Her friends laughed and told her that this was another manifestation of her snobbery, a belief in some glamour which was unreal. But she was convinced that she was on the track of something quite solid and real. When she had more time, she wrote to Vita, she "wanted to go into the matter of profound natural happiness, as revealed to me yesterday at a family party of an English banker, where the passion and joy of sons and daughters in their own society struck me almost to tears with self-pity and amazement. Nothing of that sort do we any of us know — profound emotions, which are yet natural and taken for granted, so that nothing inhibits or restrains. How deep these are, and unselfconscious."

Characteristically she turned to books to illustrate her point. "There is a book, called *Father and Son*, by Gosse, which says that all the coast of England was fringed with little sea anemones and lovely tassels of seaweed and sprays of emerald moss and so on, from the beginning of time till January, 1858, when for some reason hordes of clergy and spinsters in mushroom hats and goggles began collecting, and so scraped and rifled the coast that this accumulation was destroyed for ever. A parable, this, of what we have done to the deposits of family happiness. . . . Also, I will tell you about Anna Karenina and the predominance of sexual love in 19th-century fiction, and its growing unreality to us who have no real condemnation in our hearts any longer for adultery as such. But Tolstoy poises all his book on that support."

Clearly, she had begun to feel that there was such a thing as the Bloomsbury state of mind and that she must not mistake Bloomsbury for the world. The more deeply she lived in the world of *To the Lighthouse* the more she yearned for the old certainties, suspected health-giving qualities in the air she had found so stifling to breathe. Again one remembers that passing reference in *The Mark on the Wall* to "illegitimate freedom." But the way back to Victorianism was barred. The captive bird, once released, must learn how to live in the wild wood, or perish miserably. If it should ever find its way back, the chances are that the old cage will have been stowed away, all crooked and dusty, in an attic, no one now providing fresh water and bird seed, no one trying to coax a song at one time and at another throwing a shade over the bars and commanding sleep.

While Virginia was, at the beginning of 1926, "blown like an old flag" by *To the Lighthouse*, living almost entirely in it and only occasionally, and rather obscurely, coming to the surface, as she notes in her diary, she read *My Apprenticeship*, the first volume of the autobiography of Mrs. Sidney Webb. She and Virginia were not close friends, but they respected and admired one another. Their lives ran on parallel rather than converging lines. They had similar middle-class backgrounds. Each, though in different ways, had needed to resist father domination. They were both happily married, childless women, sharing their husbands' interests and activities; and their husbands, too, were closely associated as thinkers and workers in the British Labor movement. All four of them, the Webbs and the Woolfs, were relentless searchers for truth and fierce fighters for freedom. Both women had a strain of mysticism in their thinking, and examined this element in their make-up with a certain degree of alarm. Beatrice Webb turned it to political, Virginia Woolf to artistic, account.

Reading the extracts from Mrs. Webb's journal inevitably led Virginia to think about her own life. "There were causes in her life; prayer; principle. None in mine," she wrote in her diary. A touch of envy underlies these words. She had immense capacity for enjoying practically everything, great energy, rapid recuperative powers; and yet she felt harassed and depressed because she was always searching for something she could not define.

"Why is there not a discovery in life? Something one can lay hands on and say, 'This is it!' "

Beatrice Webb, severely practical, sternly logical, was sustained in times of trouble by an inner conviction of some essential rightness in the ordering of the universe. She could regard the plight of the unemployed miners not as a reproach and a horror but as a responsibility to be faced. She could share their belief that justice must eventually prevail and their vision of brotherhood become a political reality. And, because of this stubborn clinging to the sense that life has a direction and a purpose, she could find solace in the religion which, in some form or other, inspires the idealist and reformer.

This religion, with its remembered phrases and images, lay in wait, it seemed, for Virginia Woolf too; like the "dumb poetry" it was everywhere. But she could not, in honesty, avail herself of its consolations. She was forced to look elsewhere for a solution of her problems and an escape from the sense of futility and doom. She had her moments of ecstatic revelation. They came when suddenly, inexplicably, she had "a great and astonishing sense of something there, which is 'it.' It is not exactly beauty that I mean. It is that the thing is in itself enough: satisfactory: achieved." So she wrote in her diary at this time of stress. The same exploration of the unknown is found in the course of the agonized search for her mother which is at the heart of *To the Lighthouse*.

Here is Mrs. Ramsay, convinced atheist but no materialist, sternly resisting the temptation to accept the easy comfort of "dumb" religion. In a quiet interval before dinner, she picks up her knitting and lapses into thought:

Often she found herself sitting and looking, sitting and looking, with her work in her hands, until she became the thing she looked at — that light, for example. And it would lift up on it some little phrase or other which had been lying in her mind like that — "Children don't forget, children don't forget" — which she would repeat and begin adding to it. It will end, it will end, she said. It will come, it will come, when suddenly she added, We are in the hands of the Lord.

But instantly she was annoyed with herself for saying that. Who had said it? Not she; she had been trapped into saying something she did not mean. . . . What brought her to say that: "We are in the hands of the Lord"? she wondered. The insincerity slipping in among the truths roused her, annoyed her. She returned to her knitting again. How could any Lord have made this world? she asked. With her mind she had always seized the fact that there is no reason, order, justice: but suffering, death, the poor. There was no treachery too base for the world to commit; she knew that. No happiness lasted; she knew that. She knitted with firm composure.

And here is Mrs. Ramsay mystically identifying herself with the beam from the lighthouse as it sweeps in its revolving across her bedroom,

. . . the steady light, the pitiless, the remorseless, which was so much her, yet so little her, which had her at its beck and call . . . as if it were stroking with its silver fingers some sealed vessel in her brain whose bursting would flood her with delight . . . and the ecstasy burst in her eyes and waves of pure delight raced over the floor of her mind and she felt, It is enough! It is enough!

Or, reading poetry:

. . . then there it was suddenly entire; she held it in her hands, beautiful and reasonable, clear and complete, the essence sucked out of life and held rounded here — the sonnet.

There is the ring of truth about this. One accepts it as an account of actual experience, whether the diarist records it as happening to her when she saw the mountains of Persia in the cloudy sky over Russell Square, or the novelist relates it as occurring to another woman in a quiet room at St. Ives.

But, as the saints and mystics have testified, these moments of revelation are transient. There is no final discovery, only the continual search and the occasional glimpse, followed by drudgery and doubt. Virginia had been so sternly conditioned to moral, though antireligious, rectitude that she did more than forbid herself the luxury of calling on the Lord to ease her burdens; she even questioned whether it was either explicable or justifiable, this dedication to an unknown "it."

"I'm ashamed to say how wrapped up I get in my novel," she wrote to Vita in February 1926. "Really I am a little alarmed at being so absorbed. Why should one engross oneself thus for so many months; and it may well be a mirage; but I can scarcely do anything else. I got up on the Downs, though, and then came down to tea and sat over a wood fire and read some poetry, and a manuscript (thinking still of my own novel), then cooked an omelette, some good coffee; and wanted a little drop of wine."

Back in London again, the question of snobbery still nagged at her. One evening she dined out with a young man who had been amongst those who had maintained that her interest in lives different from her own was merely her form of snobbery. On the way home she wanted to pay for the taxi. "He said nonsense. I said you're a damned aristocrat, and I *will* pay the cab. Which I did, and gave him not only my well-known lecture upon Russells and Herberts but a new Chapter, added for his benefit, called How No Aristocrat Can Write a Book. So we quarrelled over this for a bit, and next day, oddly enough, I had to defend him from the charge of being an *arriviste*. What motive can he have in coming to Bloomsbury, etc? Well, I said, it shows his intelligence. But, they said, with that name and appearance he can't be intelligent. Damn you, I said, that's Russells and Herberts the other way round all over again. So it is. And what is worse — Mayfair snobbery or Bloomsbury?"

Exactly what she meant by "snobbery" is hard to define, since she used the word to cover not only the rivalry for social prestige between the inheritors of titles and the exploiters of brains but also her own attempts to understand the supposedly glamourous lives of penniless actresses and respectable stockbrokers. Here was the core of her problem as an artist: how to enlarge her range of outer experience while concentrating on her inner vision? Fortunately there were practical matters to keep her busy and prevent her from brooding. The Hogarth Press was busy, though "our fortunes tremble." She kept up some mechanical activity with her hands, setting type. Dinner had to be ordered; Grizzle, the dog, had the mange and a cough and had to be taken to hospital.

But, with all the comings and goings, writing a novel in the heart of London was almost impossible. She felt, she said, as if she were nailing a flag to the top of a mast in a raging gale. "What is so perplexing is the change of perspective; here I'm sitting thinking how to manage the passage of ten years, up in the Hebrides [the supposed location of *To the Lighthouse*]; then the telephone rings; then a charming long pink-cheeked Don called Lular comes to tea; well, am I here, asking him about the life of Webster, which he's editing; or in a bedroom up in the Hebrides? I know which I like best — the Hebrides."

She continued to live three lives at once, writing *To the Lighthouse*, talking to herself in her diary and to Vita in letters, and attending to practical daily affairs and the social round. She would sit half the morning, she told Vita, crammed with ideas and visions which refused to be dislodged because she could not catch the right rhythm. "Now this is very profound, what rhythm is, and goes far deeper than words. A sight, an emotion, creates this wave in the mind, long before it makes words to get it; and in writing (such is my belief) one has to recapture this, and set this working (which has nothing apparently to do with words) and then, as it breaks and tumbles in the mind, it makes words to fit it." But this interesting idea, like so many she advanced in letters and conversation with an air of authority and often prefaced with the announcement of their profundity, was merely tentative, a basis for discussion. "No doubt I shall think differently next year," she concludes airily, before going on to another topic.

This might be a piece of news, such as that Leonard had

decided to give up being literary editor of the weekly *Nation,* in order to have more time for other activities. She was delighted. "What a mercy — no more going to the office and reading proofs and racking one's brains to think who to get to write . . . this is the first step to being free, and we feel ten years younger, and please, dearest Vita, do make Harold do the same thing. One walks into one's wife's room, carrying her tray at 8.30, and says, 'By the way, I'm going to give up the *Nation* today' — or the Foreign Office, as the case may be! It's over in ten minutes. Seriously, giving up appointments (this is the fourth time since we married) is the only pleasure in the world." There was also the possibility of giving up the press, too. Anything, anything for a change, an escape from the treadmill on which she found herself. At the same time she knew that the prospect of having infinite leisure was all a dream. "This is exciting, but harasses the mind. We shall have to make five hundred pounds a year and I shall sell my soul" writing articles, but it was fun to consider.

Or perhaps Vita would like to hear about the various people she had been seeing, the ridiculous things that happened at parties. She went to one through a storm: "It was a blizzard, thunder and snow; and we had to cross London to Chelsea. Well, by the time I got there my poor old hat (I never bought a new one) was like a cabman's cape; and a piece of fur, hurriedly attached by a safety pin, flapping. And those damned people sitting snug round their urn, their fire, their tea table, thought O Lord, why can't Virginia look more of a lady: which so infuriated me, through vanity I own, and the consciousness of being better than them, with all their pearl necklaces and orange coloured clothes, that I could only arch my back like an infuriated tomcat." On another occasion she thought she heard "in the whirl of meaningless words" a mention of the Holy Ghost, whereas the speaker had actually referred to the whole coast. "I asking 'where is the Holy Ghost?' got the reply, 'wherever the sea is.' Am I mad, I thought, or is this wit? 'The Holy Ghost?' I repeated. 'The whole coast' he shouted, and so we went on, in an atmosphere so repellent that it became, like the smell of bad cheese, repulsively fascinating."

Or she had been lunching with Lytton Strachey at a fashionable restaurant. "First I was so dazzled by the gilt and the warmth that in my humility I felt ready to abase myself at the feet of all the women and all the waiters: and really trembled at the incredible splendour of life. Half way through lunch, reason triumphed: I said, this is dross. I had a great argument with Lytton — about our methods of writing, about Edmund Gosse, about our friendship; and age and time and death and all the rest of it. I was forgetting Queen Elizabeth. He is writing about her. Dear old Lytton — he was infinitely charming, and we fitted like gloves, and I was very happy, and we nosed about the bookshops together, and remarked upon the marvellous extent of our own reading. 'What haven't we read?' said Lytton. 'It's a question of life, my dear Lytton,' I said, sinking into an armchair. And so it began over again."

But "what bosh letters are, to be sure! I don't think this gives you much idea of what I have done for the last fortnight. There are immense tracts unnamed . . . I've sat with my pen in the air these ten minutes . . . One's thoughts are too transitory — if you were in the armchair opposite, you could just catch them before they fall."

In the studio the thoughts were being caught, the words were being written as the waves broke and tumbled in the mind. By the end of April she had finished the first part of *To the Lighthouse*, rather more than half the book, and begun the second part. She was amazed at her own fluency, though not sure whether what she wrote was nonsense or brilliance. "Why am I so flown with words and apparently free to do exactly what I like? When I read a bit it seems spirited, too; needs compressing, but not much else," she noted in her diary. "In the intervals of being leaden with despair," she told Vita, "I am very excited."

The book opens at once on the central situation. The story is of the utmost simplicity: an expedition is planned, but post-poned; ten years later the surviving characters reassemble, and the trip is made. This is the frame for a picture of absorbing interest and astonishing intricacy of controlled design. It is technically the most perfect of the novels in its command of the material and presentation of the different themes, and also the most revealing about the life and character of the author.

It was not Virginia Woolf's habit to open a door gently and sidle in, coaxing the reader to follow, with whispered introductions and pauses for explanations of what is to come. She flings the door wide and marches straight in. The scene is set, the characters are assembled; we catch them in mid-act, almost in mid-word, and what we see and hear is directly linked with the book's title. Long before the end — and long after — that title will have acquired other significances, but from the beginning there is no cheating.

Just as *Mrs. Dalloway* launches the reader on the adventures of a summer day in London with the announcement about buying flowers for a party, so *To the Lighthouse* begins abruptly: "'Yes, of course, if it's fine tomorrow,' said Mrs. Ramsay," continues with the joy of six-year-old James in the prospect of the next day's excursion, and is followed by his father's authoritative statement that tomorrow's weather won't be fine. "Had there been an axe handy, or a poker, any weapon that would have gashed a hole in his father's breast and killed him, there and then, James would have seized it."

For it seems to the child that his father has deliberately ordained bad weather. Mrs. Ramsay would like to indulge in the hope, at least, that the wind might change, but Mr. Ramsay is sternly opposed to such folly, and loses his temper when he finds her making preparations in case a sail to the lighthouse may be possible the next day. "She flew in the face of facts, made his children hope what was utterly out of the question, in effect, told lies." Mr. Ramsay, philosopher and reader of barometers, never told lies. "He was incapable of untruth; never tampered with a fact; never altered a disagreeable word to suit the pleasure or convenience of any mortal being, least of all his own children." They had to be made aware that "life is difficult . . . and needs above all, courage, truth, and the power to endure."

Mrs. Ramsay cannot, will not, fight her husband, even though she feels outraged by what seems to her the brutality of his insistence on dashing the children's hopes. It is an old, old argument between them, so old that it is no longer conducted in words. They can never agree; but she cannot make a final stand against him, for she loves and reverences him. When he apologizes and demands her sympathy because he is such a failure as a husband and father and philosopher, she surrenders immediately, deserting her children in order to comfort this stricken great man who is always right and always in need of reassurance.

But his son hated him. . . . He hated the twang and twitter of his father's emotion which, vibrating round them, disturbed the perfect simplicity and good sense of his relations with his mother. . . . She laughed, she knitted. Standing between her knees, very stiff, James felt all her strength flaring up to be drunk and quenched by the beak of brass, the arid scimitar of the male, which smote mercilessly, again and again, demanding sympathy.

The child, in his jealousy, senses his mother's exhaustion but cannot know her joy in being able to restore her husband's serenity. But even this fulfillment, this "rapture of successful creation," is marred by the openness of these domestic scenes, "for then people said he depended on her, when they must know that of the two he was infinitely the more important, and what she gave the world, in comparison with what he gave, negligible." She frets, too, because she is afraid to tell him the truth about household expenses. "And then to hide small daily things, and the children seeing it, and the burden it laid on them — all this diminished the entire joy, the pure joy" of their relationship. But, since "she had the whole of the other sex under her protection . . . always taking care of some man or other" — as her older daughters see it — she must rouse herself from her fatigue and her brooding to attend to the comfort and welfare of the houseguests, even when she suspects that "all this desire of hers to give, to help, was vanity."

The simple opening statement about the weather has thus led to the heart of the book. Mr. and Mrs. Ramsay are shown in characteristic attitudes, almost ritualistic attitudes. They complement each other, embody opposing principles, are rather more than life-size to their children but intensely human to one another, and vague, uncertain to themselves.

In reconstructing the scenes of her childhood and painting the careful, detailed portraits of her mother and father, Virginia Woolf did not rely only on childhood memories. She used her adult mind and her novelist's technical skill, as well as her own self-criticism, to present her characters from different angles. Her method of telling a story is anything but didactic. She does not announce, as her father (or Mr. Ramsay) did, "This is so, because I say so; these are facts which cannot be denied." Instead she shows us the characters as seen by one another. Very artfully, at precisely the moment when the reader feels impelled to protest, "Really, this is unfair," or "No, this is too adulatory," she uses another pair of eyes, takes us inside another mind, corrects the focus, and shows us the picture differently. This not only keeps the story moving, enabling her to bring in many other revealing incidents and a wider range of reminiscences, but helps to create the illusion that the reader is taking part in the story's progress, is sharing the author's task of stating not only what happened next but finding out the truth underlying the appearance.

VIRGINIA WOOLF knew the importance of enlisting the reader's co-operation. It is explicit in her criticism and implicit in her novels; both are voyages of discovery. The author knows the purpose of the expedition — whether it be to find a rare kind of butterfly or the source of the Nile. She steers the course and travels the most difficult parts alone. What she brings back is for the rest of the interested world to see, to discuss, to enjoy, to use or reject, as the case may be.

Although *To the Lighthouse* explored well-mapped territory, she found that to revisit as a woman the scenes of her childhood was a strange and enlightening experience. No life of her father can be written without being influenced by her portrait of him. It is not a complete portrait; it attempts no explanation of how he acquired his eccentricities, does not examine his religious, political or critical views, is not concerned to measure his stature or gauge his influence. Nevertheless it conveys an undeniable impression of authenticity. Here are the facts that elude the reference books or dimly lighten the pages of a critical study. Here they leap into life with a kind of savage intensity, contradicting one another and confirming a final truth which is only reached by imaginative understanding. Fierce hatred and adoring love have gone into the picture, reverence and gratitude and appreciation side by side with resentment and the need to rebel, all fused by the play of fancy, lit in turn by the roving, remorseless and rigidly controlled beam from the lighthouse which is the writer's artistic conscience.

A softer light suffuses the portrait of her mother. Virginia was thirteen when her mother died; consequently she felt less sure that she was capable of understanding her fully. But this justifiable intellectual doubt is not reflected in the novel. Mrs. Ramsay is a massive figure, though the outlines are vague. She is more mysterious, more idealized, yet more complete than Mr. Ramsay. The novelist had to detach herself from the Father in order to see him clearly, but to reach the Mother she had to immerse herself in her recollections and then go deeper and deeper in search of understanding until, inevitably, she met herself.

She presents both her mother and her father on what might be called the historical level, using evidence that could be vouched for by other people. She describes her father's habit of reciting aloud, with dramatic gestures, any verses that came into his head, regardless of his audience or whereabouts, and his equally disconcerting habit of relapsing into prolonged silence; his hospitality plus his ignoring of guests; his commanding presence and the respect he evoked; his obvious devotion to his wife and children as well as the demands he made on their forbearance; his doubts about the ultimate value of his work and the duration of his fame; as well as his insistence on having his own way and being always right in his opinions; and his never being without a book in his pocket or hand, and a pencil with which to make marginal notes and comments.

She also tells us of the universal tributes paid to her mother's beauty, charm, wit, gaiety and poise; her capability and kindness and courtesy, and the way she trained her children to be polite and considerate; the directness of her approach, which enabled her to swoop on truth like a hawk, so that she seemed to know without having learned and "her simplicity fathomed what clever people falsified"; her lack of self-consciousness about her striking appearance, how she "clapped a deer-stalker's hat on her head; she ran across the lawn in galoshes to snatch a child from mischief . . . as if her beauty bored her and all that men say of beauty, and she wanted only to be like other people, insignificant"; her tireless, but unbustling, activity; her appreciation of the arts, her interest in food; her amusing exaggerations in talk side by side with exact rightness and purity of feeling. And all these details are given to the reader not in great chunks of description, but slipped in here and there, as anecdote, or scrap of conversation, or remembered impression, coming now from this character or that, arising from a variety of situations, and leading on to other discoveries.

On the metaphysical or mythical level we are given a conception of Mr. Ramsay's splendid mind, which, "if thought is like the alphabet, ranged in twenty-six letters, all in order . . . had no sort of difficulty in running over those letters one by one, firmly and accurately, until it had reached, say, the letter Q. . . . But what comes next? . . . On, then, on to R." An artist, wishing to understand what goes on in that mind, asks Andrew Ramsay what his father's books are about. " 'Subject and object and the nature of reality,' Andrew had said. And when she said Heavens, she had no notion what that meant, 'Think of a kitchen table then,' he told her, 'when you're not there.' So now she always saw, when she thought of Mr. Ramsay's work, a scrubbed kitchen table."

As for Mrs. Ramsay, she has, like Helen Ambrose in *The Voyage Out*, the power of making men see visions. An elderly scientist, hearing her voice on the telephone, is struck by the incongruity of talking about train schedules with a woman so classically and majestically Greek. A shy and awkward young man, aggressive about his proletarian background, who has accompanied her on an errand in town, suddenly sees her

With stars in her eyes and veils in her hair, with cyclamen and wild violets — what nonsense was he thinking. She was fifty at least; she had eight children. Stepping through fields of flowers and taking to her breast buds that had broken and lambs that had fallen; with the stars in her eyes and the wind in her hair — He took her bag.

Virginia Woolf herself appears in many guises. She is in all the intimate domestic scenes where the Ramsay children are in evidence. She is one of the elder daughters who silently accept their mother's rebukes for bad behavior to guests and who disappear from the table "as stealthily as stags" when a meal is over and slip upstairs to the privacy of their own rooms to debate anything and everything and to "sport with infidel ideas which they had brewed for themselves" of a life different from that of their parents. She is among the amused listeners when Mrs. Ramsay expatiates on "the iniquity of the English dairy system,

and in what state milk was delivered, and was about to prove
her charges, for she had gone into the matter, when all round
the table, beginning with Andrew in the middle, like a fire leaping from tuft to tuft of furze, her children laughed; her husband
laughed; she was laughed at, fire-encircled, and forced to veil
her crest, dismount her batteries, and only retaliate by display-
ing the raillery and ridicule of the table as an example of what
one suffered if one attacked the prejudices of the British Public." She is also one of the younger children whom Mrs. Ramsay
hates to think of as growing up and losing their capacity for
starting every day "fresh as roses, staring, wide awake, as if this
coming into the dining-room after breakfast, which they did every day of their lives, was a positive event to them, and so on,
with one thing after another, all day long, until she went up to
say good-night to them, and found them netted in their cots like
birds among cherries and raspberries."

More specifically she is the youngest daughter, Cam the
wicked, who was "wild and fierce. She would not 'give a flower
to the gentleman' as the nursemaid told her. No! No! No! She
clenched her fist. She stamped." She is the Cam who dashes
past, "like a bird, bullet or arrow, impelled by what desire . . .
who could say? It might be a vision — of a shell, of a wheelbar-
row, of a fairy kingdom on the far side of the hedge; or it might
be the glory of speed; no one knew." She is the wild villain who
could be happy for days with the simplest, cheapest toy. She is
the child who is wide-awake and quarreling with her younger
brother, James the ruthless, hours after they should both have
been asleep, all because of an animal skull someone has nailed
on the wall, which frightened the little girl but which the little
boy would not let anyone move away. Mrs. Ramsay solves the
problem by covering up the skull with her own shawl (green, incidentally be it noted) and coaxing the child to sleep with talk
of "Mountains and valleys and stars falling and parrots and an-
telopes and gardens, and everything lovely." The scene is so
similar to one at the beginning of *Jacob's Room* that one cannot

escape the conviction that this incident relates to an actual experience, never to be forgotten, the same symbols of skull and shawl, death and mother love, recurring again and again in the adult mind.

Virginia is also Cam the girl of seventeen, who, ten years later, when Mrs. Ramsay is dead but the house has been reopened and the guests gathered, goes with her father and brother to the lighthouse. The young people have no desire to make the trip. Their father has ordered it, for some reason of his own; they go under protest, sullen, silent, united in a compact to "resist tyranny to the death." But Cam succumbs to her father's appeal, as her mother had always done.

For no one attracted her more: his hands were beautiful, and his feet, and his voice, and his words, and his haste, and his temper, and his oddity, and his passion, and his saying straight out before every one, we perish, each alone, and his remoteness. (He had opened his book.) But what remained intolerable, she thought . . . was that crass blindness and tyranny of his which had poisoned her childhood and raised bitter storms, so that even now she woke in the night trembling with rage and remembered some command of his; some insolence; "Do this," "Do that," his dominance: his "Submit to me."

It is impossible to begin to understand the character of Virginia Woolf without recognizing the passionate intensity underlying these words: the enormous capacity for love, amounting to adoration, accompanied by the equally fervent insistence that love must bring not slavishness but freedom.

In the search for her mother she used many keys that opened doors on the real past. Even the Chevalier de l'Etang is made to yield his mite, as he had done in *Mrs. Dalloway*. This time he does not display his Marie Antoinette miniature, transformed into a brooch or ring; he had become merged with the Neapolitan adventurer about whom she had written to Vita Sackville-West. She tells us Mrs. Ramsay was proud of having "in her veins the blood of that very noble, if slightly mythical Italian house, whose daughters, scattered about English drawing-rooms in the nineteenth century, had lisped so charmingly, had stormed so wildly, and all her wit and her bearing and her temper came from them, and not from the sluggish English, or the cold Scotch" — a reference to Virginia's forebears on her father's side.

It was in this same year, 1926, that the Hogarth Press issued the volume of *Victorian Photographs* by Julia Cameron, one of those "scattered daughters." Looking at those old pictures of Julia Duckworth, who became Julia Stephen, Virginia desired to remove the invisible veils from that brooding figure, to know what was behind that beauty and splendor.

For this purpose she used the eyes and mind of one of the most enigmatic and important characters in *To the Lighthouse*, Lily Briscoe, that "independent little creature . . . with her little Chinese eyes and her puckered-up face" who is on the outer rim of the circle and yet goes right to the heart of the matter. She is standing on the lawn, painting a picture, in the first part of the book. Mrs. Ramsay seated at the window, knitting or reading to little James, is an integral part of the composition, but the picture will not come right. Mr. Ramsay (whose thoughts the artist visualizes as a kitchen table upside down in the branches of a pear tree) nearly knocks over her easel when he storms across the garden reciting "The Charge of the Light Brigade." People will look over her shoulder and ask stupid questions, and how can she explain if they cannot see what she sees? Mrs. Ramsay wants her to marry, because "everyone must marry, everyone must have children," and Mrs. Ramsay is stored with knowledge and wisdom and presides "with immutable calm over destinies which she completely fails to understand," and Lily Briscoe adores her and desires to achieve some intimacy, some unity with her which seems forever denied to human beings but which, if it could be achieved, would be a miracle, a revelation of reality as exalting as capturing on canvas the vision that eludes her.

It is Lily Briscoe who, in the last part of the book, suffers the most acute anguish because Mrs. Ramsay is no longer numbered among the living, who remembers most vividly the past, who picks up Mrs. Ramsay's burden, who yields to Mr. Ramsay's demand for sympathy, even if she can only do it clumsily, without understanding, by admiring his boots. It is Lily who sees him like a king in exile, ready to fling himself "tragically backwards into the bitter waters of despair" if Cam and James show reluctance to go to the lighthouse. It is she who, while overpowered by his magnificence, admitting his greatness, feels "this was tragedy — not palls, dust and the shroud; but children coerced, their spirits subdued." It is to Lily that the great moment comes when, having found her old, unfinished picture in the attic, she evokes so clearly the memory of Mrs. Ramsay that "Some wave of white went over the window pane. The air must have stirred some flounce in the room . . . Mrs. Ramsay — it was part of her perfect goodness — sat there quite simply, in the chair, flicked her needles to and fro, knitted her reddish-brown stocking, cast her shadow on the step. There she sat."

To complete her picture and end her story, Virginia Woolf had to include Mr. Ramsay. So Lily looks across the bay and senses, though she cannot see clearly, that all is well there. Mr. Ramsay has praised James for his good sailing. Both Cam and James are willing to do anything he asks, give him anything he wishes. But he asks nothing. "He might be thinking, We perished, each alone, or he might be thinking, I have reached it. I have found it; but he said nothing." "He has landed," says Lily aloud, "It is finished." She adds the final stroke to her picture. "It was done; it was finished. Yes, she thought, laying down her brush in extreme fatigue, I have had my vision."

In these closing words we hear Virginia Woolf's own voice. Emotionally she has rejected her father's blasting pessimism, while celebrating the stark, terrible and glorious courage of his attitude and admitting that intellectually his conclusions seem to her unassailable. She has accepted her mother completely.

Through Lily, who is sexless and represents the dedicated artist-visionary, she has found the link between the two opposing but equally positive forces in the world, the woman and the man, the life-giver and the life-consumer, each in turn. Intimacy, understanding, unity have been achieved.

Chapter XIII

TO THE LIGHTHOUSE was ready for inspection by the beginning of 1927. Virginia was as nervous as a cat about how it would appear to anyone but herself. She left the manuscript for her husband to read, went off to see Vita at Knole, and when she came back managed to sit and wait until he was ready to give his verdict. Fortunately for her peace of mind he was so enthusiastic about it that he began to praise it before her control broke down. It was much her best, he told her, far more interesting than *Mrs. Dalloway,* a masterpiece, a psychological poem.

According to her calculations, it had been written in just under a year; but that was allowing for all the interruptions and the false start made in 1925, which was itself nearly a year after she had first glimpsed the Old Man. And how long before that the image of him in the boat, challenging her to accept or deny that "We perish, each alone" had been lurking in her mind, no one can say. She had resolutely kept him out of her last two novels; now she had got him safely landed on his rock, momentarily at peace with himself and his children, and she could rest. It was both a relief and a disappointment when the long struggle was over.

She was in a curious, blank state of mind. A new book was brewing, but what was it? Somewhere she saw "a fin in a waste of waters," but what it represented she could not tell. She had lost the conviction of being in touch with some sort of reality that had sustained her during the gloom of the General Strike.

During that week or so in May 1926, when it had seemed that anything might happen in England, she had been writing at full speed the short middle section of *To the Lighthouse,* "Time Passes," in which she compressed the events of ten years. The house in the Hebrides — or was it St. Ives? — stood empty, kept clean and secure against winter storms by the fleeting visits of ministering women while, somewhere else, Mrs. Ramsay died, Prue Ramsay married and died in childbirth, Andrew Ramsay was killed by a bursting shell in the war. But the house waited. That was a solid fact, something to hang on to when all was confusion and doubt in London in 1926, when, overnight, men and women who had never before disobeyed a law or risked security for a principle suddenly came to the assistance of the miners — and then dispersed when the Law, in its majesty, pronounced the solemn equivalent of the policeman's calm "You can't do that there 'ere." Stirring, sensational, incredible events shattered the routine of daily life in Tavistock Square and every household in the land. That was the reality of the world in which one lived. In the world of the mind the reality was found in the house quietly settling into decay, waiting for its rebirth and reoccupation.

The contrasts between the inner and the outer life were not often so strongly marked: "Things don't happen like that," simply, one after another, either in the world or in the mind. But the sense that the complete life is lived on several different planes at the same time was constantly with her; it recurs again and again in her diary, her letters and her books. A case in point is her visit to Thomas Hardy in his home at Max Gate, Dorset.

This was one of the interruptions to writing *To the Lighthouse* in 1926. The long diary record is curiously oblique, vaguely unsympathetic. She seems deliberately to have avoided looking at him and concentrated on Mrs. Hardy, on small domestic details, on rather inconsequential chatter. Everything is reduced in size, without producing the sharpness of a miniature. She was aware that she had not set down the essentials, as she noted later: "I was telling myself the story of our visit to the Hardys, and I began to compose it. . . . But the actual event was different." The clue to the unease she felt is found in a letter to Vita: she was excited and shy. "I'm dashing off on my chronic visit to Hardy. I shall only stay one day and drink one cup of tea, and be so damned nervous I shall spill it on the floor. And what shall I say? Nothing but arid nonsense. Yet I feel this is a great occasion. Here am I approaching the immortal fount, touching the sacred hand. He will make all of us, Leonard and me and Grizzle [her dog], seem transparent and prying. This old, wrinkled, dwindled man, who has two very little, very bright eyes."

The article she wrote about him in January 1928, after his death, might have come from quite a different woman. The agitation in the letter is controlled, the touch of acerbity in the diary has gone, but the underlying emotions and the recurrent ideas remain. The connecting link is clearly perceived at the end of the essay, when she writes of Hardy's novels, seen as a whole: "We have been freed from the cramp and pettiness imposed by life. . . . It is no mere transcript of life at a certain time and place that Hardy has given us. It is a vision of the world and of man's lot as they revealed themselves to a powerful imagination, a profound and poetic genius, a gentle and humane soul" (see *The Common Reader, II*).

In these words she expresses more than her love and reverence for a great novelist. She reveals what she sought to do in her own books. It was not to provide, either for herself or for her readers, an easy escape from daily life, or to give a bare factual record. It was to see and to convey a vision.

This was seldom attained, but was always worth the struggle, the misery, the exhaustion. The process of transmutation, something quite different from the tricks of technique, remained obscure in the extreme. Something stirred in the waste of waters before even the fin was glimpsed. What it was, how it got there, why the overmastering passion to bring it to the light gave existence a purpose and meaning, all this defied analysis. No anxious probing yielded an answer. Even casting a quick line of glancing fun into the depths brought no tangible result. One could only wait.

"I feel dissipated and aimless for some reason," she wrote to Vita at the beginning of 1927. There were several reasons. She and Leonard might or might not accept an invitation to go to America to write and lecture; it all depended on the financial arrangements and whether she could spare the time. It was exciting, getting letters and cables and feeling flattered and important enough to be able to say no. "It would be rather fun for a few weeks, and I should see some odd things, don't you agree?" Indeed, yes. She had such a capacity for seeing odd things in the familiar streets of London, such an insatiable curiosity about lives that were different from her own, such a power of investing drabness with drama and sending the searchlight of her own enthusiasm into dim places that one can only regret she never, in the event, exposed her camera eye to the cities and the plains of the United States. The proposals came to nothing in the end. Even with the offer to pay her passage and entertain her at dinners, in addition to fees for her articles, it seemed the costs involved would swallow up her earnings. "No, I think, I won't be bribed, unless it's tremendous." She and Leonard might take a quick, cheap trip to Greece instead.

Or they might buy the bookshop from Francis Birrell and David Garnett. "Leonard is like a hound with his nose to the ground. But weeks and months will pass in conversation. What fun though, don't you think — suppose we did it, and it was a great success, and I had a motor car, and we went book-buying all over England." This scheme, too, fell through; higher bidders made better offers for the business.

A deeper reason for the aimless feeling became obvious to her. "It's not writing novels; this journalising is such a thin, draggled, straining business, and I keep opening the lid and looking

into my mind to see whether some slow fish isn't rising there —
some new book. No: nothing at the moment."

A little later, however, she was writing: "I've suddenly become absorbed in a book about reading novels and can't stop
making phrases. So that's the book I see when I lift the lid and
look in. It's going to be about how to read all fiction as if it were
a book one had written oneself." At about the same time she
was toying with the idea of inventing a new kind of play, something that would be both prose and poetry, both a novel and a
play. Possibly this is a foreshadowing of *Between the Acts,* which
actually did not appear until fifteen years later.

Other ideas were beginning to demand attention. She was
journalizing freely, earning the hundred pounds she had set as
her immediate goal. "I'm well ahead with the world," she informed Vita, "and need write no more till the old fish, of whom
I've told you — he's gold, but has moulted several scales — his
tail's quite bald, by the way, and he has lost one eye in a fight
with a tench — rises to the top, and I net him. Yes, I've thought
of an entirely new book: it may be two; each more entirely new
than the other. So my fortune gilds the future for me — if my
father didn't leave me pearls, this was by the way of a make-
shift."

She was more specific in her diary, even to the title of a kind
of Defoe narrative to be written for fun. "Suddenly, between
twelve and one, I conceived a whole fantasy to be called *The
Jessamy Brides* — why, I wonder? . . . Satire is to be the main
note — satire and wildness. My own lyric vein is to be satirised.
Everything mocked. And it is to end with three dots. . . . For
the truth is I feel the need of an escapade . . . I want to kick
up my heels and be off." And when she had had her fun, there
was a "very serious, mystical, poetical work which I want to
come next" — the first reference to *The Waves,* still four years
ahead. In the meantime, before she could start on *The Jessamy
Brides,* or any other of the innumerable ideas flashing into her
head, she must get to work on the fiction book.

But first there was the trip to Europe which she and her husband managed, by hook or by crook, to fit into their tight working schedule almost every year. "I'm going to do nothing but sit in the sun, eat hugely, and watch landscapes. That's the way I travel. Looking, looking, looking, and making up phrases to match clouds. It is the passion of my life. You can't think how dry and gravelly my mind gets when I don't take it to the south where things have a dash of red and blue to them, and don't wobble in pale grease as they do here," she wrote from Tavistock Square. And, before she mailed the letter, she added: "Everybody's gone — no, there's Eddy [Edward Sackville-West] coming to tea. We linger like ghosts in a world of incredible beauty. I take back my insult to England. I've just been buying cigarettes in the Tottenham Court Road — rivers of silver, breasted by plumes of gold; omnibuses and shops equally beautiful — why go to Persia when the T. Ct. Rd. is like that?"

There were "millions" of things to be done before they left. Inoculation, which proved to be only too startlingly effective so far as the germs were concerned, was one. "How you'd laugh to see me stretched out comatose, recovering from two days' high temperature — all owing to inoculation and my principles — I know I deserve it. I urged you so lightly into it — how little I pitied you — and now you shall laugh at me." She seems to have been abnormally sensitive to any kind of medical treatment. Her doctor firmly refused to give her the second dose usually required. "So I shall go half oculated; but I stuck up for my principles all the same. I'm being as careful as a cat on eggs, in terror that I shouldn't be able to start — you know what Leonard is."

The question of buying the bookshop had started up again. A home had to be found for the puppy while they were away. "She didn't seem to mind going, Leonard said. Half laughing I said I'd ring up and ask after her. He took it quite seriously. This shows where you've led us in dog worshipping." There were all kinds of things to be bought: "skirts, hats, shoes, boxes, mackintoshes. I find myself in the wrong department. I dream, I saun-

ter. People trample on me — they inflict the most dreadful insults. It's humiliating to be in the Babes Sock Dept. when one
wants Ladies Handbags."

Eventually a family-friendly party was gathered in the south
of France, at Cassis, where she had been extremely happy with
Leonard two years before, when *Mrs. Dalloway* was finished
and awaiting publication. Roger Fry had been with them then.
One of his pictures, showing the small, rocky harbor, the square,
simple, color-washed houses of the fishermen, and the great,
bare, stony mountains behind, is reproduced in his biography. It
was a painter's paradise. "Every street corner has an elderly
gentleman on a camp stool," Virginia told Vita. "They are all
painters: austere."

She was writing her letter with difficulty, she said, on a balcony in the shade. "Everything is divided into brilliant yellow
and ink black. Clive is seated at a rickety table, writing on huge
sheets of foolscap, which he picks out from time to time in red
ink. This is the History of Civilization. He has by him Chambers' Dictionary of the English Language. We all sit in complete
silence. Underneath, on the next balcony, Vanessa and Duncan
are painting the loveliest pictures of rolls of bread, oranges and
winebottles. In the garden, which is sprinkled with saucers of
daisies, red and white, and pansies, the gardener is hoeing the
completely dry earth. There is also the Mediterranean — and
some bare, bald, grey mountains, roasting in the sun."

The work on which Clive Bell was engaged was published the
following year under the title *Civilization,* but it was at Cassis,
in April 1927, that he wrote the dedication to "Dearest Virginia." He laid it at her feet, he explained, because she alone of
his friends had been in at its birth and followed its fortunes from
its first conception in 1909. At that time it was to be his *magnum
opus;* it was to survey everything significant from the earliest
times to the present; its title should be *The New Renaissance.*
Early in 1914, inspired by the first and second Postimpressionist
Exhibitions, he had taken one section from this vast work in prog-

ress and issued it under the title of *Art*, the book which first established his reputation as a critic, a wit, a stylist, a writer who
forced one to think, whether one agreed with him or not.

Then came the war, bringing so many and such fundamental
changes. The ideas he and Virginia discussed in her workroom
at Fitzroy Square had to be re-examined. In 1919 a rewritten
chapter had appeared as a political pamphlet called *On British
Freedom*. The great work was abandoned, but the impulse behind it remained. His conception of the good life, based on his
understanding of the Greek ideal, persisted. Everything that was,
in his judgment, still valid in the old arguments about how to
attain that good life was reconsidered in the light of human limitations and the workings of political institutions shed by the
Russian Revolution, the establishment of fascism in Italy and the
collapse of the general strike in Great Britain. The resulting
book, still delightful and thought-provoking even after another
and more shattering war and its aftermath, was offered to his
friend and sister-in-law on a balcony in the south of France,
overlooking the sea which had been to the ancients, hundreds
of years before, the middle of the earth.

It is a charming scene, as Virginia depicts it. "Leonard is determined to buy a farm house here and live alone, with me, half
the year. It may be our form of religion. But then, what becomes
of friendship, love, intimacy? Nessa says suddenly, she has been
wondering why one is supposed to attend to people. Other relations seem to her far more important. That's what Vita says in
her letter this morning, I say. Heard from Vita? says Clive
(pricking up his ears, like a war horse out at grass, for he has
renounced the world and puts water in his wine and looks incredibly pink and fresh). Yes, I say. And off we go, discussing
you and Harold . . . You know what Clive is, and Virginia too,
when they get together."

She describes a visit to the home of an ex-cavalry officer
turned winegrower, living in a "divine 17th-century manorhouse,
set with cypresses, painted, tiled, with tanks of frogs and Roman

aqueducts." They sit, all silent, in the dark, listening to the frogs; they drink several different kinds of wine in a great empty room; they are given bunches of wild tulips. "And, Vita, why don't we all live like that? — and never go back to Bloomsbury any more." Their grand extravagance is wine, sold by the peasants, fetched by Clive and Duncan in great baskets. They talk for hours.

But the idyll cannot last. They are off to Sicily early the next day. And suddenly the sound of familiar English voices floats up from the courtyard; another contingent from Bloomsbury has arrived. "Shades of the prison house descend." Gone is the daydream evoked by the news that Harold is thinking about resigning from the Foreign Office, so that, if Vita can persuade Leonard not to "embrace the religion of solitude," the Woolfs and the Nicolsons may live happily ever after, in Provence. Even the thoughts about poetry and fiction, and what is more important than attending to what other people say, are banished. The conversation takes a different turn as the newcomers exclaim over Virginia's new hair style.

" 1. Virginia is completely spoilt by her shingle.

2. Virginia is completely made by her shingle.

3. Virginia's shingle is quite unnoticeable.

There are three schools of thought on this important subject. I have bought a coil of hair, which I attach by a hook. It falls into the soup, and is fished out on a fork." Her own opinion, when Lydia Keynes had complimented her on her appearance before she left London, was unfavorable. "She admires my shingled head. I don't. It's like the hind view of a frightened hen partridge."

A few days later she was back in London, bracing herself for the publication of *To the Lighthouse*, pretending that she didn't care about criticism and was more concerned about work still ahead — a paper to be read at Oxford, the book on fiction, articles to be written for money, of which she had recently begun to feel the need, though she hated the thought.

The novel sold well before publication (since she was by this time quite a commanding figure in the literary world), and even better after the critics had had their say, very much on the lines she had anticipated. There was no longer any question about whether she was negligible or not; her name was "news." She was invited to broadcast; to write for daily newspapers, not merely for stately journals; to sit on platforms and be admired or criticized on occasions such as the presenting of the Hawthornden Prize to Vita for her poem, *The Land;* even to present and to receive prizes herself.

But at this last "incessant nibbling away of my life" she balked. She had discovered that, in private life, she could take refuge in the excuse of being an invalid. She now invented a way of getting out of public appearances. She would turn to advantage her ever-recurring fear that she was not dressed properly, which she described with so much intensity in the short story, "The New Dress" (see *The Haunted House*), by firmly stating that she had nothing suitable to wear.

"My 'no clothes' dodge is working admirably," she told Vita. "I was rung up by a woman called Lady Dilke who wanted me to give the *Femina Vie Heureuse* prize to a Frenchman. So I said I couldn't. And she said you must. I said I wouldn't and she said I should. So it struck me, well, I'll say I've no clothes. At which she paled and withered and cried off instantly. It was to be at Claridge's in May. Also, I think I've got out of lunching with her on the same plea. It's true, too. Never shall I buy another skirt. Never shall I lunch with Lady Dilke. Never shall I give a prize to a Frenchman. And, by the way, for your information I may say that she said something about giving *me* the prize, and I blushed all over, holding the telephone, with shame and ignominy. This is true. Snobbish? No: instinctive; right."

Later on she tried another way of overcoming in herself the unreasoning distress she felt about her own appearance in public; she would brazen it out, purposely make herself look grotesque. "I played a funny trick. I had no hat. Bought one for seven-and-eleven-three" [that is, one farthing short of eight shillings] "at a shop in Oxford Street: green felt; the wrong coloured ribbon; all a flop like a pancake in mid-air. Even I thought I looked odd. But I wanted to see what happens among real women if one of them looks like a pancake in mid-air. In came the dashing, vermeil-tinctured, red-stopper-bottle-looking Mrs. Edwin Montagu. She started. She positively deplored me. Then hid a smile. Looked again. Thought, Ah, what a tragedy! Liked me even as she pitied. Overheard my flirting. Was puzzled. Finally conquered. You see, women can't hold out against this kind of flagrant disavowal of all womanliness. They open their arms as to a flayed bird in a blast; whereas the fashionable women of the world, with every feather in place, are pecked, stoned, often die, every feather stained with blood, at the bottom of the cage."

One can believe this story, or take it with a grain of salt. No supporting evidence confirms it. Everyone who knew her maintains that she was always elegantly and distinctively dressed, had so much beauty and grace and poise that she excited admiration in any assembly. Women testify to this no less than men. It was a beauty that defied time, that survived even when age and illness had eroded the soft curves and delicate colors of youth, because it was based on an exquisite bone structure and was lit from within. Her hair might turn gray, her cheeks grow hollow; she never mastered the art of make-up or cared for the latest styles; but she remained haunting and seductive. In her own beautiful rooms, decorated by artists, "when Virginia was there all else disappeared," wrote a great Argentine lady, Victoria Ocampo, in *Vogue*. But these tributes of ungrudging admiration made no lasting impression. To the end of her days Virginia Woolf continued to be interested in women's clothes and to be convinced that her own were all wrong. It was a complex, she knew, but one she could not control.

She made a virtue of her helplessness, asking and acting on advice from friends. "You have saved my life explaining how to buy nightgowns," she told Vita. "I have two. Now: how does one make one's hair stay firm after washing? And about chemises? I bought the stockings with lisle thread heels — you're quite right. They have existed, it seems, these thirty years. Queen Victoria wore them." This was written long before the invention of nylon, and to an inveterate walker like Virginia the tiresome but necessary business of darning was important. She could not lightly throw worn garments away, for she had been trained to be thrifty. "I bought a mixture which is applied with a sponge to shoes. They have ripened in the night to a patchy nut brown. But, tell me — when a shoe is inwardly sound, yet outwardly corrupt, what can one do? It goes against my conscience to throw them after a bride or otherwise destroy. And listen; now what am I to do about powder? Once you gave me some which didn't smell, but I don't know what it was. I bought some which permeates every pore, and I dare not stink like that. I loathe scents (except on you, when they are merely the ripeness of the apricot). Tell me quickly what to get and where. I will rise to powder, but not to rouge. So that's finished."

Her taste in clothes was not limited to the drab and serviceable. She would add to long and serious letters miscellaneous items of news for her absent friend, such as "Arnold Bennett is having a baby. Ethel's clothes are lovely — sleeves like pen and ink drawings — all one line. Princess Victoria has pneumonia:" or add a postscript, after a visit, "Could you remember to bring my waterproof (rose pink) and my gloves (scarlet)? I flung them down in the hall, I think."

Sometimes the problem of being dressed suitably for an occasion was more simply solved. "Where does one buy a black coat?" she asked. "I have to broadcast and think it should be done in broadcloth." She was not at all nervous about broadcasting, she declared. But this was a new kind of activity, not hedged around with the puritan and social taboos of her girlhood, such as those which forbade the use of rouge or perfume. No one had ever told her when she was young that "nice women" and "real ladies" did not speak on the air to complete strangers, or added that she might do it if she chose since she was naturally a perfectly free agent; implying at the same time that to take advantage of this freedom would make her feel immoral and look ridiculous.

What she did faintly fear about a radio talk was that she might be overcome by the atmosphere of respectability that pervaded the B. B. C. "I'm more likely to be deadly bored. I know what'll happen — I shall yawn and say, My God . . . this will be broadcast and ruin the chastity of twelve million homes."

Nothing bored her so much as to be listened to in respectful silence. Next to talk with friends, which did not have to be witty or profound to be interesting and entertaining, she enjoyed an audience of young people, some of whom would clearly be paying no attention, having wandered off on some mental adventure of their own, and some of whom would just as clearly be hardly able to control their impatience to find an opportunity of challenging her with awkward questions. She sympathized with both these types of listeners. They made the labor of preparing a lecture worth while. But talking into a microphone was too easy.

In the end talk with oneself was best of all. So much that other people said was apt to be irrelevant or bewildering. Arnold Bennett praised *To the Lighthouse*, but what he said was less interesting than wondering why he said it. Someone wrote to say that everything she said about the flora and fauna of the Hebrides was totally inaccurate. Well, what could be done about that? It would be uncivil to reply that her critic was no doubt quite right but she failed to see that it mattered. Secretly she was amused that she had succeeded in making it quite impossible for anyone to be sure of the physical location of her story. Did it all take place on an island off the west coast of Scotland or close to a resort town in Cornwall, on the southwest tip of England? Mrs. Ramsay, who was famous for her wild exaggerations, spoke of the house as being three thousand — or, "if one has to be accurate," three hundred miles away from Mr. Ramsay's library and lecture rooms. Assuming that three thousand miles is obviously nonsensical, says the fact-seeker, may we rely upon the second figure of three hundred? So far as Virginia was concerned, such questions might have been addressed to the winds. Have it your own way, she might have replied.

It was a different matter when she was questioned by the translator preparing the French edition. There was a query on almost every page. What were the "red-hot pokers" mentioned more than once in the garden? Were they iron spikes in a fence, painted red? No, they are familiar English flowers, so called because that is what they look like, she explained. But if a botanical expert declared that no flower of this kind would ever flourish on a Scottish island, all she could do was to admit that this statement was, for all she knew, quite correct. On the other hand, she was amused to find, some serious people seemed to take her for an authority. The Seafarers Education Society had, she gleefully reported to Vita, bought two copies of the book. "It's an awful thought that the Merchant Service will be taught navigation by me; and the proper use of foghorns and cylinders. It's a compliment never paid to you poets. I think I deserve it. The trouble I took with that Lighthouse!"

Once the book was launched on its successful career, in Europe and in America, earning enough pounds and francs and dollars to justify expenditure on a paved terrace in the Rodmell garden and the Woolf's first automobile (a Singer, affectionately known as the Lighthouse), Virginia was again attacked by headaches. She was tempted by too many ideas which refused to materialize. She could think and talk about what would be, after many inexplicable changes, *The Waves,* as she listened in the evenings to the spiralings of late Beethoven sonatas on the gramophone; but she could not write. "It's odd," she wrote to Vita, "how being ill even like this splits one up into several different people. Here's my brain now, quite bright, but purely critical. It can read; it can understand; but if I ask it to write a book it merely gasps. How does one write a book? I can't conceive. It's infinitely modest, therefore — my brain at this moment. Then my body — that's another person. No, my body is a grey mare trolling along a white road. We go along quite evenly for a time like this. . . . Suddenly she jumps a gate/. This is my heart missing a beat and making a jump at the next one. I rather like the grey mare jumping, provided she doesn't do it too often."

In August she was still in the doldrums, though physically well again. Would Vita lend her (and she stressed that she meant "lend," not "give") Mrs. Radcliffe's *Mysteries of Udolpho* and what was, in Vita's opinion, the most romantic novel by Mrs. Aphra Behn? "The truth is I'm stuck in Romance and do nothing but fabricate theories for my dull, dreary, long-winded, asinine book on fiction; and I can't get a single thing I want from the London Library." The weather was awful, an apple tree had been blown down, Pinker the spaniel had been sick; and she wanted a photograph of Vita, a snapshot. "I've only the incredibly noble and high-minded Hawthornden prize winner. Mightn't I have a blowsy scallywag once in a way?"

What was behind that last request is indicated in various entries in the diary during the next few weeks. The fish with the golden scales finally came to the surface and was netted at the beginning of October.

Chapter XIV

SHE HAD been in despair the previous morning, she wrote to Vita from Tavistock Square on October 9, 1927, trying in vain to get on with the book which, it seemed, was being extorted, drop by drop, from her breast. "Fiction, or some title to that effect. I couldn't screw a word from me; and at last dropped my head in my hands: dipped my pen in the ink, and wrote these words, as if automatically, on a clean sheet: *Orlando: A Biography*. No sooner had I done this than my body was flooded with rapture and my brain with ideas. I wrote rapidly till 12.

"Then I did an hour to Romance. So every morning I am going to write fiction (my own fiction) till 12; and Romance till 1.

"But listen; suppose Orlando turns out to be Vita — suppose there's the kind of shimmer of reality which sometimes attaches to my people, as the lustre on an oyster shell . . . shall you mind?

"Say yes, or no. Your excellence as a subject arises largely from your noble birth — (but what's four hundred years of nobility, all the same?) — and the opportunity thus given for florid descriptive passages in great abundance. Tho, I admit, I should like to untwine and twist again some very odd, incongruous strands in you: and also, as I told you, it sprung upon me how I could revolutionise biography in a night: and so, if agreeable to you, I would like to toss this up in the air and see what happens. Yet, of course, I may not write another line."

Vita said yes, there being among the "odd, incongruous strands" in her character those of fastidious, personal pride, complete honesty, and the power of recognizing a genuine creative impulse. She was perfectly willing to sit for her portrait to such an artist, curious to see how it turned out.

Two things, at least, were certain; it would not be naturalistic, and it would be quite unlike a picture by any other artist. Virginia, protesting that Vita was quite mistaken in thinking she was orderly because she kept work sheets and time schedules and sent regular letters to the right address when Vita was traveling, had asked: "Do we then know nobody? Only our own versions of them, which as likely as not, are emanations from ourselves?" Vita remembered, too, Virginia's surprising comment on her book about Persia (*Passenger to Teheran,* published by the Hogarth Press in 1926): "I kept saying, 'How I should like to know this woman' and then thinking, 'But I do,' and then 'No, I don't — not altogether the woman who writes this.' I didn't know the extent of your subtleties. Here's a brave attitude — emerald staircases, that's familiar enough, but not the sly, brooding, thinking, evading one. The whole book is full of nooks and corners which I enjoy exploring. Sometimes one wants a candle in one hand, though. Indeed it is odd that now, having read this, I have picked up a good many things I had missed in private life. What are they, I wonder, the very intimate things one says in print?" So it was agreed that Virginia should have her candle and go exploring in what she described as Vita's "rich, dusky attic of a mind."

Virginia began writing at full speed, although furtively, she admits in her diary. This was the kicking up of her heels she had promised herself, and her puritan conscience made her doubt whether anything she enjoyed so much could really be justified. "The truth is," she wrote to Vita, "I'm so engulfed in *Orlando* I can think of nothing else. It has ousted romance, psychology and the rest of that odious book completely. I am swarming with ideas."

If it were possible to trace with exactness the origin of any artistic impulse, one might offer the suggestion that *Orlando* had been growing in her mind ever since her talk with Lytton Strachey in 1925 about *Mrs. Dalloway* when he had advised her to try something wilder and more fantastic, like *Tristram Shandy.* "But then I should lose touch with emotions, I said. Yes, he agreed, there must be reality for you to start from." Observation must be precise, to the minutest detail, even if the tiny scraps of information never appeared but were consumed like the dry twigs gathered to start a blazing fire.

She knew so clearly what she wanted, though not at all so clearly how she would use it, that within a week of beginning to write the book she was again asking Vita's co-operation. "Please lend yourself to my scheme," she begged. "Look here: I must come down and see you, if only to choose some pictures." She wanted one of a young Sackville, male, about the time of James I; another of a young Sackville, female, about the time of George III. For Vita-Orlando was to start life, in Virginia's pages, as a young nobleman in the year 1500 or thereabouts, have many adventures in many reigns, and be still young and vigorous, still an aristocrat and, more important, still a poet, but a woman, in the year 1928.

How this fantasy-fiction-farce would work out, how the challenging, compelling craziness of the idea could be made to embody a central truth, this remained to be seen. In the meantime it was urgent that Virginia should refresh her racing imagination with a sight of family portraits and the living woman. "I want to see you in the lamplight, in your emeralds," she wrote. "Just to sit and look at you and get you to talk and then, rapidly and secretly, correct certain doubtful points. About your teeth, now, and your temper. Is it true that you grind your teeth at night?" No detail could be too small when the artist was working on a canvas so large.

Virginia had started on a mad gallop, she knew; but she also knew she must remain in control of her steed, must never lose the sense of the direction in which home lay. She abandoned herself to the pure delight of pursuing so tricky a phantom fox, never to be caught and butchered but always to lure one on, up hill and down dale, over familiar and strange country, while the wind tore at one's hair and the larks sang overhead, and people stood at farmhouse or inn doors or paused in their work in the fields as one swept gaily by.

The reader who is willing to suspend judgment, forsake common sense and daily routine and hearken instead to the horn of the hunter will get pure enjoyment and magical release in the lyrical freedom of this fantastic chase. He will also discover, trying to recapture the exhilaration of the passing moment, that he has seen and understood more than he realized at the time.

Virginia herself tended to underrate *Orlando* once the book was finished. Of all her brain children this was the one that got itself the most easily born and went most merrily on its laughing way, giving its conscientious parent no further cause for fret. Many critics share her view — forgetting that one should never, never trust an author about his work; he is the least likely to be capable of unbiased judgment; if he proves to be right, it will be by accident, and for the wrong reasons. So the earnest searcher for higher truths and deeper meanings, an aesthetic harder to understand and a philosophy more difficult to expound, may slowly shake a heavy head and declare the book no more than a sport, a freak, a faintly deplorable lapse, very charming and beautiful, no doubt, but of no importance.

Actually it establishes her very firmly as an inheritor of and contributor to the magnificent tradition of English letters. The book is a joke, yes. But jokes are remembered and keep one awake and understanding what is going on, whereas the solemn delivery of noble sentiments on an exalted theme too often results in the listener's wondering how much longer the speaker can stand on his feet and emit such sonorous but meaningless words. In asserting her right to play, Virginia Woolf claimed one of the basic freedoms.

She roamed where she pleased through the last four centu-

ries. Orlando, practicing swordsmanship or scribbling tragedies
or dreaming under an oak tree, is almost too late to make his
bow to Queen Elizabeth. Then he is her steward and treasurer,
a Knight of the Garter and a frequenter of low company at
Wapping Old Stairs. He is a gallant and a sonneteer at the Court
of King James, where, during the Great Frost of 1608, he loves
and is jilted by a Muscovite princess. Again pursuing poetry, he
befriends a starving writer, Nick Greene, and is mercilessly ridi-
culed in a scurrilous pamphlet for his pains. He is driven from
his home by the unwelcome attentions of an amorous archduchess. He flees to the court, catches the eye of Nell Gwyn (for by
this time Charles II is on the throne) and is sent as Ambassador
to the Turks. He is made a duke, marries a gypsy dancer named
Rosina Pepita, falls into a trance while Constantinople is being
sacked by rebels, and awakens — a woman.

Unperturbed by the embarrassing change, she gathers what
few jewels the looters missed, secretes one precious manuscript,
and is off to join the raggle-taggle-gypsies-o. With them she lives
in great content until she succumbs to the English disease, a romantic love of nature. Worse still, she desires to write, the
change in sex having in no way altered her inner character. She
arouses so much suspicion and hostility in her nomadic companions that only her decision to leave saves them the trouble of
murdering her.

Back in eighteenth-century England, after a voyage mainly
spent in accustoming herself to conventional women's clothes
after Turkish trousers and gypsy rags, she finds herself entangled in litigation. Only the law can decide whether she is alive
or dead, the ducal husband of Rosina Pepita or the nameless
mother of illegitimate sons; and other fine points. However, her
old servants and faithful dogs recognize her instantly. The archduchess has become an archduke, and remains as much a pest
as ever. In a London rebuilt by Wren after the Great Fire she
pours tea for Addison and Pope and Dryden and Dr. Johnson
and Dean Swift, and is rewarded for her hospitality and her ad-

miration for these scholars, philosophers, poets and wits by being derided and denounced by them all for being a woman.

And so we reach the nineteenth century, and crinolines and Queen Victoria, and romantic verse, and the overwhelming need for women to have husbands and wedding rings. In the nick of time, riding a great horse, arrives Marmaduke Bonthrop Shelmerdine. Instantly he and Orlando are in love and engaged and married; but he has to be off on his adventures; he must sail his brig around Cape Horn in the teeth of a gale.

The Victorian age passes, and the Edwardian. Orlando rides in trains and then drives her own car. She has a son. She meets Nick Greene, now Sir Nicholas and a respected Professor of Literature. She sees her Russian princess, now fat and aging, in Marshall & Snelgrove's store. She destroys all that is left of the innumerable tragedies, sonnets and allegories she has written in so many different styles and moods since she was a boy and caught sight of a shabby poet — could it have been Shakespeare? — scribbling away in a servant's room; but she keeps and at last completes the one poem she has carried always with her, the poem about England and Nature and everything under the sun that she loved, "The Oak Tree." And as she stands under that great oak, Shelmerdine returns, leaping from an airplane as he once leaped from a horse. "There sprang up over his head a single wild bird. 'It is the goose!' Orlando cried. 'The wild goose . . .' And the twelfth stroke of midnight sounded; the twelfth stroke of midnight, Thursday, the eleventh of October, Nineteen Hundred and Twenty Eight."

The literal-minded reader, for whose benefit the preceding summary has been made, may well feel bewildered by such obviously preposterous nonsense, particularly when it is described as a biography and the eminent author thanks a most impressive group of distinguished experts of all kinds, living and dead, for their help in her researches. The rather better informed but still serious reader who recognizes the photographs of Vita Sackville-West catches her likeness to the family portraits also reproduced in the book, and picks up the various references to the Sackville family's long history, including the lawsuit about the succession to the peerage in 1912, may concede that there is considerable point in an entertaining trifle, though possibly questioning whether such a piece of prolonged tomfoolery is always in the best of taste. Only the reader who has been enjoying the joke, conniving at the evasions and accepting the hints, will really see what riches are here displayed and understand how *Orlando* illumines what went before and what came after in Virginia Woolf's life and works.

For all the light mockery, a feeling of maturity and assurance is conveyed. She is at her ease with the Elizabethans, fine, swaggering, rollicking, daydreaming adventurers; she can be hail-fellow-well-met with any of them. With the rather smaller, neater, more niggling, pensive and learned bigwigs of the seventeenth century she is ready to crack a conceit or split a hair. Among the eighteenth-century wits she moves demurely, paying with good manners for the right to enjoy their company when they are civil and to leave them at their malicious play. As for the august beings held up for her admiration in the nineteenth century, she had at times been impelled to challenge them, fight them, deny them; now, free from their thraldom, she walks easily among them as an equal. She will prance, swagger, dip, soar, curtsy, sigh, rhapsodize, discourse with any of them, through the ages, any time.

She announces, in short, that she has come of age as a writer. Henceforward let no man patronize her except at his peril. But welcome, one and all, to my party, she says. Milton mourned Lycidas, his drowned friend; Shelley wept for Adonais when Keats died in Rome; I give you the toast of Orlando, who is living yet, and will go on living as long as the English language in prose or verse serves beauty and celebrates friendship.

The entertainment offered to her guests was a charade, a ballet to be danced to a divertimento for flute and strings, instruments whose notes can be both sweet and piercing. She uses a prose so rhythmical that when suddenly, deliberately, with a flick of the wrist, it is checked from becoming verse, the effect of the syncopation is that of a missed heartbeat. One is reminded of the calm audacity of Michelangelo's Adam negligently accepting life from the finger tip of the Creator. She lets little, silly, tinkling rhymes be heard now and again, and one sees Mozart saucily chasing a tune round a bush before tossing it high into the heavens. She puts a kitchen match to a six-penny firework, and, as the colored gunpowder sparks blaze briefly in the sky, the air tingles with stardust.

These are not purple passages, in which the words sink in velvet and the reader drowses by the fireside. They are turns of a kaleidoscope, where sometimes the lighter and sometimes the more somber chips of glass dominate the pattern; but always there is a pattern. One thinks of her friend Roger Fry insisting that all the arts are linked and can be understood in terms of one another. This annoys the musician and the painter, and sends the teacher of aesthetics into a frenzied search for the right words to make the theory plain. The reader of *Orlando* who has succumbed to the magic does not pause to have the mystery expounded; he just feels it.

BUT TWO things must be noted about this triumphant *jeu d'esprit*. Writing it was not as easy as falling off a log; and it does not stand alone.

There were times when *Orlando* was so "potent in its own right" that the thought of a coming engagement which would cut short a morning's work led her to cursing fate for the interruption. "You see," she told Vita, "when, as with us, the mind's bent one way, it's physical and moral torture to unbend." And then there were times when the radiant man-woman turned sullen, dragged his-her feet, shuffled along a dusty road, hands in pockets, with never so much as a whistle, was almost pushed into a ditch by, of all things, that patient, plodding tortoise of an idea about Women and Fiction. She must not allow so dull a creature to outrace her lovely hare. He had to be goaded out of his listlessness, made to finish the course in fine style. The situation was saved from degenerating into too Aesop-like a fable by the tortoise's hibernating; it grew a second head, and finally appeared a year later, transfigured, as *A Room of One's Own*. This was a book as different from *Orlando* as *Orlando* was from anything that had preceded it. And yet the two demand to be read together.

They are opposite sides of the same medal. Just as Shelmerdine and Orlando, two parts of one personality split in the nineteenth century, have to be reunited in the twentieth before the wild goose can be glimpsed in its flight, so Virginia Woolf had to get both the essay-pamphlet and the satire-fantasy out of her way before she was free to go adventuring on her next wild-goose chase, the serious, poetic, mystical work that would call for the exercise of the most profound creative impulse. Without the tossing in the air of *Orlando* and the extortion from her breast, drop by bloody drop, of the book on fiction or romance or "some title to that effect," *The Waves*, generally accepted as the finest expression of her genius, could never have been written.

It was because *Orlando* and *A Room of One's Own* were complementary but emerged as separate entities that Virginia did not rank either of them very highly. She gave them both all she had at the time, but was never satisfied that it was enough. The one was too private, too playful, her artistic conscience said; it celebrated love and friendship, but not enough; it praised poetry, but the allegory of the stumbling progress of the poet, rejected by one society after another as a misfit and hampered in his movements by women's clothes, was not sufficiently clear. The other was a restatement of the evaded themes; dedicated not to one woman but to all women who were cursed with the kind of imagination and love of freedom that would not let them rest; but even so she had not made her points with enough force. Both books came, she felt, from levels too near the surface of her mind to satisfy her. It was as though she had been idly skimming stones across a pond. Where they sank a ripple spread. If the eye could only follow the furthest ripple to the extremest verge, a rainbow might be seen springing from the reeds. And it was the rainbow Virginia was after.

Orlando was not finished by Christmas 1927, in spite of the Woolfs' refusing a flattering invitation to go to Russia during November, as guests of the government, to help celebrate the tenth anniversary of the Revolution. The political weather was temporarily fine, but Russian winters are invariably cold, and the Woolfs decided they could not spare the time for the trip across Europe. Virginia had innumerable questions to put to Vita. "I should hate for ever to be for an instant a burden to you," she wrote, but "The truth shall be dug out of you at all costs." The truth was not on matters of fact, which were easily established, but on points of interpretation of an elusive character; the woman she knew and didn't know.

She must have photographs, instantly; Orlando in the East; Orlando in breeches; Shelmerdine; Orlando in country clothes in a wood — Leonard might take this one afternoon if Vita had a camera handy; a bookplate or something with the Sackville arms on it; all very important, very urgent.

Vita supplied everything she wanted, and asked no questions. Hers not to reason why. Like Leonard and Vanessa and everyone else, she obeyed the unwritten law that protected the author's right to the complete privacy of her workroom. Virginia was writing; what she was writing her intimates might hear if she chose to tell them, but they would have to wait until the work satisfied the writer before they really knew what had been keeping her so busy.

The woman who was sitting for her portrait in *Orlando* actually never read a word of that book until she received a printed copy shortly before its publication. Many years later, after Virginia's death, she discovered by chance when looking through the handwritten copy that it contained many unpublished passages. She has no idea why they were cut out of the final version and can only conclude that Virginia found them redundant. The deletions were certainly not made as a result of any protest from her, since no question of what might or might not be included was ever discussed between artist and sitter. Admirable trust, and admirably rewarded.

Yet she must often have wondered what exactly was going on. Why, for instance, this renewed demand to be told what on earth an ambassador finds to do all day long? And why all these questions about the romantically beautiful young man whose portrait still hangs in her dining room and is reproduced and called Shelmerdine in the illustrated edition of the book? Who was he? Lady Nicolson wishes she knew his identity or even who painted the picture. All she can say is that she bought him in the cellar of an embroidery shop in London for fifteen pounds with a wedding-present check in 1913 and that her son Benedict, a professional art critic, thinks it possible that Sir Thomas Lawrence may have had a hand in the painting. It was enough at the time that the picture caught her fancy and caught Virginia's too.

Virginia carried the manuscript about with her, from London to the country and back, groaning and complaining that it was an addled egg, an old man of the sea; she must put it away in a drawer; she must finish it; it was an unspeakable bore; and yet appendices were blossoming in her head and she could write another three volumes easily. "It's all your fault," she pretended.

"Oh, Vita, Vita, how you have brought my life to ruin and wasted the fair taper in a sea of grease!"

A few days later, in March 1928, she wrote: "Did you feel a sort of tug, as if you were being broken, on Saturday last at five minutes to one? That was when he died — or rather stopped talking; with three little dots . . ." Those three little dots were almost all that remained from the plan for *The Jessamy Brides.*

Of course, it would have to be rewritten. It was "all over the place, incoherent, intolerable, impossible. And I am sick of it."

Motoring through France soon restored her spirits. She was not allowed to drive, and looking out of a window for eight hours a day turned her into a "revolving brute" with a mind "like a deep, irreflecting river in which facts are slowly turned." There were apt to be bugs in the hotel beds. Crossing the Maritime Alps the party encountered snowstorms, had three punctures, "changing wheels in pitch darkness on the edge of precipices." But, "This is the way to live, I can assure you."

Back in London she found that a notice she had read in *The Times* before she left was true. She had been awarded the annual prize bestowed by the French journal *Femina,* the very prize that she had declared she would never accept when Lady Dilke mentioned it to her on the telephone the previous year.

It was formally presented to her in May by Hugh Walpole, who found it as nerve-racking and depressing an occasion as she had when Vita received the Hawthornden for "The Land," so shamelessly called "The Oak Tree" in *Orlando.* Virginia was sympathetic with the poor man for having to make a suitable speech before all the lady novelists in London; so she carried him off to dinner at Tavistock Square, and everybody cheered up considerably.

This, although not their first meeting, was the beginning of a friendship that lasted all their lives. He was shy, but she encouraged him, and Vita also helped to put him at his ease. He was devoted to both of them ever after. Virginia wrote a few days later: "I hear Mrs. Nicolson and Mrs. Woolf gave some offence by coming to the prize dressed as if for a funeral. Still it *was* my funeral. Hugh has now written me an eloquent letter of affection and regret — says he was stunned. He must be a man of the tenderest heart, and so I've told him."

She understood that his modesty was quite genuine, not assumed to extort praise in protest, so it did not embarrass her to realize that he considered she had genius in spheres where he had only talent, for, as a critic, she happened to agree with him. But she valued him as a person and, although it was sometimes a ticklish problem, she managed never to hurt his feelings and praised his work when she could. "He's a dear, rosy old bumble bee," she wrote, "and as mild as a shorn lamb." So she tempered the east wind of criticism to him, enjoyed his companionship, and responded to his adoration with constant affection. He was always humble; she was always kind. The quality of their relationship is touchingly revealed in his own account of their last meeting, many years later, during the war. He told her he had always loved her, and she asked him why, and seemed pleased by the reasons he gave. A friend who joined them later, says his biographer, can never forget the glowing magic of the evening spent with these two old friends, chatting and laughing, gloom and fear temporarily shut out on the other side of the blackout curtains.

The gentle, loving side of her character was beginning to be more freely expressed. It is felt in the increased maturity and poise of *Orlando,* following the exploration of her past in *To the Lighthouse* and the courage required for *Mrs. Dalloway.* There is a geniality and good humor pervading *A Room of One's Own* which is unexpected, considering that its feminist theme used formerly to elicit anger and caustic mockery, when old wounds throbbed.

The impression gained from her books is confirmed by a diary entry in September 1928. She was amused to note that Rebecca

West, whose "trumpet calls" always aroused her admiration, annoyed her old friend Desmond MacCarthy by asserting that men are snobs. Virginia reminded him of a condescending reference in his *Life and Letters* column to the limitations of women novelists. Now, coming from an intelligent man, what else was that but an expression of male snobbery? But there was no acrimony in the exchange, she observed. Only, thinking about it, she characteristically wondered whether it might not mean that "we are now coming like the homing rooks back to the tops of our trees? and that all this cawing is the beginning of settling in for the night? I seem to notice in several of my friends some endearing and affecting cordiality; and a pleasure in intimacy; as if the sun were sinking."

It shows, too, in her letters. Vita must please never be angry on her behalf about adverse criticism of *Orlando*. It was probably her (Virginia's) own fault if critics were waspish; she stung them first. The only thing Virginia would regret would be if Vita felt the attacks were so well-founded that she and Harold thought less well of Virginia and the book. But that couldn't happen, could it? And, anyway, the public liked it. An immediate reprint was called for.

It went on selling, too. In January 1929 she reported in a postscript: "*Orlando* has now sold 13,000 copies in America; that's the last time I mention him." But she was mistaken. One of her little jokes backfired and brought an avalanche of letters upon her.

Remembering the controversy about the exact location of *To the Lighthouse* she concluded her preface to *Orlando*, which began with acknowledgments to the illustrious dead from Defoe to Walter Pater, by thanking a gentleman in America (whose name and address she pretended to have lost) "who has generously and gratuitously corrected the punctuation, the botany, the entomology, the geography, and the chronology of previous works of mine and will, I hope, not spare his services on the present occasion." The gentleman in America was, of course, a composite character, but her jesting reference to him was a direct incitement to all and sundry to write to her about anything that seemed odd or inaccurate in *Orlando*.

As usual, there was a basis of truth in her fantastification. There really was a gentleman in America. He is still living and still treasures her courteous reply when he pointed out various inconsistencies in the punctuation of the American edition of the first volume of *The Common Reader*. These variations arose from the fact that the articles had been reprinted from different English papers, each of which had its own style; hence the book reflected the prevailing confusion but not her own views about the use of hyphens, and so on. She would correct the misprints and try to impose some sort of conformity in future editions, if any were called for.

·When *Orlando* appeared he had retired, but not stopped working; the habit of correcting, line by line, word by word, comma by comma, once formed by years of scholarly and patient work as a librarian, is not easily broken. He was among those who wanted to know in what dictionary she found the word "scrolloped"; and what sort of dog was an elk-hound; and surely there were no bears in Malaya; and where was the Roumanian territory mentioned in the title of the Archduchess Harriet Griselda of Finster-Aarhorn and Scand-op-Boom? These were mysteries; but of one patent error he did convict her — she did not know the difference between "downstream" and "upstream." This she had to admit, though without feeling reduced to a state of near idiocy such as overcame Cam in the boat going to the lighthouse when Mr. Ramsay was outraged because his daughter could not tell east from west. This was one of the mistakes for which she could forgive herself and let her friends laugh at her because of it.

The letters came in such numbers that she had to ask for help in dealing with them. Admitting an error is easy, but explaining a joke is almost impossible; and she was exhausted. So she would be forever grateful to a friend who might find time to reply suitably to a batch she forwarded to Vita. "If she wrote very kindly and said (to the lady) that Knole was intended — and the climate changes in sympathy with the age — and gave her my kind regards — and then to the boy of 16, perhaps she could say that 'Elizabethans' is probably inaccurate but intentional; and that the grammar is colloquial; and give him my kind regards — Oh Lord! I cannot write any more letters about *Orlando* or anything else — so if she could — but don't let her bother — I daresay she has enough to do." Somehow or other Virginia must answer the donkeys; they were "nice, good donkeys," she hastened to add.

Orlando wasn't finished with yet. The winter of 1929 was abnormally severe. In London, where, for the most part, water pipes are outside the houses and no one does anything about it because of the conviction that no weather, however bad, lasts long enough to be more than a healthy Britisher can endure, the freezing conditions had dismaying results. "Talk of icicles!" wrote Virginia to Vita, who was shivering in the Alps. "You can see icicles fifty feet long from the top storey to the ground — in Tavistock Square. We are in desperate straits; all of us; most of us have no baths, no water closets, and some no gas fires, and the pipes are frozen. Our water closet is our glory — the plug still pulls. No bath, though. What's happened is that Nature, having read a certain description of a frost (see *Orlando*) was so taken by it that she determined to do it better. Needless to say she does it infinitely worse. Not a flounder nor an old woman to be seen at London Bridge."

Orlando had seen both, and much besides, in 1608. According to Virginia's retelling of the old chronicles, the ice was so clear that

. . . there could be seen, congealed at a depth of several feet, here a porpoise, there a flounder. Shoals of eels lay motionless in a trance. . . . Near London Bridge, where the river had frozen to a depth of some twenty fathoms, a wrecked wherry boat was plainly visible, lying on the bed of the river where it had sunk last autumn, overladen with apples. The old bum-boat woman, who was carrying her fruit to market on the Surrey side, sat there in her plaids and farthingales, for all the world as if she were about to serve a customer, though a certain blueness about the lips hinted the truth. 'Twas a sight King James specially liked to look upon, and he would bring a troupe of courtiers to gaze with him.

Londoners in 1929 who had stood in line at public swimming baths, railway termini or big hotels where hot water still flowed, crept back to their comfortless homes through streets that seemed paved with basalt or black iron; gates and doors spat to the touch with the fury of adders; and brick walls that should have been sheltering maliciously radiated an ever icier chill. They turned on their radios and heard about what fun it was in the good old days when there was a frost really worth calling a frost, when the king held court on the frozen Thames at Greenwich and the citizens enjoyed at his expense a carnival of unexampled brilliance.

Whether anyone felt warmer after this recital is unknown; but it was a valiant attempt on the part of the B. B. C.

Nature soon gave up her attempt to copy Art. About a week later Vita, doing her best to pull a longbow and arouse sympathy for her sufferings in central-European forests, received this note: "I am glad that you have escaped the wolves, though it would have been a romantic death for you and might have suggested a second volume to *Orlando*. They had to broadcast the thaw, too, the other night; for it is thawing; and on the whole we are rather less comfortable than before, as the drip is everywhere, and gas has failed. No baths again."

In the book the thaw was as rapid as the frost had been prolonged; watery ruin swept everything before it in a few devastating hours. Orlando, planning to elope, prepared to forsake everything for love-in-exile, realized as the first raindrop struck his cheek that he waited in vain for his fickle princess to keep their rendezvous. Galloping madly through torrential rain and rushing flood, he was just in time to see her ship, so long becalmed, putting out to sea. In real-life London in 1929 the thaw began stealthily at the top stories; water could get into the houses days before it could get out again. An orgy of cleansing in attic apartments was followed by most disconcerting and disagreeable results on lower floors. What was good for bath pipes freed by pressure from years of soap-slime deposits was not good for tempers. Tenants downstairs angrily assailed the sybarites upstairs. Fastidious ladies near the roof turned pale and faint when asked to see for themselves what black mud, allegedly resulting from their necessary ablutions, was oozing into their neighbors' tubs. The thaw was anything but romantic, in fact.

But the bold and dashing Orlando still held the imagination in the next big freeze, which occurred in January 1933. "Here it is freezing, freezing," wrote Virginia. "The pipes are frozen; but tomorrow the pipes will burst. Oh, and tonight they're dancing Orlando on the ice, and I shan't be there. It's a remarkable fact — the whole British peerage say they descend from courtiers I invented, and still have the snow boots which they wore in that frost, which I invented too. It's all true every word of it. They charge thirty shillings a ticket and I would willingly have gone and hired skates if you'd have come."

Vita had just crossed the Atlantic, through very heavy weather. Virginia imagined her standing on the bridge with the captain, facing waves "eighty miles high," while in Tavistock Square the only way to empty a bath was to bale it out into a bucket with a tumbler. "I tell you all this to bring you in touch with England. I daresay you're eating clams on a skyscraper at this moment. Shall you have your new novel ready for October? — it's about America and it has a storm at sea."

The presence of Orlando, as well as of Vita, was desired in the United States. Virginia had given the manuscript, together with many passages not printed when the final revision was made, to its inspirer, after having it beautifully bound in calf. In 1932 an American collector wished to acquire the manuscript, and Virginia passed the suggestion on. "For my part I think it would be a very good thing if you sold it now; you might get a hundred or two; and it seems to me far better to sell now, when the dollar is worth whatever it is worth, than to keep it mouldering at Long Barn; and it will moulder still more at Sissinghurst" (an old family castle in Kent which had been allowed to fall into decay in other hands and which the Nicolsons had reacquired and were gradually making habitable once more). "What I should like would be that you should start your library on the proceeds. So let me know. I will write another book and give you the MS instead."

Vita's reaction can be judged from Virginia's next letter, written ten days later. "I've refused the five thousand pounds for *Orlando* on your behalf. What a donkey! This would have built you a library to last for ever." But she must have been secretly very pleased that Vita valued her gift too highly even to consider parting with it, for the next month, May 1932, she added an airy postscript, apropos of nothing that appears: "Would you like to give *Orlando* to the Bodleian? Aren't I vain?"

The manuscript, far from moldering, still stands proudly, with other treasures, on the shelves of the library in the round room of the rose brick gateway tower at Sissinghurst. Its next home is already decided upon. "I have left it to Knole in my will," writes Lady Nicolson, "as I felt there was so much about Knole in it that that was the right place for it to be, with various other manuscripts that have got there from people like Pope and Dryden." This does not mean that it will be lost to the public, since Knole is now, like so many other ancestral houses of Britain, no longer a purely private home but is partly administered by the National Trust in order to preserve its historical relics for posterity.

Chapter XV

TO RETURN to *Orlando's* soberer and by no means identical twin, *A Room of One's Own*. This short, six-chaptered book is an expansion and rewriting of two papers delivered in Cambridge, at Newnham College in May 1928, and at Girton College in October of the same year. The subject of the lectures was to be "Women and Fiction." Virginia seized the opportunity to re-examine and restate many ideas which had occupied her mind for years, which had cropped up in her books over and over again in many forms, and which would continue to crop up. The more she thought about the theme the more she realized that the questions concerning the true nature of women and of fiction presented problems she was unable to solve. She had tossed many ideas about women (and men) and poetry (and prose) in the air in *Orlando*. Now she would try to explain, step by step, why all she could do was to offer "an opinion upon one minor point — a woman must have money, and a room of her own if she is to write fiction."

The phrase "a room of one's own," though not new, captured the public imagination, and is probably the title most frequently associated with the name of Virginia Woolf by people not primarily interested in literature but who like to have a convenient memory tag to hang on an author. The words could hardly be simpler, nor could her own statement of her theme be more exact. Unfortunately the reversing of the equation — "women and fiction equals a room of one's own" to "a room of one's own equals women and fiction" — led to misunderstandings. The book does not advocate, as is sometimes assumed, that all women should be given five hundred pounds a year to enable them to neglect their real womanly business of child-raising and home-keeping in order to devote themselves to writing novels.

This summary of the book's theme is patent nonsense and would not be worth mentioning if it did not still persist in criticism of the Bloomsbury Group that it was made up of people with private incomes, belonging to a privileged and expensively educated class, who thus had a totally wrong scale of values because they never had to work for a living, knew nothing about the hard facts of life, and made themselves ridiculous by imagining that they were better than anyone else.

There is a grain of truth here. Virginia did have a small income which left her free to do the kind of work for which she was most fitted. She did have her own scale of values, resulting from her education and background. She did know that in some respects she was, from her point of view, "better" than people who had not had her advantages. She also knew that her comparatively privileged and sheltered position imposed its peculiar limitations. She would have liked to escape from these bounds, to have had other experiences. She regretted the impossibility of being different from what she was, and resented the implication that it was her fault. She looked at herself in the mirror, was not satisfied with what she saw, but decided that, as it was the only face she had, she had better make the best of it.

In order to understand what sort of woman Virginia Woolf was, it is necessary to follow the argument of *A Room of One's Own*, for then one can see why she struggled to finish this book, which had such an uneasy life of its own that it was like a "creature arching its back" in her mind. Although once it was finished she regarded it as a trifle, she wrote it with "ardour and conviction." This is probably one of the main reasons why it had an immediate appeal, why it is still read and quoted, and why it is to many women the most beloved and meaningful of her works.

She begins, as usual, to make her points by telling a story. "Lies will flow from my lips," she warns, "but there may perhaps be some truth mixed up with them; it is for you to seek out this truth and to decide whether any part of it is worth keeping." So she describes an imaginary visit to an invented "Oxbridge" preparatory to delivering a lecture at "Fernham."

She is warned off the grass; this is for the feet of Fellows and scholars only; unidentified females must keep to the gravel paths. She is denied admittance to a library, because she is an unaccompanied woman. Fearing to incur a third rebuff on similar grounds, she scorns to attend chapel. She is royally entertained at lunch, however, in a magnificent hall. It is a wonderful meal, and wonderfully described. Anyone who wishes to know how Virginia Woolf felt about good food and good cooking should read the first chapter of *A Room of One's Own.*

Her dinner that evening is eaten with the students of a college for women on the outskirts of the ancient university city. She is cordially welcomed, but the meal, in contrast with that glorious lunch, is a saddening experience. Plain living and high thinking is the rule at Fernham. Wealth untold has been poured for centuries into the endowment and adornment of the colleges for men; the monastic origins of these seats of learning survive only in the picturesque ceremonial of the service. To raise the comparatively small sum required to build a college for women less than a hundred years ago had been an uphill struggle, and the amenities of life must be postponed. It was understandable enough, for the grandmothers of the young women of England who went banging and singing down corridors and up staircases in that adequate but austere building had been very busy bearing twelve or thirteen children, and until 1880 did not legally possess one penny of their own.

But the British Museum Library, that storehouse of wisdom, is open to all comers, and thither Virginia repairs to gather material for her lecture. She consults innumerable books written by men about women, for women are, it appears, the most discussed animals in the universe, but finds nothing to her purpose. All these books, having been "written in the red light of emotion and not in the white light of truth," confuse and anger her, and how is it possible, if one is angry, to discover truth? She can only escape from her anger because there is money in her purse. She can ignore the angry men who seem so afraid she will defy them and do what she wants instead of what they say. A legacy from an aunt has "substituted for the large and imposing figure of a gentleman, which Milton recommended for my perpetual adoration, a view of the open sky."

The next day she decides to consult the historians and the poets; and finds their testimony in direct conflict. Woman "pervades poetry from cover to cover; she is all but absent from history." A few names of great queens and heroines appear in the history books, but what they were actually like, what the average women did from eight in the morning until eight at night, remains unrecorded for the most part; until about the beginning of the eighteenth century their voices are seldom heard. Clearly they were not unobserved and featureless at the time they lived, or where did the poets get their models for Cleopatra, Lady Macbeth, Rosalind, the Wife of Bath? Here is the strangest paradox. "Woman dominates the lives of kings and conquerors in fiction; in fact she was the slave of any boy whose parents forced a ring upon her finger. Some of the most inspired words, some of the most profound thoughts in literature fall from her lips; in real life she could hardly read, could scarcely spell, and was the property of her husband."

Suppose Shakespeare had had a gifted sister, what chance would she have had to write plays? None whatever, concludes Virginia. Even if she had managed to make her way to London she would not have been allowed to learn the first elements of theatercraft; for in those days it was a ludicrous notion that women could act. An unprotected woman hanging about a stage door would have been the legitimate prey of any ruffian. She would probably have killed herself and been "buried at some cross-road where the omnibuses now stop outside the Elephant and Castle."

Now one understands why Orlando had to be a boy in the Elizabethan age. It is not only that most gay, healthy, intelligent, spirited girls go through a stage in their adolescence when their natural behavior is so irrepressibly boisterous and their contempt for feminine graces so marked that they are not just boys, but tomboys. It is that the Elizabethan Age was flamboyantly masculine. Whether Orlando is regarded as the poet searching for the wild goose of beauty or as an individual whose infinite variety must be expressed in terms of family history, the only form appropriate to the sixteenth and early seventeenth centuries is male.

The fact that it was a virgin queen who gave the age its name adds to the complexity of the allegory, for the first Queen Elizabeth survived only because she combined masculine vigor and ruthlessness with feminine wiles and trickery (assuming for the sake of brevity that these qualities observably characterize one sex or the other). She was a man in petticoats, a woman armed with striking power. The theme of double — or interchangeable — sex runs through *Orlando,* as does its obverse theme of the arbitrary division of the two sexes when both need to be united to form the complete and ideal whole human being. Virginia Woolf's ideas, and feelings, about man/woman and woman/man are stated explicitly and with all the clarity at her command in *A Room of One's Own.* Reading either book reveals instance after instance of how one fed into the other.

As the Elizabethan glory fades and the Augustan begins to glow a few rich women momentarily appear in English literature. They are immediately derided as "blue stockings with an itch for scribbling," driven to eccentricity, bitterness, melancholy, loneliness, despair. Men have suffered the same fate, when met with the vast indifference of the public. Women had to overcome active opposition and scorn. A half-crazed duchess might write verse, but sensible women of less social prominence knew better than to expose themselves to ridicule and disgrace for venturing beyond the limits set for their sex. A few memorable letters showing undoubted but undeveloped gifts alone remain.

But gradually, as the late eighteenth and early nineteenth centuries go on and the wits give way to the romantics, and later as the romantics are superseded by the realists (that is, writers dealing in life around them and characters unswathed in the furbelows of classical allusions), women begin to emerge from obscurity. Mrs. Aphra Behn writes high-flown nonsense, but at least she is allowed to earn money by her fluent pen. Jane Austen hides her manuscript when anyone comes into the room, Charlotte Brontë and George Eliot use masculine names; but they do get their books published and receive recognition. Dramatic and romantic poetry give way to domestic fiction as the expression of English literature, and women are accorded a place. Orlando has become a woman. The Virgin Queen, Elizabeth, has been replaced by the Mother Empress, Victoria. Petticoats abound, but they are to be regarded as a protection for modesty, not as a hindrance to free movement.

And so, at last, we come to the twentieth century. Orlando is only half herself until she can be rejoined to Shelmerdine. Virginia Stephen has to slay the Angel in the House before she can write truthfully. And men have leaped valiantly to the defense of their time-honored privileges, for the frontiers of decency have been invaded and women are swarming all over the place. Here is Sir Edmund Gosse declaring that Virginia Woolf no longer respects her father, as she tells Vita-Orlando without troubling to comment. He, Gosse, hated his father; but that is a very different matter from Virginia's openly differing in her critical opinions from her father, who recognized very clearly and properly what were masculine and what were feminine virtues and characteristics. It is a shocking state of affairs, all this wreckage and rubble left after the fury of the women's suffrage movement has spent itself.

Virginia calmly picks up a modern novel by a woman she calls, for the sake of convenience, Mary Carmichael. Not a good novel, she concludes regretfully, but what a brave attempt. It is marred by anger. The writer has been injured in the sex war, still feels frustrated, cannot apply the healing balm of humor when male gadflies sting. And yet she goes on, clambering over the wreckage, as though she had every right to go where she pleases. The eighteenth-century woman was hooted off the scene. The nineteenth-century woman kept her corner and obediently held up, though sometimes with an impudent, barely concealed smirk, the mirror in which man could see himself in full dress, with attendant females. But Mary Carmichael, clumsy and disheveled as she may be, is striding about and announcing that she really cannot be bothered with this male-female nonsense.

Suppose she is right, Virginia Woolf asks us to consider. What may conceivably be the result of ceasing to waste her time and energy and talent in continually asserting her claim to her own room in which she may without interruption, so long as she pays her due rent from her own earnings, write truthfully about life as she sees it? Suppose she is not exclusively interested in portraying women in relation to men, or men in relation to women? Suppose there is something in this discovery of hers that women get something from companionship with women which is as real and valuable as what men get from companionship with men, and that both men and women find in one another's society a solace and a satisfaction that go beyond the pleasures of the senses and replace the tensions of sex with the union of mind?

Virginia Woolf's own belief — and she admits it is a little fantastic — is that, given another hundred years or so, an income and a room of her own, and full leave to speak her mind, Mary Carmichael will be a poet; that the dead poet who never wrote a word and was buried at the crossroads still lives on. "If we escape a little from the common sitting-room and see human beings not always in relation to each other but in relation to reality . . .

then the opportunity will come and the dead poet who was Shakespeare's sister will put on the body which she has so often laid down. Drawing her life from the lives of the unknown who were her forerunners, as her brother did before her, she will be born."

THE PERIOD when she was writing *Orlando* and *A Room of One's Own* was a happy one. The first book came easily and the second was a grind, for two reasons: she wanted to get to grips with her next book, *The Waves,* which eluded her sickeningly, and so much of the material was old stuff which she thought she had got rid of long ago. It was not, as she pretended, a matter of going to the British Museum with a notebook and pencil, and then sitting by a river and concocting from her notes the amusing stories, gay thoughts, artful suggestions and neat ending which make this essay such smooth reading. She had to do something much more difficult than consult authoritative sources, catalogued and cross-referenced in a library. She had to gather up all sorts of bits and pieces lying about in her mind, and put them into order. Many of them had been used before, many of them would insist on being used again. But, on the whole, tidying up the litter was, though tedious to do, gratifying in its results.

Reading *A Room of One's Own* one gathers from it a picture of its author as a woman who had outgrown awkwardness and achieved serenity without smugness, who could be charming and witty even when she was most serious, whose smile was pleasant and reassuring even when she flashed a light into dark corners, exposing mysterious and disturbing thoughts. It is possible to glean even more knowledge about her by referring to other critical essays she had written or would write.

Dorothy Osborne, the shy girl who wrote memorable letters to her future husband, and the eccentric Duchess of Newcastle who, desiring fame and despising courts, had her verses printed, are mentioned as contrasting examples of seventeenth-century women writers. The gentle Dorothy fell silent after marriage. The defiant duchess was driven by public ridicule to melancholy and near-madness.

In the first and second volumes of *The Common Reader* the lives of these two so different women are related and their achievements assessed. As one reads these two essays another figure arises from the printed page; one catches glimpses of Virginia Woolf herself as she might have been if born in the early seventeenth instead of the late nineteenth century.

Other examples abound showing the close relation between Virginia herself and the theme of *A Room of One's Own,* and establishing that the two lectures she gave at Cambridge were based on extensive knowledge and continued thought, not on hasty research and sudden conclusions. In 1927, for instance, she wrote about two nineteenth-century women, Emily Davies, who was indefatigable in the struggle to bring Girton College into existence, and Lady Augusta Stanley, lady-in-waiting to the Duchess of Kent, to whom the slightest event in the life of the royal family was of the utmost importance. No two women, it would seem, could have been more different in background, temperament and outlook. Yet the court lady was one of the first to support the middle-class woman in the demand for university education for women in the eighteen-sixties. Part of the story of those pioneering efforts is told in the first chapter of *A Room of One's Own.* In "Two Women," reprinted in *The Moment,* one finds Virginia Woolf "tempted to imagine sprung from that unlikely union some astonishing phoenix of the future who shall combine the new efficiency with the old amenity, the courage of the indomitable Miss Davies and Lady Augusta's charm."

Again one recalls that exploration of her past which Virginia gives in "Memories of a Working Women's Guild" (republished, by permission of the Yale University Press, in *The Captain's Death Bed*), where one meets first the young, newly-married, middle-class woman, eager but uneasy among the delegates to a Women's Co-operative conference in 1913, and is then allowed to follow her stubborn pursuit of real knowledge about these practical and efficient stalwarts of the Labor Movement, and her discovery, after seventeen years of persistent, if intermittent, thought and inquiry, that in them, as in their overworked, under-paid and ill-educated forerunners, were to be found her own aspirations, the "dumb poetry that is everywhere."

One turns again to the revelations of herself in "Professions for Women" (*The Death of the Moth*) and finds her reminding her audience of the debt they owe to the often inept and doubtless ridiculous pioneer women of the past for forcing open doors once closed to their sex. Reminding them, too, of what they owe to the future.

You have won rooms of your own in the house hitherto exclu-sively owned by men. You are able, though not without great labour and effort, to pay the rent. You are earning your five hundred pounds a year. But this freedom is only a beginning; the room is your own, but it is still bare. It has to be furnished; it has to be decorated; it has to be shared.

Are these the words of a dilettante, an egoist, a snob? Did Bloomsbury breed nothing but idlers and triflers, smugly un-aware of a rougher, harsher world beyond its confines?

THERE are also references in *A Room of One's Own* to what was happening while the book was being written. Virginia saw, as not everyone did then, the menace to freedom and peace in Fascist Italy, with its glorification of male virility and martial virtues. She wanted no banners or medals for fallen heroes to decorate her room. In England, too, she noted disturbing signs of retrogression to a gloomier past, though she touched upon these lightly, for the matter was delicate.

The country was, in fact, experiencing one of its periodic flurries of excitement about morals and decency, and the storm center was current literature. A highly reputable publisher and a distinguished woman novelist who had recently been awarded two literary prizes suddenly found themselves accused of obscene libel because *The Well of Loneliness* dealt with the forbidden topic of sexual abnormality. In the resultant press uproar Leonard and Virginia Woolf were amongst those who came out on the side of frankness and freedom from censorship. They contributed money as bail for their fellow publisher. They wrote or added their signatures to letters; and in the muddle that almost always accompanies such joint efforts it appeared, Virginia told Vita, "that I write letters from the Reform Club!" This was a very far cry from the days of the *Dreadnought* hoax and would not have amused any of the elderly Stephen relatives who were so insistent at the time that, at all costs, Virginia's name must be kept out of the scandal.

When the case came to court many of the most famous writers of the day appeared to testify that in their expert opinion the book was serious, dignified and admirable. But the magistrate, Sir Chartres Biron (a name that seems to go rocketing and reverberating back to the Norman Conquest) knew his own mind and spoke it as clearly as any eleventh-century Roger Bigod enforcing law in the wild Welsh marches. He ruled their testimony out of order, and the novel was suppressed.

A little later the manuscript of some poems by D. H. Lawrence was seized in the mail by the police. Leonard Woolf immediately went to work organizing a protest against this action. "Nothing will be safe," wrote Virginia to Vita, "not even this letter."

The hunt was up. Another novel, *Sleeveless Errand*, was seized by the police. Virginia had read it and rejected it for the Hogarth Press. "But nothing in it to raise a hair," she assured Vita. "What's to be done with Morality in England? If Harold would do a man's work here, instead of a flunkey's in Berlin — but hush, hush. 'My Harold!' Isn't that what you'd say?"

This was part of the campaign she carried on to induce the Nicolsons to plan their lives according to her wishes. It was partly serious — not like her teasing of T. S. Eliot by telling him that if he'd only stayed in banking instead of becoming a poet he might have been a manager — but always expressed in this playful manner. She would not say another word; Harold's own good sense would tell him what was right. His letter enchanted her, "but shows a guilty conscience. He is ashamed of being an Ambassador. I am ashamed that any friend of mine should be married to a man who may be an Ambassador. Better be a footman — no, no, this must be written to Harold himself." He ought, in her opinion, to stay in England, write books and share in Leonard's political work. "Look here, Vita, you must wring Harold's neck, if the worst comes to the worst. You have my sanction. A dead diplomat on a dust heap. You shan't spend your entire life, or even the Marchs and Aprils of your life, in being polite in the provinces; pouring out tea; putting on emeralds. No, no, you shan't."

So long as they were only a county, not a continent, apart, it was all right, even if they were too busy to see one another often. "Yes, it does seem hard that we should make you spend all the fine weather with your nose to the pen. But I think of your glory and our profit, which is becoming a necessary matter, now that your puppy has destroyed, by eating holes, my skirt, Leonard's proofs, and done such damage as could be done to the carpet. But she is an angel of light. Leonard says seriously that she makes him believe in God, and this after she has wetted his floor eight times in one day."

Before long the puppy, Pinker, was having puppies of her own and was "a model of all the maternal vices — absorbed, devoted, jealous, cowish." The fears about morality on the one hand and censorship on the other subsided. Harold did in due course resign from the Foreign Office and take to politics and journalism, much to Virginia's delight, but while he was still in diplomacy, Vita and Virginia managed to get a week together in

Burgundy at the end of September 1928. Virginia planned the
itinerary in a very businesslike way, but imagined the trip romantically. She would prefer to travel second class, unless first
was much more comfortable, "because first-class travellers are always old, fat, testy, and smell of *eau de cologne,* which makes
me sick. . . . Being now in the pink and prime of health, I could
sit up all night. We might go to moonlight ruins, cafés, dances,
plays, junketings; converse for ever; sleep only while the moon
covers herself for an instant with a veil; and by day traipse the
vineyards."

It did not turn out exactly like this, but very close to it, as
described by Vita in an article in *Horizon* (May 1941). "She was
as excited as a schoolgirl on arriving in Paris. We went out after
dinner and found a bookseller's shop open, and she perched on
a stool and talked to the old bookseller about Proust. Next day
we went south to Burgundy. There she forgot all about Proust in
the simple enjoyment of the things we found. A fair in a French
village, roundabouts, shooting galleries, lions and gipsies giving a
performance together, stalls with things to buy; all was sheer fun.
We bought knives and green corduroy coats with buttons representing hares, pheasants, partridges. They were said to be game-
keepers' coats, but Virginia preferred to think they were poach-
ers'. The poacher would naturally be dearer to her mind than
the keeper."

But what Vita remembers most vividly is one night "when a
superb thunderstorm broke over Vezelay and we sat in darkness
while the flashes intermittently lit up her face. She was, I think,
a little frightened, and perhaps that drove her to speak, with a
deeper seriousness than I had ever heard her use before, of immortality and personal survival after death."

The occasion left an indelible imprint on her friend's mind.
She spoke about it to the present writer not as something to be
recalled with exactitude but to have been lived through as an
experience, a revelation both intimate and beautiful and, at the
same time, terrifying. She referred to it again in her review of

the diary in *Encounter* (January 1954) under the apt title, "The Landscape of a Mind." A phrase in the diary about a nightmare sense of things being generally wrong in the universe recalled, with painful conviction, moments when "physical fear released the founts of spiritual horror."

Had these founts been sealed too soon, so that when the black waters welled up there were no channels through which they could flow? Had too rigid a rationality been imposed, too stern a stoicism presented as the ideal, at too early an age? If the discarding of ancient beliefs had been a voluntary part of the challenge to convention which is normal to youth's struggle towards maturity, might not the terror have been allayed, the sense of guilt have lost its paralyzing power?

Such questions are as inescapable as they are unanswerable. If Mr. Ramsay had not insisted "We perish, each alone," if Mrs. Ramsay had not knitted with firm composure, Virginia Woolf would not have had the courage and obstinacy needed to fight ill-health and overcome the disadvantages of her privileges. She would have known neither the ecstasy nor the anguish of the artist-thinker compelled to seek the final truth that always evades, the absolute beauty that forever flies. She would not have been herself: a mystic without a religion, a philosopher without a system, a woman divided against herself, desiring but never achieving an unattainable unity.

She rested now, briefly, on the sunny upper slopes of her mountain. She seemed secure. But she knew that it was already afternoon. Renewed effort might take her to the summit. But then came the descent, and those recurrent fits of vertigo, when it would seem that shadows from the valley of death would leap up and drag her down. She would fight them to the last, but they would become more menacing and more alluring. Their victory was inevitable. Twenty more years, perhaps. But so much to be done in whatever span of fast-shrinking time might remain before the tempting peace could be fairly earned, bringing its own revelation and reward. A new illusion? A new adventure? Something positive, though inexplicable. Or a negation so complete that it conquered everything? But, in the meantime, she must press on. "It is life that matters."

Chapter XVI

I BELIEVE that the main thing in beginning a novel is to feel, not that you can write it, but that it exists on the far side of a gulf, which words can't cross; that it's to be pulled through only in a breathless anguish. . . . A novel, to be good, should seem, before one writes it, something unwriteable; but only visible; so that for nine months one lives in despair, and only when one has forgotten what one meant, does the book seem tolerable. I assure you all my novels were first-rate before they were written. If I felt I could write them easily, then I should know they were plausible and ephemeral — as indeed Mr. Swinnerton says they are."

So wrote Virginia to Vita when the book which would eventually be *The Waves* was hovering at the back of her brain, but she was postponing any start on it until she could come to terms with the "mystical feelings" she refers to in the diary. For this was the abstract, poetical work she had promised herself to do after the escapade of *Orlando*. This was the "eyeless book; a playpoem." This was the "fin passing far out, in a waste of waters," she had glimpsed more than two years before, and it refused for a long time to be netted.

It is the most complex of her books, the most complete expression of her art, the work which admirers consider to be proof of her genius, and which adverse critics point to as the supreme example of artificiality and unreadability.

There can be no question that it is as difficult for the reader to understand as it was for the author to write. It went through the most extraordinary changes in her mind. For a long while she saw its title as *The Moths,* and yet it was "an angular shape." It might be called an autobiography, but it must not be about her own childhood. She did not know how to begin it, felt no fever of inspiration but only a nagging pressure. Sometimes *The Moths* would come unbidden; sometimes she could only go "blundering on" because it was not in her head all day long as *To the Lighthouse* and *Orlando* had been. She even thought that perhaps six weeks' illness might turn it into a masterpiece.

But illnesses and interruptions never came at the right time. For a while she could hardly stop writing and then she was willing to bargain with fate for just a little illness — not a real first-class headache, a mere two weeks in bed. So it went on, in fits and starts, for nearly two years, until she could record the last exacerbations and the final intensity when, having "reeled across the last ten pages" almost as if intoxicated, she seemed only to stumble after her own voice, and could relax for a quarter of an hour in a "state of glory, and calm, and some tears."

Naturally a book that was so intractable in the making is not one that suggests itself as an easy introduction to the work of Virginia Woolf. The casual reader will undoubtedly be puzzled, baffled, irritated, and will soon give up the attempt to discover what it is all about. Who are these people? such a reader may well ask. What is supposed to be going on? Give me a good, old-fashioned story that I can make head or tail of, something I can get my teeth into or gulp down in a hurry.

But if the stranger to her work happens to be a poet (whether he is aware of it or not, and many people who regard themselves as sternly practical have a poet lurking somewhere in them), he will know at once that this book is a poem, except that it is written in prose. He will have no difficulty reading it in the subway; his trouble will be in coming back to the workaday world in time to get off the train at the right station.

It is possible to read *The Waves* many times and still not be able to give a coherent summary of its contents. It is not possible to open it at any page and read any paragraph without feeling the excitement of discovering some new beauty.

But though it adds greatly to our appreciation of Virginia Woolf as an artist, it tells us very little about her as a woman. It is a writer's book, not a human document; it yields richer material to the critic than to the biographer. Here are the same thoughts, the same symbols; only the technique of presenting them has changed. The sharp imagery of *Jacob's Room*, the glittering colors and changing rhythms of *Mrs. Dalloway* have gone; so have the pliability of the prose in *To the Lighthouse*, the extreme fluidity of *Orlando*, the neat sequences of *A Room of One's Own*. Here everything is rigid. The waves do not tumble softly on a sandy shore; they tower, frozen for awful instants, before they crash. The Ancient Mariner is not a beggar mumbling a meandering and moral tale, but a haggard stranger from another world, whose hollow eye and bony hand cannot be escaped. And yet the book is not terrifying, only exalting. Wild and strange, but solid and secure; no romantic ruin.

The basic design is simple, its working out is intricate. There are six characters, whom we first meet as children when they are together one summer in a country house. Each character has a name and an introductory tag (a solid object, a color, a sound, some childish perception) which will recur and by which they can be recognized and differentiated as, in turn, they speak. But they all use the same voice, and they never speak to one another. We learn of their actions, their thoughts, their relationships, as we follow their fortunes. Their faces are masks, so that their souls may be revealed in a series of monologues. There is no plot, no action, in the usual sense. The passing of time is indicated by short descriptions (printed in italics) of sea and sky from dawn to dark, the human life span thus linked to one day.

The boys, Bernard, Louis and Neville, and the girls, Susan,

Jinny and Rhoda, separate to go to school, and then to college, to business or to their homes. They meet in a London restaurant to say farewell to a seventh character, Percival, who is leaving for India. But Percival never speaks. All our knowledge of him is gained from the voice that uses the unmoving lips and un-blinking eyes of the six masks.

Percival dies, killed by a fall from a horse in India. His friends receive the news in different places, for their paths have crisscrossed and diverged many times. They come together again, at Hampton Court, to share their sorrow and relate their various stories.

Finally, in the deepening dark, sun and sky indistinguish-able now as they had been at daybreak, Bernard is alone, with his memories, to sum up the meaning of their lives before the London restaurant closes and he, the elderly man, has to go through the swing-door and catch his last train home.

Who are these people? The calm Susan, who loves the coun-try, marries a farmer and knows natural happiness? The bold Jinny, who dances or sits on a gilt chair to be admired in her fine and fashionable clothes? The timid Rhoda, who tries hard to conform, who has "covered the whole street, Oxford Street, Piccadilly Circus with vine leaves and rose leaves," and kills herself in Spain? Louis, who is successful in business, owns ships, and reads poetry in secret? Neville, who is delicate, a lonely scholar? Bernard, who makes phrases, tells stories, can interpret and reason and also feel?

Fleeting likenesses have suggested, to those who knew Virginia Woolf's immediate circle, possible models who may have con-tributed an outstanding feature or an odd foible to these figures. Bernard (who is perhaps partly Desmond MacCarthy, or per-haps Roger Fry) gives in his final, long soliloquy an answer that is more helpful to understanding and appreciating the book. "Who am I?" he asks. "Am I all of them? Am I one and dis-tinct? I do not know. . . . As I talked I felt, 'I am you.' This difference we make so much of, this identity we so feverishly cherish, was overcome." They are, it appears, different aspects of one character. They suffer in their separateness, only achieve reality when united in Percival.

Who, then, is Percival? As we ask this question we seem to be in a vast, empty cathedral. Light falls on worn flagstones from stained-glass windows which show the rigid forms, constructed of translucent splinters and leaden lines, of saints performing miracles, martyrs bearing the symbols of their pains and triumphs. Grinning or seductive faces are carved on the choir stalls. Exotic marble leaves entwine the pillars. Forgotten jokes and generosities tie ornamental knots in the dimness of the vaulted ceiling. Votive offerings are displayed — Jinny's crimson tassel with the gold thread, the fancy cane that Louis carried, an illuminated manuscript from Bernard, Neville's hanging globe. But where is Percival? Only in the great window, in geometric grandeur, is traced and lost and found again the glory of the Mystic Rose.

Whence came the inspiration for this ideal figure, the Whole Man, the Ordinary Man made perfect, the all-containing, incomprehensible Norm, the great Unifier, the Beloved, made safe by death from time's corruption? The answer is undoubtedly Thoby Stephen, Virginia's elder brother, who had died, senselessly, of typhoid fever in 1906, in his twenty-fifth year, his brilliant promises unfulfilled. He had replaced her father as a guide, without exercising her father's feared domination. Something of him had gone into the making of Jacob Flanders. But in *The Waves* his sister tries to give no portrait, only to convey an essence.

When she was at a low ebb in 1929, feeling the premonitions of this book but postponing the writing of it, she recalled how she had been "engaged with her anguish" after his death. She was thinking of him again as she wrote the final words, wondering if she dared put his name on the first page, and deciding not to make this intensely intimate disclosure. She had said what she had to say, and shrank from the thought of exposing herself to idle questioning.

Death is at the heart of *The Waves,* but she will not accord it the victory. Each of Percival's friends is stricken by the news of his fatal accident; each sinks briefly in unbearable emotion, but rises again to resume life's burdens and to accept its consolations. Bernard, the most articulate of them all, indulges in an orgy of suffering and protest against the brutality of fate, and then says: "But I can no longer endure extremities; I want someone with whom to laugh, with whom to yawn, with whom to remember how he scratched his head." So Virginia had noted in her diary years before, Leigh Hunt and Byron, going home after the burning of Shelley's drowned body, had "laughed till they split. This is human nature, and H. doesn't mind owning to it." So too, hearing at a party of a dear friend's death, she wrote: "I do not any longer feel inclined to doff the cap to death. . . . No leave-takings, no submission." And into Bernard's mouth she puts the final defiant words: "Against you I will fling myself, unvanquished and unyielding, O Death!" But not quite the last words. The book ends with this enigmatic sentence, in italics: *"The waves broke on the shore."*

Some readers have taken this to mean that Bernard goes through the swing-door to his doom. Others remember only the magnificent courage of his challenge, hearing Virginia Woolf's proud reiteration, "It's life that matters."

To HER surprise the book was a success. When the last re-re-retyping was done she gave the pages to her husband and waited for his verdict. "I shall be nervous to hear what L. says when he comes out, say tomorrow night or Sunday morning, to my garden room, carrying the MS and sits himself down and begins: 'Well!'"

He said it was a masterpiece, her best, though admittedly difficult for the common reader to follow. The relief she felt on receiving this honest praise was so great that she "stumped off in the rain," and was almost resigned to the fact that a goat farm and a house were being built on a slope of the downs near Rodmell.

Friends shared her husband's opinion. Winifred Holtby, who did not claim to be an intimate but who had been engaged for nearly two years on a study of her work, with the sole instruction that she should treat the subject "with the candor and impartiality applied by critics to the writings of the dead," thought that *The Waves* was a poem, and even more subtle and profound than *To the Lighthouse*. Harold Nicolson, by this time active in politics on the rebel left of the Labor Party, not only wrote about it in Sir Oswald Mosley's journal, *Action*, but made her tremble with pleasure by telephoning enthusiastically. "Ah Hah — so it wasn't all wasted then," she wrote in her diary. "I mean this vision I had here has some force upon other minds." E. M. Forster wrote that he must reread it before expressing himself about a work which he felt to be so important that it aroused in him the kind of excitement which comes from encountering a classic.

Press notices were excellent, too. The "dear old *Lit. Sup.*" twinkled and beamed, and for the first time the London *Times* itself gave her an honorable mention but surprised her by praising her characters when she had meant to have none. Provincial reviewers, who, since they were unknown to her, could not be suspected of partiality, found the book exciting. "And it sells — how unexpected, how odd that people can read that difficult, grinding stuff!" she notes. "I am in danger, indeed, of becoming our leading novelist, and not with the highbrows only."

She had, she thought, after long toil perhaps reached a beginning, might at last be "about to embody the exact shapes my brain holds." Given another ten or twenty years of life she might really do something worth while. At the moment she was carefully avoiding Roger Fry and Lytton Strachey, in case they did not approve. Strange mixture of humility and vanity, of detachment and egotism. As she told Vita, "I boast because I am modest."

Her tank was swarming with fish. A second series of articles needed to be collected for another *Common Reader* volume. A successor to *A Room of One's Own* was clamoring to be caught, something calling itself "Here and Now" or "A Knock on the Door," but eventually to be known as *Three Guineas*. Even more urgent for attention was another funny fellow, rather like *Orlando;* another biography, this time of a dog, Elizabeth Barrett Browning's spaniel, *Flush*. And lurking in the depths was something "about shopkeepers, and publicans, and low life scenes," very dim as yet but possibly the book that would become, after many changes, *The Years*.

She set to work immediately on *Flush*, "that foolish, witless joke with which I solaced myself when I was all a-gasp after having done *The Waves*," she told Vita. But the sudden change of theme and style proved to be a mistake. It was a book she never really liked, never gave a kind word to, either in her diary or in her letters. "That abominable dog," "that odious creature," "that silly book," "that waste of time," — such expressions show how she felt. Her hope was to recapture the spirit of *Orlando*, to kick up her heels once more after the strenuous effort of the serious, abstract, poetical work, but the attempt was, from her point of view, a failure. She would have abandoned it, had not Leonard thought that would be a pity, considering the work she had put into it. So she persevered and finally "despatched that stupid animal."

The spaniel which told the love story of a poet and a poetess and accompanied them on their romantic elopement became hugely popular. This further irritated Virginia, because it brought her the kind of praise she did not value. "Charming," said the public. "A piece of nonsense," said the novelist. Fortunately Vita, at least, understood that even if she did make silly jokes she was a serious writer. "That was very nice of you," Virginia wrote after a broadcast. "Pinker and I sat erect, blushing, as our praises poured forth. You soothed my vanity — there are people who say I am vain — did you know it? Anyhow, you said what I most wanted — not that I am an enchanting gossip, but that my standard is high. I loathe being called enchanting."

Fundamentally she was ashamed of the book because it was really an evasion. Elizabeth Barrett offered a great opportunity, but Virginia did not succeed in digging the truth out of her at all costs. The rugs on her invalid couch could not be snatched off by a pet dog; the curtains at the Wimpole Street window remained obstinately drawn against the light. The jealous spaniel disliked the gentleman with the yellow gloves who called so often and stayed so long; and the feeling, one strongly suspects, was shared by Virginia Woolf.

She wanted to tell the story of the woman who was motherless, mourned a dead brother, suffered from an undiagnosed illness, was inadequately educated for her intelligence and ambition, and longed to escape from the domination of an adored father. But Virginia had finished with the subject of the Victorian father. Lytton Strachey could deal with "dearest Papa" if he wished, but Virginia found him boring. Certainly Mr. Browning was a vast improvement on Mr. Barrett, but no — Virginia could not love him as Elizabeth did. And yet one ought, one really ought, if one had time and energy enough, to find the story that was smothered in those love letters, to find the real woman who floundered about in the nine volumes of blank verse comprising *Aurora Leigh*. But Flush could not be expected to do it; and, since Virginia had chosen his lowly vantage point among the shawls on the sofa, she could not do it either.

Flush's own story was distressing, too. The account of his kidnaping was very painful to relate. Three times, in fact, he was seized, crammed into a sack and starved in a cellar in Whitechapel until he could be "found" and ransomed, but Virginia compressed the three horrible events into one. It pained her to describe the spectacle of human callousness revealed by her research into this infamous trade in the pets of the well-to-do by the half-starved inhabitants of London's East End. It was fascinating to think of the lives of ants lost in a jungle of grass at Kew: it was horrible to think of human beings so brutalized by poverty that they eked out a living by exploiting the feelings of tenderhearted animal lovers and were ruthlessly indifferent to the animals they stole and then resold to their owners. No wonder Virginia did not relish being told that her story was enchanting. It is. But to her it remained trivial, superficial, basically false, a misuse of her talents.

Before she could dispose of this unsatisfactory shrimp, quite another sort of creature from her tank had to be netted. She had to clear up an argument. The younger generation was knocking at the door. She, the challenger, was being challenged, and on her own ground. The critic was being criticized, the innovator was finding something new and strange and hard to accept or fully understand. Hence she had to write *A Letter to a Young Poet.*

This pamphlet, reprinted later in *The Death of the Moth,* was one of the brilliant series of Hogarth Letters, which ranged over a wide diversity of topics discussed by different writers and included, amongst other items, a charming and poignant essay by E. M. Forster about a little black prince who was brought from Africa to England and died of tuberculosis in the eighteenth century, a serious talk to a member of parliament by Viscount Cecil on disarmament, and a passionate plea by Raymond Mortimer to a young woman to stop being alarmed by French paintings and to look at them and enjoy them instead. All the questions raised are, though with different connotations, still being talked about today. Virginia Woolf's own contribution to the series was actually continued in another essay, "The Leaning Tower," written in 1940 and reprinted in *The Moment.* Both continue to be relevant because the subject is, roughly, what ought the writer who is alive to what is going on in his world to write about, what is his raw material, and how is he to use it?

The "Dear John" to whom this letter was addressed was John Lehmann, who joined the staff of the Hogarth Press as manager in 1931, but she had other young poets in her mind as she wrote. Quite a number of them were flocking around her. They came to adore and stayed, in that encouraging atmosphere, to criticize. She liked them all. As she told Vita after getting to know one of them, William Plomer, "I'm completely bored by speculating as to poets' merits. Nobody is better than anybody else. I like people — I don't bother my head about their work. But this is my gray and grizzled wisdom. At his age I wanted to be myself." Nevertheless it was important to her to find out from their poems and their talk what they were doing, what, in their opinion, was wrong with the world and with her generation's attitude, and why, led by her nephew Julian, they assailed her for not having enough "social content" in her writing. She was becoming more and more interested in politics, both national and international, more and more aware of the threat of another war, more and more concerned to understand simple people and to grasp underlying fundamental forces. Why then did she not always find herself in agreement with the young people she so much admired?

They were right, she said, about the difficulty of conveying exactly what they felt, but wrong to despair. Catching the truth in words never had been easy, and was never likely to be. But, she advised, "Never think yourself singular, never think your own case much harder than other people's." The young poet must learn to know himself, but he should realize that in him live all the poets of the past. "For which reason please treat yourself with respect and think twice before you dress up as Guy Fawkes and spring out upon timid old ladies at street corners, threatening death and demanding twopence-halfpenny."

He should not be solemn and serious and infuriated because

his Mrs. Gape, the charwoman, insists upon attention but, like her Mrs. Brown, will not be coerced or paraded. What Virginia desired was the intuitive approach and the lyrical expression. The poet should look out of his window and let his rhythmical sense "open and shut, boldly and freely, until one thing melts in another, until the taxis are dancing with the daffodils."

She gave excellent generalized advice, wittily expressed, but the arguments between her and the young writers were not conclusive. Mrs. Gape was, John Lehmann explains in his *Pages from an Autobiography,* a fantasy from her world and represented no satisfactory symbol in his. Virginia had invented her because she still loved the "jolly old fishwives" she had described long ago in "The String Quartet": "How deeply they laugh and shake and rollick, when they walk, from side to side, hum, hah!"

She warned the young men, finally, against the allurements of fame: "the disciples and the admirers, the autograph hunters and the interviewers, the dinners and the luncheons, the celebrations and the commemorations with which English society so effectively stops the mouths of its singers and silences their songs." As she observed in "The Niece of An Earl" (*The Common Reader, II*), "Unfortunately literary success invariably means a rise, never a fall, and seldom, what is far more desirable, a spread in the social scale. The rising novelist is never pestered to come to gin and winkles with the plumber and his wife. His books never bring him into touch with the cats'-meat man, or start a correspondence with the old lady who sells matches and bootlaces by the gate of the British Museum. He becomes rich; he becomes respectable; he buys an evening suit and dines with peers."

This was a cry from the heart, for she was finding it difficult to cope with the inconveniences and interruptions of being on a pinnacle. It was, she said, using a current English colloquialism, "something chronic." She liked the experience she described to Vita of going into a confectioner's at Hampstead and being

asked if she was the Miss Stephen they used to serve twenty
years ago. That gave her a good feeling and added to the flavor
of the buns she bought for tea. But when it leaked out that
Manchester University wished to confer upon her the honorary
degree of Doctor of Letters, she shrank in horror at the thought.
"Nothing would induce me to connive at all that humbug," she
declared in her diary. She was dumbfounded that her socialist
friends drew a distinction between accepting a degree from a
university and an honor from the state. Only her sister Vanessa
agreed with her; the rest of the company made her feel "a little
silly, priggish and perhaps extreme; but only superficially." The
ironical part of this incident was that she had that day just
made a character, who would eventually be Eleanor Pargiter in
The Years, declare passionately that it was an utterly corrupt
society and she would have nothing to do with it. Now she
would have to express the refusal in her own name and in polite language.

The same fierce rejection runs all through *Three Guineas,*
where the vehemence of her scorn for the pageantry and ceremonial with which men continue to disguise the true nature of
ruthless forces and debased customs knows no bounds. In this
book she overstates the feminist case in a way that was not possible to her when she wrote, with equal ardor and conviction
but with more restraint and benignity, *A Room of One's Own.*
But the later book was written when tensions, within herself and
in the world situation, were building up to a climax. At the
time of the earlier book she could record with appreciation the
chuckle with which Sidney Webb confided: "My little boy shall
have his toys — that's what my wife says about my being in the
Cabinet." It is impossible to know whether she could at any
time have faced with equanimity the prospect of Leonard
Woolf's accepting a peerage in order to put the case for the
Labor Party in the House of Lords. Perhaps it would have
amused her, as it amused Beatrice Webb to continue to be
known as Mrs. Webb and to give as her authority for some state-

ment "the gentleman who consents to use the incredible name of Lord Passfield." Virginia Woolf would have remained Mrs. Woolf in any event.

She felt almost as strongly about accepting presents, as she frequently reminded Vita. "May I say once for all, presents are not allowed. This once will be forgiven: but never again." "I said LEND, not GIVE." "If you give me so much as a sixpenny mug from Woolworth's, I never speak to you again."

Of course, if it was Christmas time, and the present happened to be food — well! "It's not due to you that I'm alive today: I've eaten the whole pie practically myself! Heaven above, what immortal geese must have gone to make it! It was fresh as a dockleaf, pink as mushroom, pure as first love. My word, what a pie! Tom Eliot was dining with us the night it came. Complete silence reigned. The poet ate; the novelist ate; even Leonard, who had a chill inside, ate. Nothing of the least importance was said. And then the collar arrived. Out I trotted, with Virginia blazoned on my neck. Many people escorted me; others took the view that there was something sacred, like a text from the Bible, about a woman with a name on her; others — Oh, did I tell you I'd been offered an Order? I forgot — they thought I'd come from Buckingham Palace. A kind of Order of Merit. . . . But, Orlando, isn't it against our covenant to do this sort of thing? Don't you remember offering me Thackeray's wine cooler or ash tray or something, and how I said: Unhand me, sirrah?"

These two assertions of independence had different origins. Receiving presents, except on very special occasions, was apt to be embarrassing if she could not afford to be as freehanded in return — a miserable attitude to friendship, she knew, and therefore all the more irritating. A piece of gossip, a fragment of a life story, that sort of thing was delightful; but tangible gifts were forbidden to dangerous animals. "It's written all over the cage. It spoils their tempers. They suffer for it in the long run." Her inherited income, being fixed, shrank in value as prices and taxation increased. Her earned income might be comfortingly large one year — as much as £3020 in 1930 — very little another year and nothing at all the next. Then the private hoard set aside during the good years would be drawn upon, articles would be written (though she hated writing for money) and all expenses closely figured out. "I wish my cheque (for the Foundlings) had been larger," she wrote to Vita in 1936. "At the moment I am rather cheeseparing as I have earned so little this year. However, I'm getting along at last. I daresay next year I shall have no excuse for stinginess. But oh Lord, the number of letters that come (not so much to the point as yours) about the imprisoned, the insulted, the injured, the builders, the pullers down — all wanting money, poor devils."

She was not ungenerous. After the offers were made for *Orlando* she realized that her manuscripts had a definite marketable value, usually far higher than she guessed — she doubted very much that *Flush* was worth the £1000 she was assured it would fetch — but she would not sell her original copies for herself. She gave the manuscript of *A Room of One's Own* to the Women's Service Club when they were in financial difficulties, and asked Vita to help her find a collector in the United States who would buy it from them. This was a far more substantial donation to the support of the club than any amount of money she could ever have afforded to send them. She also played tricks about presents. Vita has on her shelves a handsomely bound volume which arrived with a note saying, "This is by far my best book." Eager to know what it could be, Vita opened it and found every page was completely blank. She wrote at once — some horrible mistake had been made by the binders — and Virginia had to apologize for "just another of my silly jokes."

The rejection of honors was part of her all-or-nothing, perfectionist attitude. It arose not from caring too little but from caring too much, not from indifference but from anger. The letters soliciting contributions for all manner of worthy objects formed her text for *Three Guineas*. This book is often dismissed as some kind of aberration. The fact is that it stirs a deep uneasiness in the reader. Its sixty-seven pages of notes and references are almost unbearably painful. Times have changed, one says; this statement is not true of every country; this argument is misleading because the emphasis is too great and the deduction therefore false; this bias gives the opponent an obvious chance for a crushing reply; this is too minor a point to worry about in this day and age; and so on. In other words, do not ask me to look on this distressing spectacle of a sensitive woman who passionately desires peace and is almost in despair in a world rushing towards war. Above all, do not force me to feel, as I read her protests against being patronized and denied full responsibility, how she must have suffered!

She knew her friends wouldn't approve. "Of course I knew you wouldn't like 3 gns.," she wrote to Vita. "That's why I wouldn't, unless you had sent me a postcard with a question, have given it you. You say you don't agree with 50% of it. No, of course you don't. . . . It may be a silly book — I don't agree that it's a well-written book, but it's certainly an honest book; and I took more pains to get up the facts and state them plainly than I ever took with anything in my life. . . . But oh Lord, how sick I get of all the talk about 'lovely prose' and charm, when all I wanted was to state a very intricate case as plainly and readably as I could."

But, although it might become necessary to have the matter out, "whether with swords or fisticuffs, and I don't think, whichever we use, you will knock me down," personal arguments seldom became heated. Political discussions of all kinds raged. Harold Nicolson quickly saw where Sir Oswald Mosley's fanaticism and ambition were leading. He became a Labor M. P. In the financial crisis, when Britain was forced off the gold standard, he followed the leadership of Ramsay MacDonald, supported the National Coalition and, like Keynes, preferred to call himself a Liberal. He became a journalist on the *Daily Express* and *Evening Standard,* both papers which were strongly, though erratically, Tory in politics but which were owned by

Lord Beaverbrook, who cared only to employ the best brains and did not in the least mind being personally caricatured and having his pet theories exposed to brilliant ridicule in his own pages by the cartoonist David Low.

None of these political ins and outs made any difference to the friendship between the Woolfs and the Nicolsons. Honesty and frankness were still valued by them more than conformity and agreement. Virginia went to Labor Party conferences with Leonard and accompanied him on electioneering as she did on bookselling tours of the country. "I heard you were canvassing in Leicester," she wrote to Vita. "I have to walk Brighton Pier for four hours while Leonard takes voters to the polls." In public she took little part in discussions; in private she supported her husband. There is a passage in *To the Lighthouse* describing Mrs. Ramsay, whose mind has been wandering during a dinner-table talk that does not deeply interest her, suddenly realizing that the topic has switched to the lives and wages of fishermen, and immediately she becomes alert because this is a subject Mr. Ramsay really knows and cares about. She admires him; she beams on her guests, for they must be admiring him too; she bathes everyone in her love because her husband is so wholly, unmistakably wonderful. Virginia may have seen such an expression on her mother's face when she felt she could legitimately be proud of her father. Her friends say they have often seen it on hers when Leonard was talking.

It was not passive, persistent adoration, but rather as though they were sharing a curtain call and the gallantries between the leading lady and the great actor expressed a genuine emotion. In every respect but the power to evoke feelings amounting to reverence, few men could have been more unlike than Virginia's husband and her father, few households more dissimilar than those at Tavistock Square and at Hyde Park Gate.

Mingled with the admiration and respect on both sides was a good deal of amusement. If Virginia wanted to come in on the political game, Leonard did not mind her taking the ball. One wintry day when they were visiting the Webbs, "I was launched on a six-mile walk on a cold common on a rainy morning with Sidney Webb. All my sentences leapt into the middle of the pond without a moment's reflection. Passing by a beastly pool of self-conscious beauty — Surrey is detestable — Webb said one must remember what a difference Mohammedanism had made to the negroes in Sierra Leone; whereupon, without a second, I played: made some dreadful howlers, Leonard said." No doubt, since Leonard Woolf was an expert on colonialism, Sidney Webb was crammed to bursting with facts and figures, while her knowledge of Negroes and Sierra Leone and Islam was based on old books of memoirs, travelers' tales, and the *Arabian Nights*. But what did it matter: she earned her lunch that day.

She liked to pretend that Leonard was in charge of the pets department, and that she merely took them to the veterinary or went into Lewes to buy special puppy food. Leonard was, according to her, on much closer terms with them. Mitzi, the marmoset which often went with them overseas because quarantine regulations presented fewer difficulties than finding her a really comfortable home while they were away, was perfectly well, she reported to Vita. "She sends her love. We didn't bring her because she had been feeling the cold, so L. said. She confides all symptoms to him. Today she has eaten forty worms and turned head over heels." But her letters are peppered with references to them, even if they are only curled up in an armchair and snoring. There was one dreadful day when a dog escaped her vigilance and wandered alone in the square. How she was to face Leonard and tell him the awful truth when he came home that evening, she could not think. However, the dog was aged about sixty, in terms of human life, so perhaps there would be no mongrel puppies to be explained away later. Did Vita, who knew about such things, think she ought to confess? It was bad enough that, trying to catch the delinquent animal, she had slipped, sprained a finger and scratched the tip of her nose, and that would not pass unobserved.

On another occasion she caught eczema from a dog who had the mange and whose rainbow-striped back she had been anointing. Her hair was coming out in tufts and she scratched incessantly. Vita must not come to see her. It wouldn't be safe for Vita, or, "what matters more," Vita's puppies. Then she had a tooth stopped, and she was all boils and blisters again. "When I say to the dentist, why do you do this to me? he replies, But then, Mrs. W., your skin is the most sensitive in London, at which I am flattered. But Leonard paints my skin with ointment, which I lick, and I daresay it's poison — I shall be dead. — Here's Tom Eliot ringing up."

Leonard did his utmost to guard her against herself. If she was to be away overnight she would take a little note from him to her hostess with instructions about how to care for "this valuable animal out of my menagerie." She was to be well fed and put to bed punctually at eleven o'clock. No talking after that, and no attention to be paid to anything she might try to say for herself about these orders.

After a visit to Berlin, fatigue combined with a chill and less than half the usual dose prescribed to ward off seasickness put her to bed for nearly six weeks. "Leonard is a perfect angel," she wrote to the anxious Vita when she was gradually recovering, "only more to the point than most angels. He sits on the edge of the bed and considers my symptoms like a judge. He brings home huge pineapples. He moves the gramophone into my room and plays until he thinks I'm excited. In short, I should have shot myself long ago in one of these illnesses if it had not been for him."

She regarded her physical symptoms with unusual detachment. After all, what was an illness but something that "must be let to wander about one's body like a policeman trying bolts." The doctor came, with a lovely silver stethoscope, and said there was nothing wrong with her heart except something about systolic action, which was only the latest name for an intermittent pulse. And then she had to listen to "the usual lecture about resting and never being tired and never sitting up late and never seeing too many people and never catching any single illness so long as I live. So this illness is over." But what did doctors really know, anyway? Now, if they could fix up some suitable exchange, say, her ridiculous nervous system for Hugh Walpole's diabetes, which was nothing but a simple matter of not eating sugar, she'd be more than willing, since she had the digestion of an ostrich and found that eating a chop was an excellent cure for nausea.

Her complaint about illnesses was that they never came at the right time and that they prevented her from working, and then she was unhappy. Then "I see my own worthlessness and failure so clearly; and lie gazing into the depths of the misery of human life." She had a sense of lying at the bottom of some sea, while far above her friends were going about their business as usual. She had many sharp and often ludicrous images to describe what seemed to be happening in her body, but the symbol of the sea appears repeatedly when she speaks of her mental condition. "These headaches leave one like sand which a wave has uncovered. I believe they have a mystic purpose. Indeed, I am not sure that there is not some religious cause at the back of them . . . and then one gets up and everything begins again and it is all covered over. . . . Leonard and Percy are measuring the tank with a vast tape. I must go and see what it's all about."

Shortly after this, when she was completely well and very active, she had forgotten about religion and worthlessness. It had been a good year financially and additions were to be made to Monk's House. The men were fuming to begin building, so after the Labor Party conference she would return to London "and answer the telephone as usual. I have only one passion in life — cooking. I have just bought a superb oil stove. I can cook anything. I'm free for ever of cooks. I cooked veal cutlets and cake today. I assure you it's better than writing these more than idiotic books."

Chapter XVII

SO IT WENT on throughout her life, a perpetual change from
grave to gay, from serious thought to wild exaggeration. Life
was glorious because she had seen a kingfisher over the marshes
or two of her nieces had arrived unexpectedly, the fifteen-ton
yacht which they manned having been blown into Newhaven by
a gale, and oh, how she loved this youngest and freest generation. Life was almost impossible at Rodmell because the down
above the village was, in spite of protests, to be built upon. "I'm
in such a rage — a serious rage that caught me by the throat
and constricted my heart. It's all ruined for ever and ever. I
don't see any point in living here in a suburb of Brighton. I
don't suppose there's any pleasure in my life like walking alone
in the country: no, I'm not exaggerating. My God, Vita, I wish
one hadn't picked this age to live in: I hate my kind."

She had hoped the amenities could be preserved, since, for
more than a year, so much thought and work had gone into suggesting different plans for developing the area. It was no good.
On April 1, 1932 ("April Fool's Day: and I was had completely by Leonard"), she cried out again that her happiness at
Rodmell was almost entirely ruined. "You can't think what horrors — vast galvanized iron sheds, three of them, about the size
of the Albert Hall — aren't rising right in the middle of my
marsh. The terrace is irretrievably ruined. What is the point of
staying on here? I've been walking on the Down, but everywhere one comes on the horrors, and it works a sore on one's
mind. It makes me rage and wake in a hellish misery at dawn.

I daresay this kind of outrage is among the real sorrows of life."

And then again, Vita in America was missing "the spring of a thousand years," all the birds singing and the garden full of blue and white crocuses. "We've been walking on the Down at Falmer. The woods there are like Greek horses' manes — d'you know the look? brushed red, brisk — oh, so lovely at this moment. I can only wish I were a poet, so that I could describe a team of brown horses ploughing red brown earth, a grove of trees reflected in a great pond there under the church, with two swans swimming; you must write it for me."

London was a blasted, black town, London tasted of stale face powder and petrol. But London was fun, because Vita's latest book, *Family History*, had surpassed even *The Edwardians* and *All Passion Spent* in sales. Virginia's fingers were red and waled and cut with doing up parcels incessantly for three days, while clerks panted, telephones rang, carriers arrived, and the Hogarth Press was never more frantically busy. Vita must come to London and "I will take you to the place where we once had a glass of wine in a bow window overlooking the river. Also I'll take you to the Tower. I've just been there, this dripping Sunday, because almost every day I take my walk through the City. I like it better than Kent — Bread Street, Camomile Street, Seething Lane, All Hallows', St. Olave's. Then out one comes at the Tower, and there I walk on the terrace by the guns, with the ships coming up or down, which is it? As you say, though, Spain's burning and Hitler's booming. A French politician is dining here: I have to cook the dinner and can't, as you know, talk what you would call French — (d'you remember the rough sea on the channel boat and how skilfully I christened it?)." The conviction of her worthlessness was so heavy on her that even if stretching out a hand to turn on a light would have saved her life, she could not do it. But she was still quite unrepentant about not knowing the difference between upstream and downstream or about asking a French sailor if the sea was "*brusque.*"

Rodmell was so "ridden with visitors" that Tavistock Square was a comparative hermitage. But Tavistock Square was in a state of chaos. "Your damned cousin, the Duke — if he is your cousin, disown him — has insisted that we must entirely decorate the house; and every book has to be moved, every piece of type; and here we are, for the next three weeks, camped among rolled-up carpets and tables on end. Damn all dukes! £270 to spend: and then they pull the house down." The Woolfs tried to find a house that they could buy instead of renting for a few years at a time, and thus avoid the vexations of having to meet the demands of a ground landlord, whether he was the Duke of Bedford or anyone else, for extensive repairs before the lease could be renewed; but this proved impossible.

It seemed likely that *The Waves* would not earn enough to buy them a penny bun and they would have to look upon Vita as their sole support, their breadwinner. And then there was money for a camera, for a frigidaire ("ice-cream and fresh raspberries — I must go and put my pie in the oven"). There was even a new car, "silver and green, fluid fly-wheel, Tickford hood — Lanchester 18 — well, what more could you want? It glides with the smoothness of an eel, with the speed of a swift and the — isn't this a good blurb? — the power of a tigress when that tigress has just been reft of her young, in and out, up and down Piccadilly, Bond Street. The worst of it is that we can't live up to it. I've had to buy a new coat. But what's the good? There's my hat. That's all wrong — that's a Singer Saloon hat. . . . But isn't it pathetic, the trust of human nature, to think that you'll be interested in that — with Niagara churning at your door and the wolves howling and the Indians chasing each other with tomahawks up and down snow mountains?"

She must have known better, but she always wrote about the United States in a way that would have outraged her American godfather, pretending to imagine it, in the nineteen-thirties, as she had pictured it from reading *Uncle Tom's Cabin, Martin*

Chuzzlewit, Evangeline, The Last of the Mohicans, The Old Dominion, The Scarlet Letter — with perhaps just a touch of Mark Twain and another of Ring Lardner to bring it up to date.

"For now you are travelling across America," she wrote to Vita, "with views of the Middle West racing across vast slabs of plate glass . . . and after 25 more hours the train will stop at a town like Peacehaven [a housing development outside Brighton] only 75 times larger, called Balmoralville, where you will get out, and after a brief snack off clams and iced peardrops with the Mayor, who is called, I should think, Cyrus K. Hinks — but that's a detail I leave to you, you will go to a large Baptist Hall and deliver a lecture on Rimbaud. . . . By the way, are you lecturing on me at Albertvilleapolis, Pa? If so, do send me your notes. . . . Oh, how I envy you, slipping off your skin, adventuring through fields where the flamingoes rise in flocks and the old black women stand at the doors, a baby at each breast! . . . Shall you now clear a space among the spittoons and write to me? Describe everything, down to the lace on women's nightgowns. . . . Yes, yes, it was very nice indeed to get your letter. 'I am just about to dine with the President' — those were the last words of the last chapter. I see you've learnt how to end chapters — rather as if I wrote, 'And now, darling Vita, the Prince of Wales being outside in his new streamline car, I'm off to dine with King George! — except that nobody, not even a blue snob like myself, could whip up much excitement over that. But do continue your story. What new dress? What did the President say — and what did you drink?"

While the Nicolsons were lecturing in the United States, the Woolfs had their annual European trip. Virginia wrote from Italy in 1933, "I am half dazed with travelling, so many cities have I seen and smelt. . . . We're so brown-cheeked, red-nosed and altogether dusty, shaggy, shabby — what a state my clothes are in — even I rather hesitate to wear them — for we lunch in the fields, under olives, off ham, and it's my duty to wash up, which affects my clothes."

The previous year they had fled from the desecrated downs to Greece for two weeks with Roger Fry and his sister Margery. As usual, the trip provided the most sensational contrasts. They wandered in olive woods, along cliffs soft with flowers no bigger than pearls or topazes. They saw temples and shepherds' huts. They "swam about in the Aegean, with sea urchins and anemones, all transmuted, waving red and yellow beneath our feet. The waves lapped my balcony and I looked down into the hearts of fish. The sea gets in everywhere — you come to the top of a hill and there's the sea beneath, and snow mountains beyond and bays as they were when Eve — no, it should be Persephone — bathed there. Not a bungalow, not a kennel, not a tea-shop. Pure sea-water on pure sand is almost the loveliest thing in the world — you know how many times I've said so. There, that's to make you envious. Our drawbacks — these you'll want to know — are bitter winds, stormy grey skies, and vast helpings of soft, sweet pudding.

"Have I described our afternoon on the Acropolis — when a storm rushed up from the Aegean, black as arrows, and the blue was as hard as blue china, and the storm and the blue fell upon each other and ten million German tourists rushed across the temple, precisely like suppliants, in their grey and purple mackintoshes — no I haven't described the Acropolis — you may thank your stars I know my place as a prose writer."

Their car jolted and jumped and they "crossed an appalling pass, winding round and round, every sweep higher, and one wheel or the other perpetually balancing over a precipice, three thousand feet of sheer rock beneath. How I trembled! Then suddenly swooping round a corner to come upon a flock of goats or another car, and having to back, with the hind wheels brushing the tops of lime trees. But we got through safely, and so to Delphi, where an Englishman's skeleton, the son of my oldest friend, had been found, dangling from a tree in a gorge, with a gold watch between the ribs."

But everyone was well, because Margery Fry, in addition to

being a "maniacal botanist" and an archaeologist, had "everything an invalid can want in a huge wooden box and makes
arrowroot for those who like arrowroot the last thing at
night. . . . Roger is angelic, and exudes knowledge of the most
sympathetic kind and sends his love — but is catching a flea."

There were all sorts of vexations in England. The studio ceiling fell, she had nowhere to sit and all Freud's works were ruined. After a week of "social torture" in London she retreated
to Rodmell, and immediately a large bough on a chestnut tree
in the churchyard fell off, right on top of the beehive in the
orchard. She had been sitting for a portrait bust and her eyes
were "burnt out" by the overhead lights. She was going to be
painted, stark naked, by an artist, Ethel Walker, "who says I am
the image of Lilith. She has a rough, raddled charm, has three
fox-terriers, one blind of the right eye, and lives, eats, sleeps,
drinks, in one room overlooking the river. Swans float practically in at the window. She is 73 — that is the only thing against
her — and has lived a regular herring-griller's life, which, as
you know, I love. And I've been to dine with Lady Rhondda,
because I liked so much her story of how she swam under water
when the Lusitania sank. Why do none of these adventures
ever happen to me?"

She had been to a studio party and sat on the floor eating ham and chicken, with Rosamund Lehmann and Raymond
Mortimer and Roger Fry and others, and had been' rude to
someone who said, "This is the sort of life I really love. 'Then,
my good woman, why don't you lead it?' I say, being in a trucu-
lent mood just now. . . . This brilliant wit, these flashing epi-
grams!"

She had visited the Chelsea Flower Show and bought a minute cedar tree, fifty years old, and wanted "a very small breed
of nightingale" to sing on its branches. Would Vita find her
some at Sissinghurst? The barns she could see from her garden
room at Monk's House made her think of Greek temples; and
she had been to a village wedding and seen "the bridal party

perched on kitchen chairs driven off in a great blue wagon, drawn by coloured farm horses with ribbons on their tails and little pyramids of bells on their foreheads. What an odd mixture English country life is of squalor and magnificence!"

A haystack had caught fire. She had been for a walk with Pinker, her spaniel, and had come back with five mushrooms in her hat. She had been eating mushrooms every morning, and picking blackberries — both very good. But the beagles and the huntsmen came over the field and destroyed the mushrooms. She had been measuring rooms in a great house in Gordon Square that she and Leonard would almost certainly take and would live in forever, and was preparing to devote all her time for weeks in tying up their books with string for the move; but first they were off in the fog to Cambridge to take voters to the polls; and then the "damn Duke" turned them down for the seventh time!

Touring England to sell books was wonderful, the country was so lovely, and she adored the life of hotels and overhearing conversations which made her feel England was incredibly prosperous. But its antiquity was almost too much. Not a new house, and bits of a ruin even in the hotel lounge at Taunton. What ever would it be like in another thousand years? Every inn they stayed at had been an inn since the time of Arthur or Alfred; but the bells didn't ring and the hot water was cold at Launceston, and the booksellers were often very rude and Leonard almost lost his temper. Cornwall was superb, the gorse blazing on the moors against a pure blue sea, like the flames around Brunhilde in *Siegfried;* and "I saw my Lighthouse, and the gate of my home, through tears — thinking how my mother died at my age; or next year to it."

In 1934 the annual spring vacation was spent in traveling about England, Scotland and Ireland, since her erratic heart was giving trouble again and the warmer climate of the South of France was not advised, for fear of fainting attacks. At Stratford-on-Avon her feeling of reverence for Shakespeare

caused her to write with the same simplicity as when she had
seen Montaigne's home. This was where he had sat; this was
the window out of which he had gazed, seeing what? No tourist
with a guidebook could have been more humble and direct. The
diary record of this visit is all the more moving because there
is no straining after effect, no shame prevents her from admitting that here she feels herself on holy ground. In Ireland she
and Leonard spent two days with Elizabeth Bowen, who remembers her vivid interest in everything and everybody. She
spent some time in the kitchen, talking with the old cook,
Sarah, about how to make bread. "Do you know," said Elizabeth Bowen to Sarah afterwards, "she is one of the greatest
writers in the world?" "I don't care about that," replied Sarah. "I should have known she was a lady by the stately go of
her."

That "stately go" was not at all stiff. She always kept a remarkable spontaneity of movement, a physical attribute that
corresponded with the swift and easy transitions in her mind.
Lord David Cecil remembers her as retaining to the end of her
life the movements of a young woman. Thinking of her and her
sister one recalled Yeats's line about the two girls, "Both beautiful, one a gazelle." Her fears about her appearance did not carry
over to her body and produce awkwardness or restrict her vigor
when she was well. "Oh, the joy of walking!" she wrote, "the
trance-like swimming, flying through the air; the current of sensations and ideas; and the slow but fresh change of down, of
road, of colours; all this churned up into a fine thin sheet of
perfect calm happiness."

But the happiness of walking alone, writing her books in her
mind and declaiming them aloud, painting them on the sky, did
not last. She snatched at every joy, but life was getting harder
as time went on. In addition to her cursed facility for harboring
every stray influenza germ and her equally cursed inability to
react normally to curative drugs, she suffered acutely from anxiety about her friends. If only she could stop caring about

people, stop imagining the most awful disasters if a plane
was delayed by bad weather or someone was late for an
appointment!

The only thing to be done was to make fun of it. "Lord, what
a donkey! Lord, what a donkey! Lord, what a donkey!" she
wrote to Vita, when there had been a muddle about when and
where they were to meet. "I can't ask you for the night, but
come to lunch. . . . All right, says Vita — and these were her
last words, spoken as it were at the crack of doom, I'll come to
lunch. Whereupon I ordered suet pudding. Rather hot, says
Nelly. Yes, I say, but it's Mrs. Nicolson's favourite pudding.
There is the suet pudding turned out of its basin: where's Vita?
We walk up the street. Has she been cut in two by a char-a-
banc, do you think? says Nelly. Anyhow the suet won't keep.
Pinker is sick. They say when a dog is sick it means someone's
in agony, says Nelly. I had an aunt that dreamt of a dog being
sick and her husband fell from a ladder next morning. So we
ate the suet. And then in I go to Lewes, all trembling with the
char-a-bancs a-cutting you in half, and you say, as cool as cu-
cumber — Look here: no nonsense: lunch, Thursday, 1 o'clock
sharp. Please don't go and be a donkey again." The scolding
tone, the transference to the old servant's mouth of her own
mounting anxiety, both reveal, rather than hide, her underlying
tenderness.

And then there was all the tiresome chatter about Bloomsbury. Pay no heed to it, Leonard advised, and she tried hard
not to be irritated. "I don't feel Bloomsbury: do you feel Mary-
lebone (or Chelsea, Kensington or Hampstead)?" Rose Macaulay reports her as saying (*Horizon,* May 1941). What on earth
did it matter what her postal address was? And why did anyone
think she would trouble to complain about the sniping? "Not a
bit, not a bit," she told Vita, "only of young men who insist on
coming to dinner, and then go away and send me articles in
which they deride Bloomsbury but haven't the courage to name
names. If Bloomsbury could only smell so strong that nobody

would come near Tavistock Square, I should be oh, so happy."

When she wrote this in 1936, the sneering at Bloomsbury as the home of highbrows had already been going on for some years. Leonard had written an admirable little book in 1927, *Hunting the Highbrow*, not referring specifically to Bloomsbury but dealing with attacks on intellectuals, as though having brains and using them were a social crime, and stupidity and prejudice were praiseworthy. But a hundred books, a thousand arguments, would not be enough to deflect the tide that still flows so strongly and is so hard to explain in a society that sets a high value on education and culture, trains experts and technicians to the utmost, but scarcely misses an opportunity to deride the thinker and the artist and to exalt to the seats of the high and mighty not the humble and meek but the pompous paraders of ignorance and bad manners.

The annoyance caused to Virginia by the Bloomsbury-baiters was not publicly expressed, but her diary for 1935 shows how the jeering allusions to herself and her friends increased the difficulties she had to contend with at that time, the physical disabilities, the mental discouragement and the personal sorrows which she had to overcome. She was goaded into writing a spirited letter to the *New Statesman* but took Leonard's advice and did not send it in for publication. Now that "Bloomsbury" has ceased to provide an occasion for cackling and "highbrow" is long outmoded as a term of contempt, this letter has gained in value as an expression of her feelings and a declaration of her standards. It can be read, under the title of "Middlebrow," in *The Death of the Moth*.

In it she defines a highbrow as "a man or woman of thoroughbred intelligence who rides his mind at a gallop across country in pursuit of an idea." A lowbrow is a "man or woman of thoroughbred vitality who rides his body in pursuit of a living at a gallop across life." Highbrows and lowbrows, she contends, like and respect one another, get along well together, in fact cannot get along without one another. But for the middlebrows, "the go-betweens, the busybodies who run from one to the other with their tittle-tattle and make all the mischief," she has nothing but contempt. She is proud to be called a highbrow, she intends to go on associating with lowbrows whenever she gets an opportunity, but "If any human being, man, woman, dog, cat or half-crushed worm dares call me 'middlebrow,' I will take my pen and stab him, dead."

No doubt she felt better after writing this, as she did when recording in her diary her rage at learning from E. M. Forster that her name had been suggested for the committee of the London Library but it was decided that "ladies are quite impossible" on committees. She was going to write a book *On Being Despised;* "pail of offal" was one of the mildest terms that came to her mind. "God damn Morgan for thinking I'd have taken that. . . . And dear old Morgan comes to tea today." And poor Morgan, who loved and honored her, and cannot have guessed from her manner at the time what a furious storm devastated her, so that her hand trembled even as she wrote about the incident. But "these flares up are very good for my book: for they simmer and become transparent: and I see how I can transmute them into beautiful clear reasonable ironical prose."

This diary entry is so revealing that it defies comment. One does not know whether to laugh at the display of temper, sympathize with the deep resentment underlying the outburst, applaud the way it was not allowed to interfere with her affection for the old friend who was the innocent cause of the anger, or admire the artistic impulse that immediately began to turn it to good account. But one cannot help noting how these repeated exacerbations were gradually destroying the calm benignity and good humor of *A Room of One's Own.* She had so few reserves to draw upon. The wires were stretched so tight that they might snap at any moment. Her friends sensed this. The closer they were to her the more they co-operated with her husband to shield her as far as possible, without unnecessary or

fussy solicitude, from undue excitement or extravagant spurts
of energy.

She knew that she needed to be protected against herself,
although her vulnerability often caused her to feel ashamed.
Sometimes, as after *To the Lighthouse,* she turned to Vita almost as though the younger woman were her mother. She implored her for help in devising some means of preventing the
"rats" from nibbling away at her life. But why should she
put her burdens on Vita? It must be some deep psychological
impulse, she concluded. But "Vita, Vita, why have you taught
me this piercing cry?" A few days later she would recover her
gaiety, would relate with the customary embellishments some
ludicrous episode and ask, "Why didn't you warn me about sus-
penders?" almost as though she were a baby; and in the next
breath she speaks with the voice of a mature woman, a discerning critic, and a generous helper of any other human being in
need of sympathy and support in a crisis.

Her relations with the tempestuous and eccentric composer
Ethel Smyth are a case in point. Leonard Woolf could hardly
control his impatience with this overwhelming egotist, whom a
lifelong struggle to gain recognition on an equal footing with
men in the world of music had turned into an aggressive nuisance
in her old age. Uproariously funny she might be, particularly to
those who saw the grotesque rather than the tragic aspect of a
woman who was loaded with honors still complaining that she
was persecuted and discriminated against; but she was too
much like a thunderstorm to be welcome in a house where
peace and calm and orderly schedules of work and rest were
imperative.

Virginia knew quite well how her husband felt, admitted that
an hour or two of Dame Ethel's ranting was enough to leave
anyone stunned and exhausted, but she could not resist the
temptation to listen to her stories, even if they were so fantastic
that she could not believe more than half of them. "D'you
think it can be all nonsense — the prison?" she asked Vita, when

old Ethel (as she called her, to distinguish her from Ethel Sands, the painter) was writing in one of her volumes of memoirs about her experiences as a militant suffragette. "If so, isn't nature odd, keeping an old woman in a state of frenzy for weeks, if it's all nonsense, what she writes. I daresay I am just the same, with my moths and waves. I wander over the Downs declaiming, making up, and altogether working myself into a frenzy, too. And what's the good of it?"

Old Ethel might so nearly drive her to distraction that she would write: "Ethel's new dog is dead. The truth is, no dog can stand the strain of living with Ethel. I went down one day and found it on the verge of a nervous collapse, simply from listening to her conversation." But immediately she would regret being so malicious. "Well, well — if we all weather as red and roaring, we shan't do so badly." It was deafness, she guessed, that made Ethel so intolerably rough and rowdy. "It's the solitude; she can't get rid of her mind in talk."

She had just had a stormy visit from Ethel, she told Vita. "Storm of nature and grumblings from Ethel, and she dragged me to the top of the Downs in a hurricane, talking about God and *The Wreckers*. Which is which? I don't know." So, "think of me, who hate opera, sitting under five hours of Wreckers, with her beside me." The idea of refusing to go to the performance of the opera does not seem to have occurred to her. She let Ethel take her to a party at the Austrian Embassy where one of her works was performed. "A triumph, you must admit, for a woman of 73. She in a sweater and mouldy fur coat; I almost smart by comparison." And in the slow movement the composer made such clearly audible and gleefully indecent remarks about the effect the music was meant to produce that everyone was scandalized. Yes, old Ethel was a termagant, but she was also a magnificent oak. She talked without stopping, until the veins on her forehead were swollen. "But she is a game old bird, and I respect her to the point of idolatry."

For Ethel Smyth was pursued by the same furies that drove

Virginia Woolf. "What if she should be a great composer? This fantastic idea is to her the merest commonplace: it is the fabric of her being," she wrote in her diary, describing Ethel conducting a rehearsal. "She thinks this is about the most important event now taking place in London. And perhaps it is."

Also, Ethel loved her; and for affection Virginia was grateful. Ethel believed in her, though she did not believe it was anything but ridiculous humbug when Leonard said firmly that Virginia was not well enough to see her. Ethel respected her judgment, wrote her last book of reminiscences (*As Time Went On*) at Virginia's suggestion, and dedicated it to her. So the least Virginia could do was to help give Ethel a birthday present she would really most appreciate; a public performance of her choral Mass. This was given with due pomp and ceremony in March 1934, at the Albert Hall. "Heaven be praised," wrote Virginia to Vita, "Ethel's Mass has been played — but it was a joke to see her sitting in her triangular hat by the Queen's side in the Royal Box, among all the Court." Afterwards the composer led a cohort of distinguished — but not courtly — friends to the nearest branch of Lyon's teashops, greatly to the astonishment of the regular customers quietly eating cream buns. It was an entirely unrehearsed affair. The invaders swarmed all over the place, making a great deal of noise, appropriating every available seat at the marble-slabbed tables, exhausted singers and musicians "all eating thick bread and butter, but a little out of their harmony: and Ethel bellowing, as red as the sun, entirely triumphant and self-satisfied."

To the old woman this impromptu tea party provided the greatest enjoyment of the day, but Virginia had lost her zest for such affairs. She was finding it more and more of a strain to live the double life of the outer and of the inner worlds. "I want only walking and perfectly spontaneous childish life with L. and the accustomed when I'm writing at full tilt; to have to behave with circumspection and decision to strangers wrenches me into another region," she wrote in her diary in August 1933, when she was struggling to master *The Years* and evade the menace of headaches and collapse into the twilight of nervous exhaustion.

She had to contend with more serious disturbances than the temporary turmoil created by Dame Ethel. Death was striking down beloved friends and admired acquaintances. "The air is full of funerals," she wrote to Vita, and again, "I've been rather submerged in tragedy." D. H. Lawrence, Arnold Bennett, John Galsworthy, Stella Benson, George Moore, Lowes Dickinson, one after another they disappeared; some much older than she, others her contemporaries; none fully appreciated or understood by her, she felt, and now the possibility of knowing them better was lost forever.

The first of the really bitter bereavements she suffered in the nineteen-thirties was the death of Lytton Strachey. He was taken ill at his home in Wiltshire at the end of 1931. For more than a month his relations and close friends gathered in the nearest inn or waited at the end of telephone wires for calls, helpless and unhappy, while doctors fought for his life. One day it was thought he was dying, the next it seemed there was a possibility of his recovering. "I should mind it to the end of my days if he died," she wrote to Vita in January 1932, "but they think he may get through now. Like all the Stracheys he has a fund of Anglo-Indian tenacity, besides which remains perfectly calm, collected and cheerful and likes to argue about truth and beauty — you must admit that this is admirable. I wish one's friends were immortal — I'm greatly at their mercy."

But one's friends are not immortal. The ulcerated colon proved to be a malignant cancer. Death won. Not long afterwards Lytton Strachey's most devoted friend, Sibyl Carrington, killed herself. "The day after we were there. I don't think anything could have stopped it — still —" Even to Leonard Woolf, not given naturally to melancholy, the loss brought the feeling of something's being wrong with the universe. The simplicity of Virginia's words tells more of her suffering than could be conveyed by any attempt to describe it more eloquently.

In the summer of 1933 the gay and lovable Francis Birrell, who ran the famous bookshop with David Garnett, fell ill. At first it was thought that a growth on his brain was small, not in a vital spot, and that an operation would enable him to recover from the threatening paralysis. But the operation was not successful. By November he was only just able to haul himself about, with assistance from Desmond MacCarthy and a male nurse. He lingered on for more than a year, "transacting his death," as Virginia wrote in her diary in December, 1934, "facing a peculiar lonely sorrow . . . looking at it, at 45 or so: with a great desire to live," but without hope, asking every hour how long before the end. "He was exactly as usual; no wandering, no incoherence. A credit to Athens. The soul deserves to be immortal, as L. said."

But Virginia was numb, still crushed by an even heavier blow that had struck in September 1934. She and her sister were together at Rodmell one day. They were anxious for news about Roger Fry, who had fallen and broken his thigh — a serious matter for a man aged sixty-six — so they telephoned the London hospital to which he had been taken, for reassurance that he was continuing his progress towards recovery. To their stupefaction they learned that his heart had suddenly failed. Roger Fry was dead.

"It was an awful shock," she wrote to Vita, using the inadequate words of utter grief. "It's been a horrid time. It was very nice of you to understand how much I should mind. I wish you had known him better. He was so extraordinarily alive — I still find myself thinking I shall tell him something. And we all lived so much together — dear me, why must one's friends die? But it's far worse for Nessa than for anybody. That I find very difficult to think of in the future."

In her diary she attempted to record her feelings, not without some shame that a part of her stood aside and observed and

analyzed the anguish that devoured the other part. "I feel very
dazed; very wooden. Women cry, L. says: but I don't know why
I cry — mostly with Nessa. . . . I think the poverty of life is
what comes to me; and this blackish veil over everything. Hot
weather; a wind blowing. The substance gone out of everything.
I don't think this is exaggerated."

She dreaded going to the funeral, in case, as at other funerals,
the need to protect oneself caused her attention to wander. But
she was glad she went. There were flowers and strollers in the
garden during the simple and dignified service. Roger would
have liked that. "It is a strong instinct to be with one's friends.
I thought of him too, at intervals. Dignified and honest and
large — 'large, sweet soul' — something ripe and musical about
him — and then the fun and the fact that he had lived
with such variety and generosity and curiosity. I thought of
this."

Again she tried to put it into words. "I had a notion that I
could describe the tremendous feeling at R.'s funeral: but of
course I can't. I mean the universal feeling; how we all fought
with our brains, loves and so on; and *must* be vanquished." A
fear came to her then, seeing herself dead. "But then, next day,
today, which is Thursday, one week later, the other thing began
to work — the exalted sense of being above time and death
which comes from being again in a writing mood. And this is
not an illusion, so far as I can tell. Certainly I have a strong sense
that Roger would be all on one's side in this excitement, and that
what ever the invisible force (death, the vanquisher) does, we
thus get outside it."

His sister and friends begged her to write his biography. It
was a task from which she shrank, but she could not resist
their pleading that she take this burden upon herself. Perhaps
it was true, what they said, that there was no one in the world
better fitted to tell his story.

But first *The Years*, the novel that was going through so
many changes, that was alternately so exciting and so extraor-

dinarily difficult to write, must be finished, and "On Being Despised" got out of the way. And fun must not be forgotten; tears must be dried and despair refused its victory. So in January 1935 she wrote a little comedy which was privately acted at a party by Vanessa, Julian and Angelica Bell, Adrian Stephen and Leonard Woolf. It was called *Freshwater;* the scene was the Isle of Wight, and the chief characters were Lord Tennyson and her Great-Aunt Julia Cameron. Virginia decided she would hire a donkey's head to take her curtain call in, to indicate what nonsense it all was. But it was "good to have an unbuttoned laughing evening once in a way."

There was a macabre incident during a rehearsal. "Roger's ghost knocked at the door" — his portrait of Charles Sanger, the mathemetician, an old friend from Cambridge, was delivered. "And how Francis would have enjoyed this, Leonard said. These are our ghosts now. But they would applaud the attempt."

The biography of Roger Fry was not completed and published until 1940. If it had appeared at any other time than after the outbreak of World War II, if it had been written by anyone else than Virginia Woolf, it would have been hailed as a classic work, a model of what a biography should be, solid and factual yet intuitive, lyrical, beautiful. But the public had come to expect something quite different from Virginia Woolf — though each book she wrote was a surprise, unlike anything she had done before — and the world had something else to think about, wanted something more stirring and martial and more immediately to the point than art and criticism.

Reading it now, one has to admit there are pages where the writer has found progress very difficult. "All those letters!" Leonard protested as they continued to arrive and had to be read and sifted and appraised. And "All those facts!" as Virginia said when Vita was writing her study of Joan of Arc, "how can anyone lift a pen among them?" Or, as she wrote when she wanted to think about *The Waves* but had instead to concentrate for the time on an essay about Fanny Burney, "One can't simply invent the whole of Chelsea and King George III and Johnson and Mrs. Thrale, I suppose? Yet after all, that's the way to write; and if I had time to prove it, the truth of one's sensations is not in the fact, but in the reverberations. When I have read three lines, I re-make them entirely, if they're prose, and not poetry; and it is this which is the truth."

No, the straightforward biography, with every date checked, every source noted, every fact verified, was not the kind of writing at which Virginia Woolf excelled. She needed to be able to give freer flight to her fancy, to listen for an echo, to see an image in a mirror at an odd angle. This creative impulse could not be denied expression, even when she tried to curb it in the interests of strict accuracy. She found that she got to know Roger Fry even better in death than she had during their long years of intimate friendship together. And those "intimate things one says in print" revealed him to her; and also reveal her to us.

It is not merely that she had been with him on many of the journeys to France and Italy and Greece which she describes; nor that some of the letters she quotes may have been written to her, or discuss points they may have talked about together. It is far more than that. She recalls an occasion (without mentioning that she was present) when he was asked for an expert opinion about whether a picture was an original or only a copy. "His eyes fixed themselves with their very steady and penetrating gaze upon the canvas. Again they seemed to carry on a life of their own as they explored the world of reality. And again, as if it helped him in his voyage of discovery, he turned and laughed and talked and argued about other things. The two worlds were close together. He could pass from one to the other without impediment. He responded to the whole vibration — the still life and the laughter, the murmur of the traffic in the distance and the voices close at hand." But of whom is she speaking? Roger Fry stands before us; and by his side is Virginia Woolf.

"His presence seemed to increase the sensation of everything in the room. But at the centre of that vibration was a gravity and a stillness, as in his face too there was that which made him look so often 'like a saint in one of the Old Masters.' But he was a saint who laughed. 'Whereas piety or holiness make goodness stink in the nostrils,' he once wrote, 'saintliness is the imaginative power to make goodness seem desirable.' He made goodness seem desirable, as he sat laughing with his friends and looking at the picture. . . . Those who knew him best will attempt no summing up of that sensation. They can only say that Roger Fry had a peculiar quality of reality that made him a person of infinite importance in their lives, and add his own words, 'Any attempt I might make to explain this would probably land me in the depths of mysticism. On the edge of that gulf I stop.' "

But this is almost exactly the impression she made on her friends. Her presence heightened one's awareness of everything in a room. She vibrated, but there was gravity and stillness at the center. She laughed, and goodness seemed desirable. She had a peculiar quality of reality that made friendship with her a vital experience. This is the testimony of those who knew her personally: it is also the emanation of herself that comes from reading her books.

Not that any of her friends thought of her as a saint. The mere suggestion would have been greeted with hoots of laughter in Bloomsbury, "a place where lowbrows and highbrows live happily together on equal terms and priests are not, nor priestesses, and, to be quite frank, the adjective 'priestly' is neither often heard nor held in high esteem." Curiosity was more valued than reverence. "Only once did I ever call her a genius," said Elizabeth Bowen. "That was one day when there had been some sort of crisis about potatoes. Virginia could not boil a potato, but that evening she produced a wonderful omelette." For that achievement she was willing to accept praise.

As for mysticism, her expressed attitude was the same as

Roger Fry's. "Mystical was perhaps the last epithet we should ever have expected Virginia Woolf to apply to herself," wrote Vita Sackville-West in her review of *A Writer's Diary*, "but it is the operative word."

In daily life Virginia involuntarily hid her deepest secrets from her most intimate friends; and from herself too, despite all her probings. It is when she writes of others, in love and understanding, that we see her most clearly. When she makes what she thinks is a discovery about herself one is frequently astonished; the reader of her books has known it for a long time.

Chapter XVIII

THERE was an interval of six years between the publication of *The Waves* and that of *The Years*, the novel which was the hardest to write, the least artistically successful and the best seller of them all.

She had the most grandiose plans for it. It was to be a first cousin of *Orlando*, a combination of *The Waves* and *Night and Day*. It should have "immense depth and intensity . . . millions of ideas but no preaching . . . a summing up of all I know, feel, laugh at, despise, like, admire, hate, and so on." There should be plenty of facts and plenty of story, a one-volume family chronicle quite unlike Hugh Walpole's *Herries Saga* or John Galsworthy's *The Forsyte Saga*, because it should not plod but "come, with the most powerful and agile leaps, like a chamois, across precipices, from 1880 to here and now."

To this design she doggedly stuck. As with *Night and Day* she was determined that this time she would be right; and as with the earlier novel, the signs of strain show. "Wasn't it my conscientious grind at *The Years* that killed it?" she asked herself in her diary in 1940, recalling some of the horror of the struggle to bring it to an end. She was ill during and after its writing. Day after day she would get up with a headache, force herself to her workroom, sometimes in her nightgown, battle for half an hour or so, and be compelled to rest. The headaches would win, and there would be weeks when she could do no work at all.

Naturally, the book lacks the bold adventurousness with

which she first attacked it. She forced it into a mold, but it came out shapeless. The twelve episodes of which it consists, although concerned with the same people or their children and grandchildren, remain disconnected. Each section has its date and an introductory passage describing the time, the weather, the scene; but the choice seems arbitrary. All the necessary clues are given so that the reader can understand what has been going on in the intervening years, who has married, died, had children, become disillusioned or achieved success. The story is coherent and logically developed, though intricate and hard to follow because so much of the action takes place off stage. The links hold; but the book has no emotional core.

We are looking at a great altarpiece, but our attention is distracted from the central figure of almost inconceivable majesty because some child angel has arrived late and is only pretending, by opening his mouth extremely wide or puffing his cheeks to the bursting point, to be singing or trumpeting; the donor's little dog is up to mischief; a rose has poked its head round a pillar; through the window there are seen glimpses of landscape, ships at sea, peasants at work in fields pausing to quaff ale, knights are riding, rabbits — or are they monkeys? — peep out of rocky crannies, play unconcernedly on the barren sides of mountains that are vast, precipitous and vaguely threatening. It is with an effort, and a sigh, that we remind ourselves that we should be concentrating on — what? An Annunciation, an Assumption, a Nativity, a Crucifixion?

The truth is that the artist has tried to give us all these different pictures on one canvas. Her real theme is not the ostensible one, inspired by simple devotion. She has to display her virtuosity, her skill in composition, the balance of masses, the direction of lights, the picking up of colors, the flow of lines. No restraint she imposes on herself can conceal her absorbed interest in these technical problems. Her picture shows her constant preoccupation with the rhythmic interplay of life and death.

As always, she has to assert that life shall, must, win. But she is losing her confidence. She will go on fighting to the end. She will be defeated; she knows that. But she will rise again, she who cannot possibly believe in immortality. "If I'm persuaded to anything," she wrote to Vita, "it is of mortality. Then why this sense that death is going to be a great excitement, something positive, active?" Can it be? She suggested, when writing in praise of Vita's life of Joan of Arc, that in other times people "believed where we can't. Or rather, our belief is hardly perceptible to us, but will be to those who write our lives in 600 years. I agree, we *do* believe, not in God though: not me, anyhow. And I can't lay hands satisfactorily on your 'unity.' Perhaps I mean belief is almost unconscious. And the living belief now is in human beings."

So her living belief in life conquering death had to be expressed by being gay and welcoming the ghosts of Lytton Strachey and Roger Fry and Francis Birrell to parties they would have enjoyed.

It is expressed in *The Years,* a book laden with heavy symbols of death, always followed by some new affirmation of continuing life. Delia, in 1880, looks into her mother's grave, and is "possessed by a sense of something everlasting; of life mixing with death, of death becoming life. For as she looked she heard the sparrows chirp quicker and quicker; she heard the wheels in the distance sound louder and louder; life came closer and closer." And when she hears the preacher's words about being delivered from the miseries of this sinful world she cries to herself, "What a lie! What a damnable lie!" It is not a miserable, sinful world.

Sometimes the symbols are reversed, but they are always juxtaposed. In 1891 a pregnant woman, gathering ripe fruit and discarding what the wasps have attacked, hears shooting in the woods, learns that Parnell has died and with him so many hopes of a peaceful end of the troubles in Ireland. In 1918, the war is over but the guns still boom and the sirens wail as the news

of the armistice comes through. But in most cases it is life that
has the triumphant last word.

Sally, who is sick and has a crooked back, sings and dances
and laughs, puts aside a Greek tragedy and wants to know all
about the party that is going on while she has to lie in bed.
Eleanor, who had been her father's housekeeper and then devoted herself to social work, sees in 1917 a man she might have
married, thinks of a younger sister's happy marriage, and is surprised to find that she has forgotten the Zeppelins have been raid-
ing London.

In the long last section, headed "Present Day" — that is 1936-
1937 — when the Second World War was imminent and the
dragon's teeth were already turning into armed men in Spain,
the images of the incessant struggle between death and life
come thick and fast, as the Pargiters come together and talk.
Eleanor, very old now, thinks of the endless dark that awaits
her. "But something baffled her; in fact it was growing light."
Night had been conquered by dawn.

The caretaker's children come to tea. The slices of cake cut
for them are thicker than would be cut for the children of the
Pargiters' personal friends. They are too shy to speak. "The
younger generation don't mean to speak." They sing a song,
however; verse after verse, completely unintelligible, but extraordinarily beautiful.

An old man tries to make a speech at a party but is always
interrupted. "Now for the peroration," he begins again, and
interrupts himself. There will be no peroration, he declares, because there was no speech. "But the dawn has risen," says another man.

The party breaks up. How are they to get home? All the
tubes and omnibuses have stopped. "We can walk. Walking won't do us any harm." And Eleanor, who is being offered
roses, looks from the window and sees in the square a young
man and a young woman alighting from a taxi and fitting a
latchkey to a door. (Years before Virginia Woolf had used this

image of a man and a woman setting off together in a taxi to express her idea of the harmonious union of the sexes.)

And then the end. "The sun had risen, and the sky above the houses wore an air of extraordinary beauty, simplicity and peace." These are almost the very words she had used in *Jacob's Room* to describe the fruitful land seen from the barren sea.

The Years is extremely moving, even to a reader who comes fresh to it and fails, therefore, to catch the echoes from the writer's past books. At the time of its publication it was possible to miss many of the references that show her keen forebodings of world disaster, her ever-renewed faith in a new world to follow the old. The critic of literary form may deplore that the novelist has taken a backward step, has ceased to surpass her previous achievements as an artist. The reader mainly interested in following her thoughts may regret that she has found no solution to the problems she set forth, has failed to offer a systematic philosophy, does not qualify as a constructive thinker, merely reiterates old themes, and this time with a stronger emphasis on disillusion. Yet, with knowledge of her life at this period, the book gains poignancy as a record of continued courage in the face of increasing odds.

Even without this knowledge the novel enjoyed a popularity that seems, to the purist, out of proportion to its literary merit when judged by the standards of its predecessors. Its sales, both in England and in the United States, cleared that invisible hurdle which publishers know so well and which marks the dividing line between the regular readers who wait patiently for the next work of their favorite writers and the huge reading public beyond. Something unexpected had happened. Virginia Woolf had managed to insinuate herself into the affections of people who had never heard of Bloomsbury and were unconcerned with both the higher and the lower forms of literary criticism. Maynard Keynes probably put his finger on the explanation of the book's appeal when he told its author that he found it very moving, tender, beautiful and human.

This novel gave her so much trouble in 1936 (when her health was atrocious and she could sometimes work no more than ten minutes at a time) that she would have been "delighted to tie a stone to it and drop it into the Atlantic." But it headed the list of best sellers in the United States for more than three months in 1937 and went on being bought steadily for months more. It is not, however, the book most likely to be mentioned when people, hearing her name spoken, unexpectedly confide that they read something of hers at least every year, have just finished *Orlando* or *To the Lighthouse* for the fifth or sixth time, are now starting *Mrs. Dalloway* or *The Waves* again, mean to go back to the earlier novels, always keep the two volumes of *The Common Reader* or the posthumously published collections of essays and stories close at hand. The vital spark which glows so strongly in most of the later works is dimmer in *The Years*. But it may be the book which, because of the human appeal Keynes discerned in it, laid the basis for the feeling (again unforeseen and met in the most unexpected quarters) that leads people to speak of her as though she were still alive, almost as though she were a personal friend who might pop in at any moment and hold the baby while the older children are put to bed, so that one can have a quiet talk.

This kind of easy, unquestioning reference to her is not confined to women or related only to the domestic scene. Her name crops up in all sorts of memoirs and autobiographies and critical studies by men distinguished in various fields. The more sober and elderly speak of her as a formative influence in their lives; the younger and less restrained do not blush to describe their first reading of her books as a vital experience. Her name is linked with acknowledged masters, such as Flaubert and Henry James. She has definitely not been put in the "file and forget" category. "Her and Shakespeare!" whispered a young nurse to a patient in a New York hospital not long ago, and then continued her routine tasks, blushing all over at having revealed something that was of tremendous importance to her.

And yet the woman these different people speak of or write about had a difficult life made more difficult by attacks because she lived in Bloomsbury, worked in an ivory tower, was aloof and snobbish and perversely unintelligible and, having a private income, could know or care nothing about the lives of ordinary men and women. Who is right? Each reader, each generation, must decide; the evidence is conflicting, the witnesses on both sides are numerous.

NOT LONG after the publication of *The Years*, death struck again, still nearer home. Virginia's favorite nephew Julian Bell, elder son of her sister Vanessa, went to Central China to teach English in Wu Han University. She loved him dearly, for his own sake and because he reminded her of Thoby and because he talked to her as though she were his own age. He returned to England in March 1937. A month later he announced that he must go to Spain, where the Civil War was raging, the tide already turning in favor of Franco, the beleaguered Republicans needing every scrap of help they could get. He was not a Communist, and although he had given up his former pacifist views, he was not a soldier: he would serve as an ambulance driver.

In June Virginia saw a sad procession of Spanish refugees "impelled by machine-guns in Spanish fields to trudge through Tavistock Square, along Gordon Square, then where? — clasping their enamel kettles," homeless beggars, asking alms. In July she was thinking of Julian near Madrid. The thoughts were melancholy, for both she and his mother were consumed with anxiety for his safety and had implored him not to go.

She was sad, too, because she had just heard that a very old friend, Janet Case, was dying. She was asked to send an obituary

notice to the London *Times*. "A curious thought, rather: as if it
mattered who wrote or not. But this flooded me with the idea of
Janet yesterday. I think writing, my writing, is a species of me-
diumship. I become the person." She was carried back in memory to the old days at Hyde Park Gate, when Janet was teaching
her Greek.

She had loved her teacher, and stood in awe of her long after
she used to go hot and cold on her way to take lessons at Windmill Hill, Wimbledon. But the love was unspoken on both sides.
Janet had played a great visionary part in Virginia's life, "till
the visionary became a part of the fictitious, not of the real
life." Only at the end, in her last letter, could the old woman
bring herself to write "My beloved Virginia" — a breakdown of
rigid reserve that had its hint of farewell. How much the shy
and lonely girl would have valued such words if they could possibly have been spoken at the time. But forty-odd years had
passed, and Virginia had to go to her funeral.

Two days later, on July 21, came the dreaded news from
Spain. Julian was killed. Virginia wired to Vita immediately
and sent a hurried note: "Nessa likes to have me, so I'm round
there most of the time. It is very terrible. You will understand."
Later, when she had a spare moment, she wrote more fully: "It
has been an incredible nightmare. Lord, why do these things
happen? I'm not clear enough in the head to feel anything but
dull varieties of anger and despair. He had every sort of gift —
above everything vitality and enjoyment. Why must he get set
on going to Spain? But it was useless to argue. And his feelings
were so mixed. I mean, interest in war, conviction, and a long-
ing to be in the thick of things. He was the first of Nessa's babies, and I can't describe how close and real and always alive
our relation was. As for Nessa — but, as I say, I'm so stupid,
generally doing odd jobs, I can't think, nor, as you see, write.
So forgive this egotism. . . . And dear old Clive — he is such a
pathetic and always honest man, cracking his jokes to try and
make us all laugh. Oh, I admire!"

But something precious was saved from this tragic loss. Among Julian's pupils in China was the young wife of another professor at the university. So few people spoke English that Julian often felt lonely and homesick, and he became very friendly with the Chinese couple. He talked to them about his life in England and particularly about his family, his mother and father and aunt. After about a year of almost daily conversations, the young woman began to feel that she knew them all quite well. When he was about to return home she went with him to help choose the presents they would most like. He promised to get her from England some of his aunt's books so that she could discover for herself, as she read, more than he could tell. He kept his word, and probably referred very warmly to his new friends in his letters home, for his mother wrote to tell her of his death, and she also received a parcel containing *The Waves, The Years* and *A Room of One's Own,* with a note from Virginia saying that they had been sent at his request.

At this time this young woman was in the deepest distress, for war was devastating China too. The Japanese were invading her country, spreading ruin everywhere as they advanced. She went to help the wounded, and they cried, "Give us arms, so that we can fight back!" Far away, in another part of China, her mother was killed. The literary weekly she was editing had to cease publication. She felt helpless, alone, near despair and madness. Then, out of the darkness of her misery, she wrote to Virginia for advice.

She received in reply a letter that might have come from an old friend, it was so full of sympathy and understanding. The advice was sound, also. "Work," wrote Virginia. That was the only cure, the only thing she knew that was of the slightest help when one's life seemed to be shattered. It was the advice she tried to take herself. She encouraged the girl to write, to put down exactly what she thought. She continued to send her English books, mostly eighteenth- or nineteenth-century volumes of letters, biographies, novels, poems. Some of the choices may seem odd. What kind of a picture of English life and thought could a Chinese woman gain from Sir Walter Scott's and Jane Austen's novels and Mrs. Gaskell's *Life of Charlotte Brontë?* But Virginia was a natural, not a trained, teacher. She assumed that what interested her would interest any other like-minded woman. Therefore she sent Cowper's letters and poems, because he had "a dash of white fire in him . . . what I call central transparency," as she once told Vita. No "cat-sat-on-the-mat" nonsense, no talking down to someone who, being a foreigner, could not be expected to understand anything about England.

She also wrote of her home life in terms that would interest a painter, knowing that in China writing words and painting pictures are closely linked. "It is full spring here; and our garden has blue, pink, white flowers — and all the hills are deep green; but very small. Our little river is about the size of a large snake; Julian used to wade across it; and sail a tiny boat." And she was trying to visualize China from the letters she received: "a large, wild place, with a very old civilization. I get hints of it from what you write."

She described the troubled air in Britain, too, the threat of war, the awful waiting to know what Hitler would do next, the great and terrible cloud that was hanging over Europe. But always she conveyed her belief in work and her love for life. "Her letters expressed her warm feelings," said this Chinese lady. "They are like sunshine which goes straight into the heart of a half-dead plant, with a kind of power to recover it to life again. From *The Waves* and *The Years* I learned much about life. Then I made up my mind to write in spite of all sorts of distress."

The book Virginia encouraged her to write about her childhood in a great house in Peking, when her father was a rich nobleman and the mayor of that city in the days of the old Dowager Empress, was recently published by the Hogarth Press, under the title of *Ancient Melodies*, with the author using part of her name, Su Hua. It richly justifies Virginia's faith in her.

The two women never met in life, but communicated in spirit. By a strange coincidence Su Hua asked another friend, whose work she admired, to write the introduction to the volume. She had no idea at the time she made the request that this woman knew Virginia intimately. The poet and gardener to whom she appealed was none other than Vita Sackville-West.

Su Hua has visited Rodmell, has painted a sketch of Monk's House as seen from the orchard, with roses blooming and birds in the sky, thinking of Virginia all the time, noticing in her room many of the things she had helped Julian to buy in the market place and the fair in a temple at Peking long ago.

So Julian and Virginia live on, unforgotten by their friends, evoking memories of joy and tenderness and beauty.

There is another link with Julian and Spain. An Irishwoman back from that country, intensely indignant about what was happening there, was taken to meet Virginia, at her request because of something she had written in the *New Statesman* on the subject. Virginia sensed what this passionate and frustrated woman was suffering. Instead of offering sympathy she did something very practical and of immediate therapeutic value. "She used to make me read James Joyce to her because she said that the intonation of my Irish voice lived with the rhythm of his prose. I don't know what she did to me. She introduced to me a whole world of ethical and literary values, and she told me to regard tolerance as the daughter of doubt, and respect the lineage. I loved her as I have loved few people, and for me she is more permanent in my life than my mother or father. I say is, for I cannot use the past tense for one so all-time. Her suicide struck me as a personal loss, but greater than that; it was the taking away of a certain kind of sunlight from the scene. But never a defeat for her."

The Irish voice speaks. Virginia smiles. She hardly seems aware that the words are spoken of her. What matters is that they express something she would have recognized as truth.

Chapter XIX

DAMNED BULLY!" The words burst unexpectedly from the lips of that elderly Victorian lady, Eleanor Pargiter, in the last chapter of *The Years*. Her niece is amused, and shocked, for such an expression, coming from such a woman, meant much more than the same words uttered by anyone of the younger, more careless and more free-spoken generation. What had provoked this fury and caused her aunt to tear the evening paper in two and fling it on the floor? It was the picture of "a fat man gesticulating."

The man could have been Mussolini or Hitler; it really makes no difference. What Virginia Woolf was expressing in this incident was her own hatred of Fascism and force, her steadily mounting fear that the world was heading for another war, her growing resentment against her helplessness to do anything effective to prevent the headlong plunge into disaster.

It was not a purely personal matter. In *Three Guineas*, which is as closely related to *The Years* as *A Room of One's Own* is to *Orlando*, she strove to express her detestation of all the false values and wrong attitudes that threatened to destroy human lives and wreck the hopes of achieving something that approached her idea of civilization. She offered suggestions for ways in which women could use their new freedom from complete economic dependence upon men and so help to check the destructive tendencies in modern society.

At first sight these suggestions seem nebulous and negative. She asked women to reject honors from institutions that had succeeded in breeding neither "a particular respect for liberty nor a particular hatred of war"; to beware of pageantry that was an excuse for strutting and trumpeting and self-advertisement; not to seek wealth or distinction at the expense of becoming aggressive and combative and of losing their capacity for enjoying the beauty of the world; to show disapproval by indifference to emotional appeals which increased possessiveness, jealousy, pugnacity and greed; to become, in fact, "outsiders," unregistered members of a secret society "without offices, meetings, leaders or any hierarchy, without so much as a form to be filled up, or a secretary to be paid," individuals content to remain obscure, united by a common faith in human values and real loyalties.

But this abstention from parades and fights had its positive side. It called for a constant critical and informed analysis of the passing show, a resolute direction of influence towards the pursuit of reason, happiness and peace, a determination always to face light and life, not darkness and death.

These were the ethical and moral standards by which she lived and which she consistently expressed. They were not always easy to uphold. There were times when expressing disapproval by indifference was not enough to express the murderous hate she felt for the "damned bullies," whose idiot ravings glorifying war filled the newspapers so regularly in the late nineteen-thirties that they hardly excited comment or were accepted as the words of responsible and reasonable human beings. Eleanor Pargiter's action in swearing aloud and tearing the paper in two was symbolical of what all "outsiders" would like to do with these dangerous lunatics at large and unchallenged.

There were other times, as during the Munich crisis in 1938, when she felt helpless. "Complete ruin of civilisation . . . Quentin conscripted, etc. One ceases to think about it — that's all. What else can a gnat on a blade of grass do?" But she would like to write the new novel that was forming in her mind — and other things, too, as soon as the biography of Roger Fry was completed.

It was impossible to settle to work with this feeling at the back of the mind that at any moment Europe might be flung back to the hideous nightmare of 1914. So one talked about new chairs and new books, or played bowls; and noted how one's share in village life had increased in depth — new roots being put forth to hold one a little more firmly in a reeling world.

No: war was imminent, but at the same time war was inconceivable, like death. "All that lies over the water, in the brain of that ridiculous little man. Why ridiculous? Because none of it fits; encloses no reality. Death and war and darkness representing nothing that any human being . . . cares one straw about. Not liberty, not life . . . If it were real, one could make something of it. But as it is it merely grumbles, in an inarticulate way, behind reality." So she wrote in her diary, feeling an individual helplessness but also the beginnings of the herd impulse, the gropings for protection and support.

She compared the dead Roger and the living Hitler, and blessed Roger "for giving me himself to think of — what a help he remains in this welter of unreality." Roger, as she first knew him at Gordon Square in 1910, was more real to her than the crisis. "Nobody in their senses can believe in it. . . . Much better to play bowls and pick dahlias." Work and play, one's books and one's garden and one's friends — these existed and made sense. But all "these grim men . . . like grown-ups staring incredulously at a child's sand-castle which for some inexplicable reason has become a real vast castle, needing gunpowder and dynamite to destroy it" — no, she could not stretch her mind to take in such nonsense. It was from this puppet world that she was an "outsider."

The Munich crisis passed. Politics became a mere matter of saying "I told you so," or trying to believe that peace might have been secured, for a while at least, without any inner conviction that the important and permanent things in life, the ordinary things, would be allowed to prevail over the rubbishy, tawdry, nonsensical beliefs in abstractions that actually meant nothing but death and disaster. These are not the thoughts of a politician. They express the typical attitude of a woman clinging desperately to what she most loves and values in the human scene.

She re-established some rhythm in her life, reading now this, now that, working at the biography or articles, and occasionally taking a "frisk" at the novel which was to become *Between the Acts* after a long period of being known as *Pointz Hall* or simply *P. H.*; playing bowls, cooking dinner, seeing friends, listening to music, walking on the downs; going through the usual fluctuations when *Three Guineas* appeared and was wildly attacked or enthusiastically praised.

Death continued to call away her personal friends. Lady Ottoline Morrell died suddenly early in 1938. "I miss her," she wrote to Vita, with her usual simplicity when faced with loss. "I mean Gower Street looks to me dumb and dismal. I used to go round there between tea and dinner." But Ott turned up and had to be written about in her place in Roger's biography. In November 1938 Viola Tree, daughter of Beerbohm Tree, died. "Two years younger than I am. . . . How out of place, unnecessary." For she had been, although never a very close intimate, valued for her buoyancy and liveliness; "bold and courageous . . . a great hand at life." Also, she "could transmit something into words," and the Hogarth Press had published her memoirs. Her overflowing vitality there had caused Vita to consider her expansiveness rather vulgar, and Virginia had replied, "You are utterly wrong. Why read memoirs as if they were poems? Don't you see Viola's vulgarity is *not* vulgar; her irreticence is *not* unashamed; an aroma — she aims at that; life, in fact. . . . Try reading it as if you were catching a swarm of bees; not hunting down one dart-like dragonfly."

Mysterious word, "vulgarity," as elusive as "snobbery" in its meanings. But both words in Virginia's lexicon were always linked with her endeavors to know more and more about other people's lives.

As time went on and it became more and more clear that the Munich pact was nothing but a snare and an illusion, she ceased to wonder whether she was a snob because she saw glamour and romance and some kind of nobility in lives different from her own, or whether she would have had a fuller understanding if her education had been less private and she had learned in a girls' school to be passionate about hockey instead of lady-like about Greek. What was left of the Bloomsbury Group was rapidly thinning away. The time for parties was over.

She was no longer an "outsider." Her popularity as a speaker had grown, but instead of going for a week end to Cambridge or Oxford to talk to undergraduates, she was more likely to be spending an evening session at a polytechnic or addressing a meeting of the Workers' Educational Association. The activities of the Women's Institute in Rodmell interested her; as did the opportunities for learning cookery in Brighton. And there were more and more refugees, from Spain, from Germany, all needing help to rebuild their lives, all with a story to tell.

Her delicate antennae were picking up other, more generalized signals, too. The thought of imminent war made all private plans meaningless, but the sense of being thus cut off and separate was followed by "the community feeling: all England thinking the same thing . . . at the same moment." She shared this feeling as she had not been able to share the community feeling in the First World War or the peace celebrations in 1919. When the actual crisis came in August 1939, the Woolfs were in the thick of moving to a flat in 37 Mecklenburgh Square, retaining their tenancy of 52 Tavistock Square for the Hogarth Press.

The atmosphere was very different emotionally from that which prevailed the previous September, when everyone was keyed up and expectant. It was different from the feeling when

Hitler celebrated Easter by marching into Prague, and one almost heard in one's own throat a low British growl. Now, stunned by the Russian-German pact, the public showed no excitement; no crowds, nothing of the hysteria of August 1914. "It's fate," said the foreman of the movers. "What can you do against fate?" Deep pessimism below; on the surface something that might almost be indifference. "Rather like a herd of sheep we are. No enthusiasm. Patient bewilderment. I suspect some desire 'to get on with it.'" wrote Virginia in her diary. Was the country at war or not? Perhaps the broadcast that evening would be able to settle that question — for the time being. Terrible as it was to think of the mothers who would suffer as her sister had suffered when Julian was killed, the private fear was submerged by the common feeling that, sooner or later, the "damned bullies" would have to be called to account.

Was she a coward? she asked herself, after the first air-raid warning sounded in Rodmell in September 1939. "Physically I expect I am. Going to London tomorrow I expect frightens me. At a pinch enough adrenalin is secreted to keep one calm. But my brain stops. I took up my watch this morning and then put it down. Lost. That kind of thing annoys me. No doubt one can conquer this." But, as in August, when there was all the discomfort of the moving to distract her, there was always something to do. Evacuees from London were arriving and coals needed to be carried to a cottage that would house eight women and children. Other refugees had already decided to return home. Blackout curtains had to be fitted to windows. And between interruptions she would work. "This little pitter-patter of ideas is my whiff of shot in the cause of freedom. So I tell myself. Thus bolstering up a figment — a phantom: recovering that sense of something pressing from outside which consolidates the mist, the non-existent."

During the period of the "phony war" she was tired and depressed. She decided to begin reading Freud and thus "enlarge the circumference . . . defeat the shrinkage of age." She was determined to do all she could to avoid taking life in very small sips, "testing one's little bits of strength and setting its easy tasks so as to accumulate years." Her way must be to keep off "the settling down and refrigeration of old age" by not letting herself be tied in future to any prolonged task. "Violently turn the pillow; hack an outlet." These were her hints for the future, the "traveller's notes which I offer myself should I again be lost."

So in 1940 she began again to write *Between the Acts*. This was a book that, according to her diary, gave her pleasure and relief. In 1938 she devoted odd moments to composing the scraps of verse which would be used in the historical pageant of England upon which the story pivots. She was not sure whether anything would come of the plans she had made, but by the end of that year she had written one hundred and twenty pages and knew she needed a hundred more to complete the novel. Early in 1939 she recorded that she was in full flood, and then "One day's happiness with *P. H.*," and then she put it all away again for fifteen months. From May 1940, when it was "bubbling," until its completion in February 1941, it was her great consolation, her escape into her own "reality" from the outer reality of the horror of the Battle of Britain.

If she could have solitude — no men driving stakes, digging gun emplacements at the garden gate of Monk's House, no neighbors — then she could "expand and soar into *P. H.*," she wrote, when invasion was expected. Back from London and a protracted air raid, one day in August, she had her first solitary morning; felt so light, free and happy that she was able to write more *P. H.* poetry. In September the Mecklenburgh Square house was hit during a heavy raid, but she forged ahead with *P. H.*, all the same. In October the Tavistock Square house was demolished; but she returned to *P. H.* In November, floods and bombs burst the banks of the River Ouse, destroying most of her favorite walks across the marshes; but she was working on *P. H.* in spurts, and so gaining relief and freedom. When the book was nearing completion she recorded that she had enjoyed writing almost every page of it.

In the last entry but one of the published extracts from her diary she noted, "Finished *Pointz Hall,* the Pageant: the play — finally *Between the Acts* this morning." Until that day, February 26, 1941, it would appear that she had not recognized her underlying theme. When she first began to write this novel in April 1938, she had not only the title, *Poyntzet* or *Pointz Hall,* but the ending. The book was to contain anything that came into her head, serious things discussed alongside "real, little, incongruous, living humor," and it was to close with an evocation of all these big and little things, all the "waifs and strays — rambling, capricious but somehow unified whole." During the three interrupted years of work to complete it, the title and the central conception persisted, the idea of "orts, scraps and fragments" in a continuous flux, coming together, dispersing, and again uniting, in effect another variation of her old theme, night and day, darkness and dawn, death and life. The title remained the same until almost the last moment. The evocation, as such, disappeared, though it may be clearly heard in the last scene of the pageant and at intervals throughout the rest of the book. Only at the end was the real title made plain to her; and with it came the last words, less defiant than usual but equally electrifying as well as baffling in their significance: "Then the curtain rose. They spoke."

When *Between the Acts* was published a few months after her death, with a note from her husband that, in his view, she would have made only minor revisions had she lived to pass the final proofs, this end struck a somber note. It seemed evident that she had seen an apocalyptic vision. She had looked back through time to the creation of the world, seen the primeval forests and the monsters which emerged from the ocean to flourish there, seen prehistoric man, half brute, half ape, leave his cave and establish his uncertain dominion, seen the beginnings of history and concentrated on her own country, finally focused on one small country house and one day in the first half of the twentieth century.

In the garden of that house the annual village pageant is performed, in aid of funds to supply electric light to the church. The villagers act successive scenes from English history, in crude verse and comic speech, while a gramophone plays now this classic, now that popular jingle. The audience of local people, mainly middle class, knows perfectly well that England is little Phyllis Jones, Queen Elizabeth is Mrs. Clark, licensed to sell tobacco, half the donkey is played by Albert, the idiot, and the cockney policeman directing traffic at Hyde Park Corner in 1860 is really Mr. Budge, the keeper of the village tavern. But they do not know what the play is about, even when the actors present mirrors to the audience and through a megaphone comes a harsh voice asking them to look at themselves before they disperse. The rector cannot explain — he is reduced to getting the collecting boxes circulated — and the author, the strange, disreputable Miss La Trobe (otherwise known as "Bossy") refuses to come forward.

The argument about the pageant's meaning continues in a desultory way when the visitors have gone home and the family living in Pointz Hall resume their usual evening occupations. Old Bartholomew Oliver reads his evening paper and falls asleep in his armchair. His widowed sister, Lucy Swithin, reads further in her *Outline of History*, seeing mammoths and rhododendron forests and swamps in Piccadilly. His son Giles, the stockbroker, and his daughter-in-law Isa, mother of two young children, retire to bed. "Before they slept, they must fight; after they had fought, they would embrace. From that embrace another life might be born. But first they must fight, as the dog fights with the vixen, in the heart of darkness, in the fields of night. . . . The window was all sky without colour. The house had lost its shelter. It was night before roads were made, or houses. It was the night that dwellers in caves had watched from some high place among rocks. Then the curtain rose. They spoke."

In 1941 the meaning seemed plain enough. Virginia Woolf was describing Britain between the two World Wars. She stopped at the point where the curtain rose on the Second World War. The cave men, or perhaps the ancient gods, spoke. But what they said, no one heard. What they decreed was unknown. All the trappings of the pageant had been put away. A new scene had not yet been written. There must be fighting and darkness before, perhaps, a new life could be born. Come rain or shine for next year's pageant, come swallows or death-dealing airplanes in the sky, now the house had lost its shelter, now night ruled, and the unknown speakers took the stage.

But even in 1941 they did not prophesy doom, except to those for whom the bells toll every quarter of an hour. The Battle of Britain had been fought; it might have to be fought again; and again. The new historic scene might prove in retrospect as ludicrous and paltry as the old, or as beautiful and heart-stirring. The same old characters would reappear, the same people but wearing different clothes. The mirrors and the megaphone voice would tell nothing except what one wanted to see and hear

In Britain during the war despair was a luxury not to be afforded; and no defeatist message was gleaned from *Between the Acts,* even by readers who understood that its final words meant that the curtain was rung up on a World War of which the outcome was still in doubt. Today it is even less possible to gather gloom and misery from this book. Its exact meaning remains oracular. The allegory may be interpreted in different ways. The various characters may be understood to symbolize different things. We can see now that the author's vision extended beyond the dark days in which she wrote. It may well be that future generations will see other significances, as yet hidden from us and as unguessed by her as the interpretations now read into *Don Quixote* or *Hamlet* and *The Tempest* would have been incomprehensible to Cervantes and Shakespeare in their time.

The book has a lambent quality; light flickers over it, and it contains light. Something of the ease and freedom the writer gained from it breathes from its pages. It is not massive or solemn or rigid or portentous, though it is full of portents and symbols and signposts. The balance between comedy bordering on knockabout farce and exaltation reaching an ecstatic point is extremely delicate, but firmly held. The characters, not fully realized or psychologically dissected, are boldly sketched and consistent with themselves; moreover, they communicate with one another as they do not in the abstract pattern of *The Waves* or the representational chronicle of *The Years*. They have a life of their own apart from their life in the author's mind, as a nonprofessional critic observed. "They seem to move and speak of their own volition. I cannot say exactly what *Between the Acts* means. I only know that I feel I understand it more than any other of Virginia Woolf's books — and I think I have understood them all."

This apparently confused but fundamentally revealing and acute criticism conveys a not uncommon impression. It is as though, at the end of her life, the author had, by releasing some of her controls, gained a mastery of her material never before achieved; almost as though a child, relaxing in sleep, had opened her hand, let go her tight clutch on a cherished toy and could, with a last faint smile, allow it to be taken from her, securely confident that it would be close by when she awoke.

Chapter XX

AM I AFRAID? she asked herself in 1940, when the Battle of Britain was raging and invasion was expected any day. Yes, intermittently, she concluded. But the worst of it was that one's mind didn't work well next morning. She tried to imagine what death might be like, being flattened by a bomb. She had got it fairly vivid, she wrote in her diary. Painful? Yes. Terrifying? She supposed so. But for once she wouldn't be able to describe it. And after one very bad day in August ("Two raids in London. One caught me in the London Library"; followed by confusion at Rodmell, not knowing whether the plane that came down over Lewes and the other planes that swooped and dived and then made for London were British or German), she concluded that "It would have been a peaceful matter-of-fact death to be popped off on the terrace playing bowls this very fine cool sunny August evening." She thought she was a coward for suggesting it was not a good idea to stay two successive nights in London, and was much relieved to find that Leonard and Miss Perkins at the press agreed.

But the fact that they had somewhere to go outside London, and the means of leaving that assaulted city, even though their refuge was still in the area under attack, did not prevent her from realizing that she was more fortunate than millions of others. "The people I think of now," she wrote, "are the very grimy lodging-house keepers, say in Heathcote Street; with another night to face; old wretched women standing at their doors; dirty, miserable."

In September a bomb, aimed at the port of Newhaven, dropped so close that it made the pen jump out of her hand and she cursed Leonard for slamming the window. But, she thought, how peaceful and happy life was, marooned at Rodmell. "A life that rings from one simple melody to another." Why not enjoy it after all the crowded, busy years in London. Breakfast in bed, walking, reading, writing, playing bowls, cooking dinner, listening to music, doing embroidery, getting to bed early; no interruptions, no society. But — what about Miss Perkins and her day, cleaning up the mess at Mecklenburgh Square, helping to get what was left of the press transferred to Letchworth after the bomb wrecked the house? She could not forget the hands that fluttered as they swept up the litter, the outwardly cheerful girls in pants and overalls, with turbaned heads, fighting the all-pervasive filth of fallen ceilings and crumbled walls.

And then there was the day in London ("A lovely September day — tender weather") when the time bomb that had fallen in Brunswick Square exploded. "I was in the baker's," she notes. "Comforted the agitated, worn women." Only a very courageous woman, unaware of her courage, could make so simple, so matter-of-fact a statement about her conduct in an emergency. What she did she took for granted as normal behavior. What remained in her mind was the feeling of sympathy for the other women, more exposed than she to continued danger, more exhausted by unremitting strain.

She was right, too. In those days, when everyone was in danger, no one could say who in a group would be the helper or who the helped, least of all could the temporary lionheart guess. There was no merit in it; it just happened. Tomorrow, half an hour later, it might be different, roles reversed. But over and over again the same thing might be observed. More often than not, in fact, it was the frail, the sensitive, the handicapped, the stricken and bereaved, whose imagination (not will) overleaped the barriers of strangeness and supplied the calming word, the maternal gesture that let the tears flow and the shuddering tremors subside in the stolid and the strong.

It was the same need to be stronger than circumstance, to defy fate, that led Virginia, walking on the marsh and inspecting bomb craters the day after Lewes had been hit in October, to keep close by her husband's side, cracking the grim, private joke of "prudently deciding that two birds had better be killed with one stone." It was the same instinctive sympathy with others, combined with detachment about herself, that caused her to note in one diary entry the queue, mainly children and women, lining up during the day outside an Underground station to secure shelter for the family during the night's expected raid ("which came, of course"), the fact that the only surviving relic in the ruin of their old home in Tavistock Square was an ancient basket chair, and then the odd feeling of relief at losing possessions. "Rubble where I wrote so many books. Open air where we sat so many nights, gave so many parties." And the new home in Mecklenburgh Square, wrecked, almost certain to be destroyed, with the complete loss of so many books and chairs and carpets and beds and pictures she had worked and saved to buy, one by one; all probably doomed. Nevertheless the queer feeling of relief, exhilaration, in fact, persisting; the dream rising of starting life bare, unburdened, unfixed to one spot.

The Woolfs never lived in London again. In Europe whole populations were being moved, not by their own free will, unless they were homeless wanderers trying to survive in forests and caves, hoping to elude the dictators who would put them in armies or prisons or camps or gas chambers and mass gravepits. But in England one did not wander, or not far from home, at any rate. There was, for one thing, nowhere to go; for another, no one to force you to roam. One "carried on." So Leonard and Virginia, with no gas for their car, trains to and from London uncertain, remained at Rodmell, becoming more and more a part of the communal village life around them.

But it cannot be said that the corner that held them knew them no more. Elizabeth Bowen, who saw a great deal of Virginia in London in the last years of her life, had a strange experience in a new hotel in Mecklenburgh Square after the war. Although everything around had changed, she suddenly felt that this must be where Virginia had lived. She went upstairs to check. Yes, there, out of a back window on a staircase, was the same view over roofs. Well, not quite the same, of course — gaps here, new buildings, or new chimneys at least, there. But this, indubitably, was the same spot where they had sat and talked and laughed and drunk tea and eaten cake so many afternoons; until Leonard, ever watchful lest his wife become too excited or overtired, would put his head inside the door and give the unobtrusive but quite unmistakable signal that now would be a good time for friends to leave and for Virginia to rest. A true ghost story, without a shadow or a shudder; a companionship so strongly remembered, a personality so continuing to live on in the mind, that time was annihilated and space refilled.

Nor did the fact that the Woolfs had no London home mean that they were completely isolated or absolutely tied to Rodmell. There were visits to Cambridge and to Letchworth; not long journeys, since nowhere in England is a vast distance from anywhere else, but tiresome enough at any time, particularly when the trip involved getting into, across and out of London, Lewes being south and Letchworth north of that county, city and capital.

During the war this gigantic knot in British transportation presented extra and unexpected problems to the traveler. The rigid censorship regarding bomb damage prevented one from having advance information about what roads or bridges were blocked or why it was impossible to proceed further in any particular direction. The reason might be a huge gap or minor repair work to ensure safety, the collapse of railway or river embankments, demolition of dangerous structures, the digging out

of time bombs and rendering them harmless, the need to give
priority to military traffic.

The situation was, of course, nothing like so dreadful as in
France and the Netherlands. The roads and fields were not
swarming with refugees and armies; if you were halted by a
policeman or air-defense worker, he spoke your language and
was civil; if your train was shunted for hours into a siding, it was
not boarded by men demanding to see your papers; if a bus conductor advised you to get out and walk, it was a suggestion, not
an order. All the same, traveling was far from pleasant and easy.
Nevertheless, people moved about.

Leonard Woolf was lecturing, and that sometimes meant as
many as fifteen people arriving at Monk's House, and also meant
that Virginia had to go into Newhaven to get the inevitable fish
and cook it, for Mabel (their sole remaining servant) had decided that if you were going to be killed you were going to be
killed and so had decided to join her sister in London. Virginia
could not blame her and was, indeed, glad to have the house to
herself. But entertaining of any sort was difficult, with so little
possibility of getting even part-time domestic help from the
busy villagers. Virginia did not complain, except for an occasional "this chops my day up." She found it hard to maintain
any rhythm in her reading-writing work; and she continued to
like cooking.

She continued, too, to be interested and active in the Wom-
en's Institute. There were afternoon meetings, followed by tea
and biscuits. She told them on one occasion about the great
Dreadnought hoax. They were probably slightly scandalized
("Such goings on!"), or pretended to be, and laughed more freely
when they got home, for the English village remains to this day
the stronghold of respectability. The most horrific things may
happen, and everyone knows about them; but one does not talk
about them, at least not in public, these countrywomen, whom
Virginia so much admired and respected and sought always to
understand, being realists who are not in the least cynical.

Virginia's niece Angelica Garnett came in January 1940 to lecture to them on the theater, with illustrations from photographs shown by an Epi-dia-scope, "Greek for looking through and over, I think," Virginia wrote to Vita, having some difficulty with the spelling of the name of this contraption, and adding that she had "run mad hunting one down in Lewes" for the occasion.

The next month's event was another gala occasion at the Women's Institute. For in December 1940, when they celebrated their twenty-first birthday and actually had chocolate cake to eat, Mrs. Chavasse, the president, was able to announce proudly that "Mrs. Harold Nicolson, equally well-known as Vita Sackville-West, has consented to lecture to us on Persia in February!!!"

"Loud cheers," Virginia reported to Vita. "General enthusiasm. A vote of thanks was then given to Mrs. Woolf for having secured you. You can't think how they beamed and boomed over you. They've all heard you on the wireless. You can't think how excited they were — never having been beyond Lewes in their lives. And you, whose voice they know, whose husband's voice they know!"

The lecture was to be illustrated with pictures of Vita's travels. Unfortunately the Epi-dia-scope, so hardly obtained, took only photographs, and the Persian travel pictures were on slides. That meant that a magic lantern must be found. But where? Such things, so familiar in premovie days, had become practically extinct. So there was more running mad. But Virginia enjoyed it and laughed over the adventures she had in tracking the "lanthorn," as it became in her later letters. The Queen of the Highbrows, the Princess in the Ivory Tower, the Quintessence of Bloomsbury, who was supposed to know nothing and care less about ordinary folk, was as determined as a child to show her great friend off to her village friends. The magic lantern was secured, and the imperturbable, the ever-generous, the beautiful Mrs. Harold Nicolson found her way across country in the dead-darkness of an English wartime winter to bring the sunshine of Persia and the warmth of her personality to a remote village.

Vita's generosity and thoughtfulness brought other joys into Virginia's life at Rodmell about this time, too. Sissinghurst had long been more than the pink tower with the doves which appealed so much to Virginia's imagination; it was a working farm in all earnestness. Now the great point about a farm, as city dwellers all over Europe discovered during the war, is that, unless a ravaging foe has destroyed everything, there is usually something extra that can be found and made use of, something that can be given to the less fortunate and yet not deprive the farm worker of what he needs to continue his unending toil. Sissinghurst yielded such extras, and the castle in Kent sent gifts to the cottage in Sussex.

In October 1940 a parcel arrived at Rodmell containing "masses and masses of the finest wool." This was a most exciting present, for wool had been one of the first shortages of the war, and one that had been particularly felt in a country whose prosperity had once been founded on wool, where the production and use of wool was so essential to the national economy that Sir Thomas More, looking out of his window in a troubled time, could see sheep feeding on men. Now, with an army needing to be clothed in wool and with blankets and coats and underwear to replace those destroyed in the blitz, there was an abrupt end to those cascading skeins of deliciously colored yarn that used to brighten so many small shops in back streets and gladden the hearts of so many women knitters. Virginia did not knit, but she felt the cold. And here was wool from a Sissinghurst sheep, great soft, foaming heaps of it.

"How can you say it wants dyeing?" she wrote in her letter of thanks. "It's a most harmonious mothy colour; and Louie says you've sent enough for a jersey for me and for socks for Leonard. Oh, how can we ever thank you sufficiently — the two old Wolves dressed in real sheep's clothing — not ordinary sheep either, Jacob's sheep which came in before the conqueror. Dear me, dear me, we were so exhilarated we hardly rolled into work all day."

The woman who hated receiving presents certainly tempted anyone to send her gifts, when she knew so well how to return thanks.

In November she had a further occasion to show this talent. "I wish I were Queen Victoria. Then I could thank you — From the *depths* of my *Broken* WIDOWED heart. *Never* NEVER NEVER have we had such a *rapturous* ASTOUNDING GLORIOUS — no, I can't get the hang of the style," she wrote. "All I can say is that when we discovered the butter in the envelope box, we had in the household — Louie that is — to look. That's a whole pound of butter, I said. Saying which I broke off a lump and ate it pure. Then in the glory of my heart I gave all our week's ration — which is about the size of my thumbnail — to Louie — earned undying gratitude; then sat down and ate bread and butter. It would have been desecration to add jam. You've forgotten what butter tastes like. So I'll tell you — it's something between dew and honey. Lord, Vita! — your wool; and then on top your butter!!! Please congratulate the cow from me, and the dairymaid, and I would like to suggest that the calf should be known in future (if it's a man) as Leonard, if a woman as Virginia.

"Think of our lunch tomorrow. Bunny Garnett and Angelica are coming. In the middle of the table I shall put the whole pat. And I shall say: Eat as much as you like. I can't break off this rhapsody, for it's a year since I saw a pound, to tell you anything else. I don't think anything else seems important. It's true all our books are coming from the ruined house tomorrow; all battered and mildewed. It's true I've been made Treasurer of the Women's Institute; also I want to ask you about lantern slides of Persia and will you come and talk. But this is mere trifling. Bombs fell near me; trifles; a plane shot down in the marsh; trifles; floods dammed — no, nothing seems to make a wreath on the pedestal fitting your butter."

This may sound extreme to anyone who has never suffered shortages. But those who have had to go short confirm that, of all food substances, butter was the most stimulating. After complete deprivation of it, the effect of even a small quantity can be far more intoxicating than alcohol.

In December the noble Sissinghurst cow, whose Leonard-Virginia calf had been weaned, was able to yield yet more milk for another present. On Boxing Day, the day after Christmas, 1940, she wrote: "If my admiration for you could be increased, it would be by the fact that your divine butter arrived on Christmas morning. Anybody else, that is, would have sent it any other day. As it was, Leonard and I, economising with a duck this year, had such an orgy of butter eating, it was worth ten turkeys. Oh what a gift! Oh Vita, what a Cornucopia of Bounty you are. . . . And I never give you a thing — I wonder why that is. Then I have to add about £2000 from your books [published by the Hogarth Press] let alone the meaning of 'em."

She goes on to write about books. She would like to borrow, if possible, a life of Bess of Hardwick, a life of Lady Anne Clifford, which Vita had suggested as themes and which Virginia was considering as possible *Common Reader* articles. And "Yes, of course we'll get the Lantern." A postscript gave the latest information about the number of copies sold of the latest Sackville-West book. And a final postscript, which gives the last touch to the picture of confusion and excitement of the time: "Must tell you, Lady Oxford sent her chauffeur here with her legacy for me — a bronze bust of Voltaire." No doubt that was appreciated; but it was not put in the middle of the table, nor weighed in the balance against ten turkeys.

In February 1941, shortly before the lecture on Persia, "dearest Vita" was once again "an overflowing Cornucopia." Virginia's letter of thanks gives a most revealing picture of the times.

"How you pet, pamper and spoil me! Nothing could have come more pat than your pat. I'd shaken a bottle of milk for an hour; at last a yellow lump appeared; I put it on the kitchen table. The cat ate it — so when the post came, it was like the voice of God in answer to our prayers. . . . Yes, I'm a butter woman now, and it takes the devil of a time. Also: what am I wearing at this moment? Jacob's Ram. Louie made me a thick warm jersey. It's saved my life. I live in it. And it's a lovely colour — the whole county envies me. Dear me, how you rain blessings. . . . Yes, we'll get the Lanthorn. I'm going to London tomorrow to walk among the ruins. Did I tell you all my books are to bits? — So, if you have Lady Anne Clifford or any other Elizabethan biographies — dear me — I'm asking another favour: could you bring them? It's the very devil writing when every book lies at the bottom of a vast pile up at the blacksmith's. Many are utterly ruined. So goodbye till 18th [the date of the lecture] to which I look forward as a drowning sailor to a Spice Island."

And the almost inevitable postscript, "Who is the Countess of Gall?" These last-moment additions to letters, showing how her mind ranged from the domestic harassments that every housewife shared to her preoccupations with writing, are often extremely poignant. In January 1941 there is a note scribbled at the top of a page, evidently just before she sealed and mailed the letter: "My blue envelope I bought from a bombed shop in Chancery Lane. Cheap. Lord, what chaos in the Temple! All my lovely Squares gone."

And then, after this orgy (a pound of butter a month for two people, arriving unexpectedly) she reproached herself for her greed; noted in her diary that she made up imaginary meals. As though everyone else in Britain was not doing the same.

Another friend who visited Rodmell in 1941 was Elizabeth Bowen. The old routines were followed. *Between the Acts* was almost finished, and Virginia put in her usual two hours of work in the lodge at the end of the garden. "I have spent the whole morning trying to move a party from the dining room into the hall," she said; and the two authors groaned and laughed over the obstinacy of characters, the technicalities involved, the differences between writing novels and plays, and so on. Virginia was gay; in fact, Elizabeth Bowen remembers the hilarious account of the "running mad" to get the lantern for Vita's lecture; not the details, but the fanciful decorations and the robust merriment of the story. And yet, were not the intervals of abstraction more frequent, the look of sadness more pronounced?

Although it was mid-February, the weather was warm, the sun shone. It was one of those false dawns of spring, so enchanting and so misleading, sheer magic. They sat in the bright, sunny room upstairs, and Virginia brought out an old shawl she and Leonard had brought back from Spain long ago. It had been used as a portiere, but was now tattered and worn almost to shreds, though still lovely. They spread out the glowing, tawny silk on the floor, trying to decide what use to make of the fragments, too dear and too precious to throw away. They laughed and talked, and reverted at intervals to the problem: what was to be done with the curtain. In the end, nothing was decided. It was a wonderful afternoon. But was it happiness or unhappiness that inhibited their work? Elizabeth Bowen cannot be sure.

She left before lunch on a Saturday. Virginia pressed her to stay, but not quite with the old spirited formula, "Go, if you're bored!" Elizabeth explained that she had an engagement with a very young man, had, in fact, promised to go with him to a theater. One must not disappoint the young. Virginia understood and agreed. But was there not a touch of resentment in the agreement? Again, Elizabeth is not sure.

At the last moment she remembered that she had left in her bedroom a small jar of cold cream — already a rare article in those days. "I'll send it on," said Virginia. "No, I won't. I'll keep it, as a sign that you will come back." And on that teasing-tender note they parted; forever.

The fluctuations which her friends noted in her moods are reflected in her writing. They are naturally more clear in the diary entries during the war years, where, on page after page, one sees her straightening her back, squaring her shoulders, striding off to do something practical — such as cleaning out a room, cooking a meal, bicycling into Newhaven or Lewes to buy food — or deliberately switching her thoughts to another subject, another kind of book, either to read or to write; in short, remembering to take the kind of medicines she had prescribed for herself to keep age and melancholy at bay.

The darkness of London depressed her, so "Standing in Whitehall, I said to my horses, 'Home, John' and drove back in the grey dawn light" to the brightness of her workroom at Monk's House. "What shall I think of that's liberating and freshening?" In London, there would always be the River Thames, walking along the Strand, "letting each face give me a buffet." Or she could imagine her next trip with Leonard to sell books, seeing lovely farmhouses, enticing lanes, flowers in the hedges. At Rodmell she could garden a little; "oh, and print; and change my bedroom furniture. Is it age, or what, that makes life here alone, no London, no visitors, seem a long trance of pleasure? . . . I'm inducing a state of peace and sensation feeling — not idea feeling." She had been planning the lecture to the Workers' Educational Association which became "The Leaning Tower" (an article printed in *The Moment*), and continues the old argument with John Lehmann about modern poets and poetry. But now she would relax and enjoy reading an Elizabethan, "like swinging from bough to bough." She would "dream a poet-prose book; perhaps make a cake now and then. Now, now — never any more future skirmishing or past regretting. Relish the Monday and the Tuesday, and don't take on the guilt of selfishness feeling: for in God's name I've done my share, with pen and talk, for the human race. I mean young writers can stand on their own feet. Yes, I deserve a spring — I owe nobody nothing. Not a letter I need write, nor need I have weekenders. For others can do that as well as I can, this spring."

These were her moods before the Germans took the offensive, and swept through Holland and Belgium and France. "Apple blossom snowing the garden. A bowl lost in the pond. Churchill exhorting all men to stand together. . . . Duncan saw an air battle over Charleston — a silver pencil and a puff of smoke. . . . So my little moment of peace comes in a yawning hollow. But though L. says he has petrol in the garage should Hitler win [for Leonard Woolf, being a Jew, a Socialist and a well-known intellectual, had no illusions about the Nazis] we go on. It's the vastness, and the smallness, that makes this possible."

The war was like a desperate illness. "For a day it entirely obsesses; then the feeling faculty gives out; next day one is disembodied, in the air. Then the battery is recharged." So one listened to the words of the leaders as they were broadcast — words which seemed to her to come so easily, since words were her stock in trade, but which were also a vital part of the protection against invasion. One read and talked under the apple trees, or played bowls; because life must go on.

She saw her first hospital train. That is to say, she felt it: "laden, not funereal but weighty, as if not to shake bones: something — what is the word I want? — grieving and tender and heavy-laden and private — bringing our wounded back carefully through the green fields at which I suppose some looked." She could not see them, those weary men escaped from the holocaust across the Channel, but in her imagination she could feel that some of them were not too heartsick or body-broken to gain renewal of strength and purpose as they saw the fields and the hills of home. She felt "the slowness, cadaverousness, grief of the long heavy train, taking its burden through the fields. Very quietly it slid into the cutting at Lewes. Instantly wild duck flights of aeroplanes came over head; manoeuvred; took up positions and passed over Caburn."

As the Battle of Britain continued, her thoughts naturally became more and more somber. She heard "a kind of growl behind the cuckoos and t'other birds. A furnace behind the sky." Moreover, there was the curious feeling that "the writing 'I' has vanished. No audience. No echo. That's part of one's death." But

immediately she checked this line of thought. She went on working. "But it is a fact — this disparition of an echo."

She walked, thinking sometimes "this may be my last walk."
Then she must get home and cook the dinner. She picked cur-
rants and gooseberries in the garden, went to see her sister at
Charleston for tea. But "there is no autumn, no winter. We pour
to the edge of a precipice . . . and then? I can't conceive that
there will be a 27th June 1941."

And then her will to live would revive strongly. "I'm aware of
something permanent and real in my existence." She was rather
proud, she was surprised to find, of having done "a solid work"
in her biography of Roger Fry. It was almost as though, in her
vision of him, she had given birth to a child born of their intimate, inner life together. So strong was this feeling that it carried over in a curious way. When she heard the British planes
overhead going to fight over the sea, she had "I think an individual, not communal B. B. C. dictated feeling. I almost instinc-
tively wished them luck."

While invasion was daily, almost hourly, expected, she continued to write, sometimes when requested, as in the case of an
American magazine wanting to know her "Thoughts on Peace
in an Air Raid" (*The Death of the Moth*), and sometimes only
in her journal, which she found useful when she had the fidgets,
when planes fell before their eyes and they could see smoke
over the racecourse at Lewes; when the windows rattled and a
dull thud far off meant that London, "majestic London," was under heavy attack while she embroidered and Leonard made cigarettes and they remarked to one another, "They're at it again";
when it was too dangerous to cross the garden; when amid the
roar of planes and the rattle of machine guns there would crop
up the question of whether they would have their fish fried or
boiled; when she had been beaten at bowls or the howling ban-
shee of the siren warning made her doubt whether her *P. H.*
poetry was any good; when she told Leonard she didn't want to
die yet; when every day was "seen against a very faint shade of

bodily risk," and one only thought, pulling the curtains, who might be killed tonight? "Not us, I suppose. One doesn't think of that — save as a quickener."

But when the stimulus and strain of the immediate danger had passed and there would be as many as six successive nights without a raid, then there would be "moments when the sail flaps," and she would feel again the detested hardening of old age, would have to resist the insidious temptation to be introspective, would need to seek refreshment in the thought of her growing detachment from "the hierarchy, the patriarchy."

There was a continual seesawing of her thoughts. She reminded herself of Walter de la Mare's line, "Look your last on all things lovely," and Goethe's invocation to the eternal moment, "Stop, you are so fair"; thinking that at her age, fifty-nine, all life was so fair, "without much more of it, I suppose, to follow." Then she would go on copying *P. H.* So long as she could write, "feeling in my fingers the weight of every word, even of a review, need I feel guilty?"

Her last two articles, written when only the final drudgery of completing *Between the Acts* remained, concerned two women, Ellen Terry, the great actress, and Mrs. Thrale, the friend of Dr. Johnson. Both of these sketches can be read in *The Moment*, and they are worth comparing, because they show how quickly the shadows were lengthening around her in 1941.

Ellen Terry was Virginia Woolf's sort of woman, although their lives were so different. The actress was an artist, a fighter; she played many parts on and off the stage; and she will be remembered because she was herself. The account of her life, written in January 1941, is as vigorous as anything Virginia wrote at any time; it would be impossible to deduce from it any of the circumstances of its composition.

Reading it, one catches echoes from the past. One recalls Virginia's imagining, years before, what would have become of the British Empire if Ellen Terry instead of Victoria had been born to rule as Queen. One remembers that Ellen, at sixteen, married

the elderly artist G. F. Watts, who admired Virginia's mother
when she was a girl and painted a portrait of Virginia's father.
One turns back to reread, in *The Death of the Moth*, the lyrical
passage Virginia wrote when she went to the Old Vic in 1933 to
see a performance of *Twelfth Night*, in which her friend Lydia
Lopokova, wife of Maynard Keynes, was cast as Olivia. Virginia
noted how the personality of the woman usurped the part she
played in Shakespeare's comedy. "She has only to float on to the
stage and everything round her suffers, not a sea change, but a
change into light, into gaiety; the birds sing, the sheep are garlanded, the air rings with melody and human beings dance towards each other on the tips of their toes possessed of an exquisite friendliness, sympathy and delight."

So Virginia's personality transforms what she writes about into
something else as one reads. The allusive character of her prose
links picture to picture in the mind. The dancer's name may ring
up for many readers the curtain on the ballet. Mention of the
ballet may have recalled to Virginia the time when her old friend
Duncan Grant composed one but fell when he himself tried to
dance. What thoughts crowded in on her as she wrote about Ellen
Terry can, of course, only be guessed. But one cannot doubt that
she enjoyed writing that article in 1941, although when it was
surprisingly returned by the American magazine which had asked
for it, she formed a low opinion of its merits. She fought against
the depression caused partly by the rejection in a very practical
way. She sent the article to another editor, she gave two more
days to *Pointz Hall*, and she cleaned out the kitchen. "This trough
of despair shall not, I swear, engulf me," she wrote in her diary
in January 1941. She would not think about James Joyce dead —
two weeks younger than herself — but of T. S. Eliot's rapt enthusiasm for *Ulysses*, her various attempts to appreciate it on its
own terms. And she would avoid introspection; see the snowdrops
in the garden, even if "we live without a future . . . with our
noses pressed to a closed door."

The case was altered, however, in the following month, when

she came to write a review of Mrs. Thrale's life. In this sketch she has noticeably lost her resilience. One would expect the subject to arouse her sympathy, for Mrs. Thrale was another woman who had had her ups and downs, had fought for her freedom and happiness, and had danced till dawn on her eightieth birthday. But, whether or not the ghost of Dr. Johnson had put its heavy foot down as Virginia Woolf wrote, the article is without her usual spring. It conveys a sense of a woman's life gone somehow awry. And yet, her diary shows, it was begun with some glow. But she was depressed, she could not remember why, exactly, only that a Charlie Chaplin film had failed to amuse her.

The last entry in the diary, dated March 8, 1941, reveals that she was still fighting for her life. It was a fine spring day. She went with her husband to hear him speak at Brighton. She saw a pretty hat — "how fashion revives the eye!" She admired the bright checked cotton of the waitress's dress. "No, I intend no introspection. I mark Henry James' sentence: observe perpetually. Observe the oncoming of age. Observe greed. Observe my own despondency. By that means it becomes serviceable. Or so I hope. I insist upon spending this time to the best advantage. I will go down with my colours flying."

She made plans, for occupation was essential, if fatal brooding was to be avoided. She noted that it was time to put the diary away and cook dinner. "Haddock and sausage meat. I think it is true that one gains a certain hold on sausage and haddock by writing them down."

And then came the day in April when her husband walked through the garden to her lodge to remind her it was lunchtime. She was just finishing something, she said, and he went back to the house. Five, ten, minutes passed, and she did not come. He went to see what was detaining her. On her table was what she had just been writing: a letter to her sister and a letter to him. He ran through the orchard, across the meadow, to the river. There on the bank he found her hat and her stick. But it was nearly two weeks before her drowned body was recovered from the waters of that muddy, tidal, seaward-flowing and ebbing stream.

"I have the feeling that I shall go mad," she had written in her farewell letter to her husband. "I hear voices and cannot concentrate on my work. I have fought against it, but cannot fight any longer. I owe all my happiness in life to you. You have been so perfectly good. I cannot go on and spoil your life."

These were terrible times; she would not make them more terrible by putting on those who loved her and whom she loved the extra burden of caring for her, guarding her against herself when the desire for death overwhelmingly asserted itself. They had recalled her to reality before. Now she felt it was too late; this time she was too old to recover. She was not willing to live, at the expense of their heartbreak, in a world of illusion. If she could not know the truth of the world around her, then she must seek it beyond the veil of death.

So, it seemed to her with the pitiful and perverse logic of the suicide, she would go down with her colors flying, giving what was left of her life to prove the sincerity of her vision, to carry her quest for truth and reality to its utmost limit.

Those who knew and loved her as she walked the earth had long faced the possibility that the delicate balance of her mind would, sooner or later, be fatally disturbed and then she would yield to the morbid tendencies within herself. Yet this foreknowledge could do nothing to soften the blow when at last it fell. The merest amateur cannot fail to note the psychological danger signals along her road: to the trained observer they are all too clear. But when those who know and love her because they have roamed with her in the realms of the imagination cry out that her self-sought death seems a betrayal of everything she stood for, and then that they refuse to admit she could go down to defeat, they assert that though the singer's lute is broken, her song shall still be heard. She has attained the kind of immortality she strove for, the seizing and sharing of the mystic moment.